THE

MAKING

OF

CABARET

SECOND EDITION

THE
MAKING
OF
CABARET
SECOND EDITION

KEITH GAREBIAN

OXFORD
UNIVERSITY PRESS

OXFORD
UNIVERSITY PRESS

Oxford University Press, Inc., publishes works that further
Oxford University's objective of excellence
in research, scholarship, and education.

Oxford   New York
Auckland   Cape Town   Dar es Salaam   Hong Kong   Karachi
Kuala Lumpur   Madrid   Melbourne   Mexico City   Nairobi
New Delhi   Shanghai   Taipei   Toronto

With offices in
Argentina   Austria   Brazil   Chile   Czech Republic   France   Greece
Guatemala   Hungary   Italy   Japan   Poland   Portugal   Singapore
South Korea   Switzerland   Thailand   Turkey   Ukraine   Vietnam

Published by Oxford University Press, Inc.
198 Madison Avenue, New York, New York 10016

www.oup.com

Oxford is a registered trademark of Oxford University Press.

Library of Congress Cataloging-in-Publication Data
Garebian, Keith.
The making of Cabaret / Keith Garebian.—2nd. ed.
p. cm.
Includes bibliographical references and index.
ISBN 978-0-19-973249-4; 978-0-19-973250-0 (pbk.)
1. Kander, John. Cabaret.   2. Isherwood, Christopher, 1904–1986. Goodbye to
Berlin.   3. Van Druten, John, 1901–1957. I am a camera.   4. Ebb, Fred.   I. Title.
ML410.K163G37 2011
792.6'42—dc22   2010017299

Printed in the United States of America
on acid-free paper

FOR HAROLD PRINCE
great artistic innovator
whose version was the first

A NEW PREFACE

In his book *Harold Prince and the American Musical Theatre* (2005: 1), Foster Hirsch recalls a woman who left the opening night performance of *Cabaret* in Wilmington, Delaware, declaring: "It's more than a musical!" Her exclamation suggests that the Broadway show had gone beyond European ethnicity and history on its way to success. As the musical's librettist Joe Masteroff maintains, *Cabaret* is probably "the most imitated and influential" of Prince's musicals (Hirsch 2005: 68). For one thing, the Emcee's opening number ("Willkommen") has become embedded in our cultural vocabulary, for example, leading Mel Brooks, in his film *Blazing Saddles* (1974), to have Madeline Kahn, playing a German chanteuse in the Dietrich *Destry* manner, greet every knock on her door with the trilingual invitation: "Willkommen, Bienvenue, Welcome" (Steyn 1997: 20). All joking aside, even on the surface *Cabaret* is not *just* a musical. The Berlin of the Third Reich, diluted for Broadway audiences, provides a symbolic edge that tips the show into the realm of fascinating metaphor. *Cabaret* is set in garish, sleazy, raucous, nervous, pre–World War II Berlin, but is it simply an American musical pretending to be German in the way that *My Fair Lady* (1956) thinks of itself as British? Certainly *Cabaret* does embody American showbiz, but it is very much defined by the German cabaret world. The Emcee literally beckons the cabaret's cosmopolitan clientele with a greeting in three languages (German, French, English), and once inside we see the larger, outer world as in a mirror with ourselves reflected in it. John Kander and Fred Ebb keep faith with Harold Prince's concept, giving the musical its special sound—actually a double score, one for book scenes, the other for cabaret numbers—and every artistic collaborator in the production helps in establishing the milieu and characters. In the musical's first two Broadway incarnations, Ron Field's choreography was flashy but unromantic, playful but unsentimental. Just as *Chicago* (1975) defines itself by vaudeville (especially in the razzmatazz murder trial of Roxy Hart) and *West Side Story* (1957) by its repertoire of movement for the two rival gangs, *Cabaret* defines itself by the seductions of the Berlin cabaret world and Prince's resistance to many conventions of musical theater: his use of a symbolic frame, music as social comment, filmic devices, and expressionistic motifs (tilted mirror, blinder lights, black box setting, and spiral staircase).

At the time *Cabaret* arrived on Broadway, the musical was facing severe challenges to its health. As Carol Ilson explains in her book on Prince, the genre was in real peril. Times Square, the main area adjacent to the theater district, was getting sleazier with porno shops, prostitutes, and derelicts, "and there were perceived possible dangers to the theatregoing crowd" (Ilson 1989:136). As ticket prices kept rising, producers reduced the number of performers in choruses as well as the budgets for costumes and sets. Meanwhile, following their television appearance on the *Ed Sullivan Show*, the Beatles had become a sensation, and their new musical sound was having an immense impact on American showbiz. Gerald Bordman (1992: 643) has pointed out, "As far as memorable melodies went, the American Musical Theatre had suddenly become not very musical. With rare exceptions audiences rarely left new musicals singing their music." Songwriters were losing status to librettists and directors, and the trend was toward directors with "strong personalities and imaginative and artistic visions" (Ilson 1989: 136). In this context, *Cabaret* broke new ground. According to Scott Miller (1996: 27), it was "Hal Prince's first experiment in making a concept musical—a show in which the story is secondary to a central message or metaphor—a form he would later perfect with *Company, Follies, Pacific Overtures, Kiss of the Spider Woman,* and other musicals." As Ilson (1989: 136) maintains, "Its unusual content and form, as well as its use of stagecraft, influenced the shape of the American Musical Theatre for decades afterward." Martin Gottfried (1984: 29) concurs, explaining further, "Since the concept musical was still in a formative stage this was a schizophrenic show. One-half of it was an orthodox musical play whose story unfolded in dramatic scenes with duly integrated book songs. The other half, however, startled and changed Broadway." But are these claims extravagant?

It has become the custom to see any innovative Broadway musical as a trendsetter, especially from the time of *Show Boat* (1927), through the debuts of *My Fair Lady* (1956), *West Side Story* (1957), *Gypsy* (1959) and, more recently, with the advent of *Sweeney Todd* (1979) and *The Phantom of the Opera* (1986). Certainly special claims can be made for these remarkable musicals, and there is no doubt that each left its important signature on the popular art form. As the world changes (along with technology and musical tastes), so do the best of Broadway musicals. The new millennium has seen the emergence of Michael John LaChiusa, Adam Guettel, Jonathan Larson (lamentably gone too soon), Jason Robert Brown, and their close collaborators. A new generation is extending and transforming the serious musical. Artistic categories have become increasingly blurred, and it is sometimes difficult to tell if a production is actually a musical or an opera or something in between. In fact, some theater professionals (such as Wiley Hausam) believe we have entered the age of the antimusical. This is not to say that the new, highly personal form of the musical is not a part of lyric theater but that it has taken on a postmodern character. The musical landscape has undoubtedly been changed by such shows as *Passion* (1994), *Floyd Collins* (1996), *Rent* (1996), *Parade* (1998), *The Wild Party* (2000), *Passing Strange* (2008), and *Next to Normal* (2009).

Cabaret is nonetheless a foster parent of this new generation because of its themes and clever form. "*Cabaret*," writes Stacy Wolf (2002: 240), "is meant to unsettle." Wolf draws attention to the fact that "most things in it can be read in two opposing directions, the result both of specific strategies and of long-standing Broadway conventions that have encouraged double readings, most notably through double entendre and camp." Even well into its previews, the show was thought likely to fail. As Mitchell Morris (2004: 145) asserts: "With its seedy characters in *louche* entanglements, luridly placed against the scene of a declining Weimar Republic and a rising Nazi party, the show seemed to violate many of the most central conventions of the musical during its post—World War II heyday." Broadway entertained little discussion of whether the musical genre could accommodate this show's dark material. The producers and publicists dropped the names of Bertolt Brecht, George Grösz, Otto Dix, and Marlene Dietrich with such frequency that it became quite apparent that they were attempting to justify *Cabaret*'s distance from the standard model of the musical (Morris 2004: 146). The show was bruited to be a cautionary tale or parable, and its method of expression was said to consist of analogies, parallels, and metaphors rather than direct statement (Jones 2003: 242). Certainly by the time of Sam Mendes's Broadway version, it was clear that *Cabaret* was a production that made deep, dark connections between Weimar and the present day because much of current popular culture has its roots in a peculiar brand of German aestheticism.

So, *Cabaret* is cognizant of many things in society and also aware of its own methods of expression. It is actually a metatheatrical musical—the first of its kind to set a trend—and though ultimately its narrative does have a split personality, it has a power and unpleasantness not commonly found on Broadway. The metatheatrical devices analyzed in this book are well known by musical lovers as much for their presentational force as for their ingenuity. These devices consist of a dramatic personage, a detail of decor, a peculiar kind of "doubleness" or duality, and the very audience of the musical itself. The Master of Ceremonies is both a detached chorus and a character in the story. He is a true *Master* of *Ceremonies* in that he introduces, interrupts, participates in, and extends the meanings of the songs and the club's novelty acts while exhorting the clientele to sit back, forget their troubles, and enjoy the deliberately lewd performances. He knows, of course, that what transpires onstage reflects what is occurring in Berlin society so that, in a sense, patrons of the Kit Kat Klub end up as voyeurs of their own public lives. The Kit Kat Klub is both cabaret setting and symbolic microcosm, and thus the performers onstage and the audience members (both in the club erected onstage and in the theater auditorium) are all incorporated within a single raffish, contaminated world on the verge of extinction. No less a distinguished musical scholar than Raymond Knapp (2006: 114) underlines this duality by claiming that *Cabaret* "has its cake and eats it too, on the one hand celebrating the Kit Kat Klub's festive escape from reality and using it as a ready platform for social protest, and on the other also suggesting that its decadence makes it directly accountable for fostering the then-incipient horrors of Nazi Germany." Knapp possibly exaggerates, for it is highly questionable to blame sexual license and decadence for fostering Nazism, though there is no question that the cabaret decadence of Berlin introduced some people to a type of freedom they had never enjoyed before and that this freedom was both scary and deadly. Berliners and other Germans were desperate for change, especially from things they perceived as injurious to their way of life (Miller 1996: 29). So, Knapp's view cannot be minimized.

Cabaret does not pound home its points about Nazism or complicity. It does not forget its roots in the entertainment world. But it does combine provocative subtleties with sheer showmanship. Although there are no singing nuns or dream ballets, there are Broadway compromises in the characters of Clifford Bradshaw, Sally Bowles, and Fräulein Schneider that don't go the entire way of their Christopher Isherwood models. And there are distinctly American elements, to be sure: in the glitzy show numbers with Las Vegas touches and in the sentimental pairings of Fräulein Schneider and Herr Schultz, of Sally and Cliff (conforming, as Hirsch claims, to the structural conventions of *Oklahoma!*), just as there are identifiable ethnic elements in the Yiddish idioms of Schultz and in the German anthem sung by the cabaret waiters and reprised by Ernst Ludwig and others. *Cabaret* is a celebration of its own energy, skill, and cleverness, and it demonstrates how Prince, for all his expertise in metaphor and metatheater, honored what Hirsch (2005: 4) calls "the performance impulse" by selling spectacles of the trashy and the sophisticated, of soft sentimentality and hard barbarism, of cold exploitation and warm vulnerability.

So, *Cabaret* is a rare balancing act that is both entertaining and instructive and that manages to make music, dance, dialogue, and decor part of the action rather than restrict them to serving as mere *divertissements*. This musical has given theater two of the finest major characters that many a performer has yearned to play. Sally Bowles has been interpreted by many actresses, from Jill Haworth, Liza Minnelli, Jane Horrocks, and Natasha Richardson to Joely Fisher, Molly Ringwald, Andrea McCardle, Jennifer Jason Leigh, Brooke Shields, Teri Hatcher, Gina Gershon, and Anna Maxwell Martin. The Emcee has been brought to various degrees and textures of life by Joel Grey, Barry Dennen, Alan Cumming, Brent Carver, Norbert Leo Butz, Raul Esparza, Neil Patrick Harris, Brad Oscar, James Dreyfus, Bruce Dow, and others. The Emcee and the Kit Kat Klub are an enduring legacy to American musical theater, for they leave an indelible mark on audience consciousness. Who can forget Grey's Emcee in top hat and tails, looking like a *compère* eager to please while also serving as satirist in his own right? As Hirsch (2005: 64) has suggested, Grey's embodiment was a case of Al Jolson becoming Bertolt Brecht. Who can forget the heavy, vulgar chorus line—surely the most unprepossessing one in Broadway history—kicking into a Nazi goose step led by the Emcee in drag? Who can forget Sally Bowles's private world becoming increasingly absorbed by the cabaret world or that same cabaret world materializing and then dematerializing before our very eyes?

From the first incarnation of the musical down to the Bob Fosse musical version and subsequent stage productions that have had the liberty of carrying Berlin decadence as far as the modern theater and social tastes allow, this musical has had the distinction of using sex (in its various permutations) as a way of indicating what was happening politically in Germany of that era. In her book *Vice Versa* (1992), Marjorie Garber discusses this point in detail, with special reference to the Fosse film, and I shall take up the matter in a later chapter, but it is important to declare that the first manifestation by Prince really cued the subject by practicing—for Broadway of its time—a truly daring form of theatrical sexual expression. By Isherwood's standards, of course, the original version was tame stuff, distorting the ambiguous sexual politics of its source to become, as John M. Clum (1999: 277) maintains, "the heterosexual romance Broadway audiences of the time expected." But as the script was revised and theater tastes developed, the story delved into bisexuality—most convincingly suggested in the 1972 Fosse film and culminating in the brilliantly daring Mendes production of 1998 that painted a lurid picture of what Clum calls "omnisexual desire."

Of course, for many audiences the stage spectacles have been outstripped by the images in Fosse's movie version, which was far more daringly tawdry and sexual even though the nucleus of the film—Minnelli's Americanized Sally—was a radical transformation, actually a betrayal, of Isherwood's material. And it is important to remember that Fosse's movie would not, perhaps, have come so startlingly to life without retracing the contours and impressions left by Prince's original musical production.

If *Cabaret* the stage musical no longer seems daringly innovative in comparison to, for example, *Hedwig and the Angry Inch* (1998), it is still sexually suggestive and eminently playable, thriving as it does on its intrinsic form as a self-conscious, deliberately theatrical musical. Mendes, who presented the show in England's small Donmar Warehouse Theater in the winter of 1993, refocused the musical on certain songs that originally had been throwaway numbers and added a psychological dimension to Sally Bowles, showing her in the process of having a nervous breakdown during her climactic title number. This small-scale chamber version took risks in emphasizing the darker facets of the musical and underscored the point that no matter how much a contemporary director or actress alters the grain and texture of Sally Bowles, the musical triumphs as something much larger than a star vehicle.

Even Prince's own 1987 revival, though less theatrically satisfying than the original Broadway production, revealed that despite the softness at the heart of its libretto, *Cabaret* could bear reinterpretations that seek to release levels of meaning and feeling not usually explored in a commercial enterprise. This is probably because of the visual and thematic vocabulary that Prince and his collaborators created back in 1966. How this vocabulary developed is the story this book seeks to tell by means of a narrative that luxuriates in miscellaneous details. Knowing full well that a musical's spirit and meaning are best released in performance rather than in critical analysis, I have sought to balance the descriptive with the analytical. My text revels in the imaginative power and dynamic forward thrust of the many artists who created the original show yet tries to maintain an objective examination of the form and content of the musical that glowed with a zeal for theatrical originality. The material from Isherwood's Berlin stories and their stage adaptation by John van Druten, Prince's struggle to subordinate the heroine to the larger concerns of his musical, and Fosse's celebrated movie version should be regarded as the stuff of cultural history, for the genesis and evolution of Sally Bowles, the Berlin of her day, and the overall form of the narrative comprise an integral part of Prince's own fundamental engagement with culture and history in the very process of artistic creation.

This book is a stage history of a great American musical, and it tells many back stories of what went into shaping the show. It chronicles the genesis, evolution, and culmination of the work in its first Broadway incarnation. It aims at capturing some of the collaborative excitement expressed by the creators of this production as they struggled to construct the musical, and it also analyzes the show's artistic achievement in theatrical and cultural contexts. The real stars of a musical are its elements: libretto, score, production design, choreography, performances, and director's vision. So, this book examines these elements without seeking to murder as it inspects. A stage musical leaves many and various traces that new artists follow while leaving shades of their own, which is why this book takes note of some of the most significant revisions or reinventions of *Cabaret*. Although it draws on the work of many theater scholars and critics and uses every resource available to me (drafts of the libretto, print, radio, or video interviews, original set and costume designs, videotaped performances, production photographs, program notes, biographies, and academic essays), this book is not a textbook, but a compendious reference for any theater enthusiast or reader.

My original production history of the show, published in Canada in 1999, did not have the benefit of some important later scholarly works in musical theater, such as those by Knapp, Wolf, Morris, and others. Thus this second edition has been enormously enhanced by the insights of these scholars and by James Leve's excellent study of Kander and Ebb. It has been enriched also by new discoveries I made in the Prince, Ebb, and Boris Aronson archives, the three versions of Masteroff's libretto, and various videotapes featuring Prince, Aronson, and Kander—all through the graces of the New York Public Library for the Performing Arts. The addition of large amounts of new material has allowed me to excise much of the extraneous biographical background on the major collaborators in order to concentrate more sharply on aesthetic and sociocultural issues that did not receive much discussion in the first edition.

Time tends to make revisionists of us all, and certainly this trend prevails in musical theater, where even the biggest hit musical can undergo radical transformations to mirror the changing zeitgeist. *Cabaret* is no exception, especially because it continues to be a popular show more than forty years after its Broadway début. This second edition emphasizes this pattern of revisioning but always with the purpose of showing that no matter how significant a new version, it never truly obscures the original signatures of the first Broadway production. While a generalist can read this second edition as a full-length biography of a show, a specialist can read it for its evocation of artistic process and as a modest attempt to show how a great musical mirrors social and cultural history, its lens changed with each major reincarnation and thereby what is reflected in it.

Keith Garebian
May 2010

ACKNOWLEDGMENTS

The following institutions, organizations, and individuals proved helpful
to me during my research and completion of this book: Billy Rose
Collection, New York Public Library for the Performing Arts; Jonathan
Hiam at the New York Public Library for the Performing Arts; the late
Patricia Zipprodt for correspondence relating to her costume designs for
the two Hal Prince productions; John Kander for his sympathetic ear and
cooperation; Hal Prince for his generous permission to quote from his
memoir and private papers; the Performing Arts division of the Toronto
Public Library; Antoni Cimolino (general director), Anita Gaffney
(administrative director), and Ellen Charendoff (archives coordinator)
of the Stratford Shakespeare Festival of Canada; Amanda Dehnert for an
interview about her Stratford version; Bruce Dow; Ron Mandelbaum and
Photofest, Inc. for their time, efficiency, and eager cooperation in the
matter of archival photographs; Professor Stacy Wolf for her encourage-
ment of my writing; Leslie Watkins for copyediting the manuscript; Norm
Hirschy, my editor at Oxford University Press, and Liz Smith, Production
Editor, for guiding this book to completion.

CONTENTS

THE

MAKING

OF

CABARET

SECOND EDITION

CHAPTER I

SALLY BOWLES AND BERLIN

IT SEEMED AS IF NOBODY SERIOUSLY BELIEVED THAT CHRISTOPHER
Isherwood's semiautobiographical Berlin stories or John van Druten's
stage adaptation of the "Sally Bowles" story could be made into a
Broadway musical. Isherwood's *Goodbye to Berlin*, published in 1939, was
a loosely connected sequence of diary entries and sketches of some of
his experiences in Berlin before Hitler's rise to power. It took him
almost four decades to reveal (in *Christopher and His Kind*) that he had
gone to Berlin for homosexual fulfillment. Feeling inhibited in England
because he could not relax sexually with boys of his own class or nation,
he went to Berlin, where it was easy "to be infatuated" by such figures as
"Bubi" (Baby), a pretty-faced, blue-eyed, blond beauty with a hard,
almost hairless, muscular body (Isherwood 1976: 10–11). Isherwood
frequented the Cosy Corner in a working-class district where small
clubs catered to rough clients and where many gays felt more comfortable than in high-class bars of the West End. He also came to know
Magnus Hirschfeld, sex researcher, expert on sexual deviancy, and tire-
less opponent of Paragraph 175—the German law that forbade sex between men. The pornographic and erotic fantasy pictures drawn by
Hirschfeld's patients at his Institute for Sexual Science (Institut fur
Sexualwissenschaft) awed Isherwood, as did its museum of whips,
chains, and torture instruments "designed for the practitioners of plea-
sure-pain; high-heeled, intricately decorated boots for the fetishist;
lacey female undies which had been worn by ferociously masculine
Prussian officers beneath their uniforms" (19).

What remained with him from those early years, after he had burned some of the diaries to save himself and others from embarrassment and legal sanctions, were an almost hallucinatory sense of the reality and unreality of Berlin and the fictional figure of Sally Bowles and, beside her, "like a reproachful elder sister," the real Jean Ross, on whom Isherwood had based Sally and who remained his friend (in a "brother and sister" relationship) until her death in England in 1973 (Isherwood 1976: 51). *Goodbye to Berlin* portrays the soul sickness afflicting an entire society while telling four stories and presenting two diaries written in a deft prose style that avoids ideology. The material is concomitantly political and psychological, fusing (an often decadent) sexuality with insights into the flawed human spirit. Despite the documentary tone of much of the writing, the book uses a "dummy" persona ("Christopher Isherwood" being "a convenient ventriloquist's dummy, nothing more"—Isherwood 1939: preface) who expresses the moral and political implications of textured realities. But what results ultimately, as various characters cross over from piece to piece and as a narrow chord of time binds the pieces together, is a seriocomic and chilling sense of unreality, a sort of

Christopher Isherwood,
1955 (Photofest)

phantasmagoria of what is remembered about events that occurred sometimes so quietly, so swiftly as to have become virtually incredible in retrospect.

This interplay of reality and unreality, as unsettling as a nervous dream, begins in the opening piece ("A Berlin Diary: Autumn 1930") with a scrupulous description of decor that suggests a tarnished, degenerate way of life. The scenic interior, consisting of a small room smelling of "incense and stale buns," a tall, tiled stove looking "like an altar," a washstand built almost "like a Gothic shrine," and a favorite chair suggesting "a bishop's throne" (Isherwood 1939: 14), evokes the sense of something abnormally unreal. The big-bosomed, shapeless landlady, always peeping, spying, poking about, and her old lodgers—Bobby, "a pale, worried-looking, smartly-dressed young man who wears a hair-net," Fräulein Kost, a florid blond prostitute with "large silly blue eyes," and Fräulein Mayr, a music hall performer who is aggressively anti-Semitic—contrast with the rich Germans in a millionaire's slum, for whom the political situation is quite unreal (21).

The rest of the book intensifies the dialectic of reality and unreality in notes that are darker and more disturbing than Sally Bowles's colorful caprices. "On Ruegen Island" is an interesting summer portrait of a tense triangular and homoerotic relationship between Christopher and a group of "beautiful blond boys who are principally interested in body-building" (Garber 1995: 487) while "The Nowaks," which documents life in a slum tenement, evokes a depressing feeling of grinding poverty and dehumanization. "The Landauers" provides flashes of insight into neurosis and describes a sour political climate that, despite the very evident tyranny, is "a little unreal" and which prompts victims to lose touch with existence. In short, this section is a "hallucination of the non-existence" of people, such as the prosperous but besieged Landauers (Isherwood 1939: 275–76). The final piece, "A Berlin Diary (Winter 1932–33)," has a depressing political moral: people can be made to believe in anybody or anything, as shown when Hitler becomes master of the city and as Isherwood finds the reality of his past experiences receding from him.

It was the Sally Bowles section, however, that fascinated most readers. The Sally of the novella is an English girl, an aspiring actress who sings at a club called the Lady Windermere, "an arty 'informal' bar, just off the Tauentzienstrasse," named after a character in an Oscar Wilde comedy of manners (*Lady Windermere's Fan*) but trying to resemble Montparnasse (48), with girls doing classical figure tableaux behind gauze, a large dance hall with telephones on the tables, an orchestra in Bavarian costume whooping, drinking, and perspiring beer, and couples dancing "with hands on each other's hips, yelling in each other's faces, streaming with sweat" (65). Sally has a deep, husky voice and sings badly, "without any expression, her hands hanging down at her sides." Yet "her performance is, in its own way, effective because of her startling appearance and her air of not caring a curse" what people think about her (49). Sally had come to Berlin with a girlfriend (Diana), an actress older than her and "the most marvellous gold-digger you can imagine," who had been there before and believed they would both get work with the UFA (International Center for Culture and Ecology) that oversaw movie palaces in Weimar Berlin. Sally receives a small allowance from her wealthy parents at home, but her mother threatens to cut it off unless she returns soon. Consequently, Sally is willing to do anything to make money and get rich. Neurotically restless, she has a string of lovers, including the German Klaus (by whom she gets pregnant but then has an abortion) and the wealthy American Clive. Sally believes she is "a sort of Ideal Woman...who can take men away from their wives" but can never keep anyone for long. She remarks of herself: "I'm the type which every man imagines he wants, until he gets me; and then he finds he doesn't really, after all" (84–85). Their initial amusement with each other eventually palls, especially after she accuses him of being a dilettante without energy or ambition. Christopher confesses to feeling jealous about her success with men and writes at the end that his novella is a tribute to her (121).

But the Sally of fiction is not fully Jean Ross. The latter, raised in luxury in Egypt, was the daughter of a Scots cotton merchant, had "a long, thin handsome face, aristocratic nose, glossy dark hair, large brown eyes," and was "more essentially British than Sally; she grumbled like a true Englishwoman, with her grin-and-bear-it grin. And she was tougher" (Isherwood 1976: 52). She never seemed sentimental or felt sorry for herself, and, like Sally, she boasted continually of her lovers. She sang occasionally in a nightclub and shared lodgings with Isherwood for a while in Fräulein Meta Thurau's flat in Nollendorfstrasse 17. After Berlin, Ross returned to England, joined the Communist Party, and had a daughter out of wedlock with Claud Cockburn, whom she never married. Her daughter, Sarah, later became a crime novelist writing under the name Sarah Caudwell. Isherwood transformed Jean into Sally, giving her a surname taken from Paul Bowles, an American composer and writer best known for his novel *The Sheltering Sky*, later turned into a movie by Bernardo Bertolucci. Isherwood had met Bowles fleetingly in Berlin in 1949 but only became his friend years later. Ross and Isherwood enjoyed each other's company, but both were selfish and often quarrelsome. Jean, unlike Sally, never tried to seduce Christopher, though they did sleep together once, when their flat was overfilled with friends (York 1991: 236).

The story of Sally Bowles fascinated a number of readers, including Speed Lamkin, a gay American novelist and playwright whose only previous play of note (*Comes a Day*) had enjoyed a short run on Broadway in 1958. Isherwood's friend, he decided to adapt Isherwood's novella in collaboration with Gus Field, a young, self-assertive, self-glorifying Jewish screenwriter whom Isherwood had probably met when both were working at MGM. Their script outline (titled *Sally Bowles*) was thin. In the first scene, their "Christopher" is discovered in his Berlin room finding it impossible to write because of the loud noise coming from a party next door. Sally enters as the party giver and next door neighbor, and she asks for a loan of glasses. He is charmed by her, as Sally claims that their rooms are really two halves of one room and suggests that if the flimsy partition wall were torn down there would be more room to dance. Sally and her guests volunteer to help. Curtain. The second scene opens with Christopher awaking from a drunken sleep to find the wall down and rubble all about. Sally is in bed on the other side. He is at first horrified, then amused. Sally claims both will be much happier, and he accepts that he is now involved in her life (Isherwood 2000: 266).

Isherwood's close English friends Dodie Smith (playwright, novelist, and former actress) and her manager and husband Alec Beesley disliked this script intensely, objecting that breaking down a wall would be unworkable in actual performance. They contrived a plan. On a visit to John van Druten's ranch in the Coachella Valley of southern California, Alec (by prior arrangement) poked his head out of the swimming pool and asked, "Why not make a play out of Sally Bowles?" then quickly dove down into the water, leaving his wife to go to work on van Druten and convince him to take on the project (284). The friendly and charming van Druten had met Isherwood in New York in 1939, and they forged a friendship based on their shared belief in pacifism, a creed also shared by Alec Beesley. Of Dutch parentage, the English-born van Druten had a law degree but took easily to writing light comedies, making his mark on Broadway with *Voice of the Turtle* (1943), *I Remember Mama* (1944), and *Bell, Book and Candle* (1950). Van Druten quickly produced a first draft, reading it aloud to Isherwood and Walter Starcke (American actor and theater producer) on May 28, 1951. Isherwood was not taken with everything: he disliked the character of Christopher, many of the jokes, the playwright's treatment of the landlady, and most of the speeches about the persecution of Jews. Isherwood made the playwright change the landlady's name because he felt her real-life model, Fräulein Thurau, would be deeply hurt by some of the satire. Van Druten had wanted to give his Christopher a chance to rebuke her and show an awakened conscience. Despite his misgivings, however, and because of friendship, Isherwood accepted this element as well as the fabrication of Christopher's fistfight with Nazis (Isherwood 1976: 102). A more serious problem with this script was its Sally. Van Druten made her humor both cuter and naughtier.

Although lively and radiant at times in its portrait of Sally, the play betrays much of the tone and flavor of its literary source. In its urge to frame the picture of Sally and to convey Isherwood's development as a

John van Druten, ca. 1933 (Photofest)

writer and young man, it invents melodramatic incident and sentimental-
izes its seven characters in a way that is painful to anyone familiar with the
subtle observation and wit of Isherwood's Berlin stories. Where the
original material is set in a variety of slum tenements, sleazy bars, and
extravagant villas, the play is confined to one room in an anti-Semitic
landlady's flat, allowing for a relatively static scrutiny of the characters
rather than the more dynamic view provided by Isherwood's roving dia-
rist's eye. The play does have a comic and dramatic life, but its narrator is
apparently quite content with mere snapshots of figures and incidents,
prompting Walter Kerr's (1951) pun "Me no Leica." Isherwood himself
recorded in his diary for November 8, 1951: "This isn't my own child. But
it certainly is a milestone" (Isherwood 1996: 441).

   Any adaptation, of course, has the freedom of invention, but van
Druten's play betrays rather more than it actually adapts. To begin with,
Fräulein Schneider (a name change from Schroeder) does retain her big
bosom, but where Isherwood's Schroeder has a ladylike distaste for
modern sexual mores, her stage counterpart is openly vulgar and delights
in the bawdy: "I sit at my window in my fur coat and call out, 'Komm,
Susser.' Komm to the third floor. And then I open the coat a little—just
a little—and what do you think I have on underneath? Nothing!" (van
Druten 1952: 12) Schneider is unequivocally anti-Semitic and, so, loses
the cumulative vulnerability that her counterpart has in Isherwood.
Another surprise (and a most unwelcome one) is the appearance of
Mrs. Watson-Courtneidge, an incarnation of Sally's mother but one so
palpably false to her original model as to seem a mere stereotype of a
middle-aged, very sentimental, and conventional English woman in
tweed. In Isherwood's novella, the mother is "an heiress with an estate"
and the wife of a snobbish Lancashire mill owner who does not care "a
damn for anyone" (Isherwood 1939: 55). Easily scandalized and upset,
she is hardly like Mrs. Watson-Courtneidge, who is sentimental to a fault
and, what is worse, appears to have passed on this trait to her bohemian
daughter. This goes absolutely against the grain of Isherwood's Sally, who
plays a very significant role in the life of the narrator for, despite her
eccentric dress and manner (a small cape over her shoulders, silk dress,
little cap stuck jauntily on one side of her head, emerald green fingernails, long, thin face powdered dead white) (Isherwood 1939: 45), she is
not simply an impetuous practitioner of free love, but a foil for the narrator's own reality. Able to separate herself from the politics and death
around her, she forfeits "all kinship with ninety-nine per cent of the

population of the world, with the men and women who earn their living, who insure their lives, who are anxious about the future of their children" (82–83). Sally casts a spell of unreality on Isherwood, which deepens his feelings of being lost existentially. (Interestingly, Isherwood later explained that Sally—like his Otto Nowak and Mr. Norris—was "lost" in the sense of being doomed or being a moral outcast.) It is through her lascivious alliances that he meets Klaus and Clive, two men who first charm and then disappoint Sally and him. Sally comes to see herself as "a sort of Ideal Woman," the type "who can take men away from their wives," but who can "never keep anybody for long" (84–85). This self-idealization is, of course, sadly unfulfilling.

Isherwood's Sally increases the flux and unreality in the novella by her own inconstancy. She becomes pregnant, decides on an abortion, suddenly breaks off communication with Isherwood, and then is found sharing a flat with stingy Gerda in an artists' colony. As she continues to fall capriciously in love with some of the most unreliable of men, she provokes Isherwood's anomalous love and hate, loyalty and denunciation. In a scene that bristles with psychological tension, she touches a raw nerve in him, and both of them discover hurtful truths about each other. This scene is missing from van Druten's play, which, to be sure, does not avoid many of Sally's contradictions—her flamboyant champagne moods followed by spasms of conservative dignity—but the deeper, darker notes are not explored.

I Am a Camera is best when it borrows heavily from Isherwood—whole passages of dialogue, for instance, and the characterizations of Fritz Wendel (the gigolo who does not admit to being Jewish), Natalia Landauer (the beautiful Jewish heiress), and Clive (an eccentric American who fails to live up to his promises to Sally of extravagant gifts and world tours)—but even here things go wrong, as when Fritz decides to forcibly seduce Natalia or when Clive proves to be implausibly ignorant about differences between Jews and Nazis. Van Druten is also much too reticent in his suggestions of Nazi barbarism, for he offers only slender evidence: mention of the public funeral for a dead leader and a bruise on the cheek of a Jewish girl, caused by a rock thrown by some of Hitler's hoodlums. Boris Aronson, who designed the stage production (and later *Cabaret*), praised van Druten's style but found the treatment of anti-Semitism superficial. He noted that the playwright/director could spend four days of rehearsal perfecting a cocktail with two eggs (Sally's Prairie Oyster) but could come up with only a Band-Aid for the Jews. In a March 1975 interview, Aronson complained to Garson Kanin: "If you look at it from a social point of view, the whole beginning of Nazis, the beginning of anti-Semitism is not really covered as effectively and as real as, oh, a lot of other things are." Aronson certainly had a point. The writing is sometimes too casual, and van Druten misunderstands Isherwood's method. As his title indicates, he takes the point of photography out of context. Van Druten's Christopher compares himself to a camera that records what it sees: "I am a camera with its shutter open, quite passive, recording, not thinking." In other words (as Isherwood noted in a souvenir program note for the play), "he is collecting mental photographs which he will later develop and fix as stories and novels." Isherwood explains in *Christopher and His Kind*, a memoir written to correct the deliberate falsifications in *Goodbye to Berlin*: "Taken out of context, [the phrase 'I am a camera'] was to label Christopher himself as one of those eternal outsiders who watch the passing parade of life lukewarm-bloodedly, with wistful impotence" (Isherwood 1976: 49). When Isherwood introduces the phrase, it is meant to suggest two things: his narrator's self-consciousness in "playing to the gallery" and a kind of *technical* objectivity. "The camera would record only outward appearances, actions, and spoken words—no thoughts, no feelings, nothing subjective" (50). This kind of storytelling is meant to be a game played with the reader in which the author, by giving the reader all the necessary objective data, "challeng[es] him to interpret it and guess what will happen next." It is "the technique of the classic detective story."

Van Druten, however, admitted to being weak with plot, one of the fundamental elements of a detective story. "I simply cannot think of one. And I have never been a man for messages, either. All I really know about is people. If people can make a play, that is fine," he wrote in an essay for the *New York Times* (and reprinted in the souvenir program). Taking inspiration from Chekhov, Tennessee Williams, and Carson McCullers, he did not mind when people referred to *I Am a Camera* as a "mood play." "My aim was that the whole thing should become one portrait, taken camera-wise, of the life in Berlin in 1930, and of the handful of people selected as its protagonists."

Premiering at Broadway's Empire Theatre on November 28, 1951, the play, under van Druten's own direction, ran for 214 performances. With set and lighting by Boris Aronson and costumes by Ellen Goldsborough, it starred William Prince as Christopher, Olga Fabian as Fräulein Schneider, Martin Brooks as Fritz Wendel, Marian Winters as Natalia Landauer, Edward Andrews as Clive Mortimer, Catherine Willard as Mrs. Watson-Courtneidge, and Julie Harris as Sally Bowles. Divided into two acts spanning almost four months in Berlin in 1930, it was set in a single room in Fräulein Schneider's flat, thereby giving it an unavoidably limited physical environment. Despite its flaws (including a lack of focus and a melodramatic compression of incidents in the final act), the play received generally strong reviews. While the *New Yorker* faulted its tendency to be "a little obvious and immature" and complained that a couple of speeches about racial tolerance, "while incontrovertible, have a florid and editorial quality rather at variance with the mood of the play," John Mason Brown (in *Saturday Review*) praised its small details of anti-Semitism for being "enormously touching." Walter Kerr (writing in the *New York Herald Tribune* of December 9) was an even bigger fan, complimenting the playwright for being "rigorously honest" in not taking sides over Sally Bowles, "a girl of arrogant wantonness, of charming unpredictability, of imminent tragedy." The play asks "for neither sympathy nor contempt" as it merely records "this arresting and disturbing little figure...for a fleeting moment" before closing the shutter as "No conclusions are to be reached, no tears to be shed."

The play won the New York Drama Critics' Circle Award on April 2, 1952, over Mary Chase's *Mrs. McThing*, Joseph Kramm's *The Shrike*, Paul Osborn's *Point of No Return*, Maxwell Anderson's *Barefoot in Athens*, and Truman Capote's *The Grass Harp*. It lost the Pulitzer, however, to *The Shrike*, and there was no doubt that its success was due chiefly to Julie Harris's glittering performance, which wove chameleon colorations into the character of Sally, who (in the words of John Mason Brown) "never stops acting," living as she does "on a diet of self-sustaining lies." Isherwood himself was impressed by the "exquisite ambiguity" of her sex life, her vulnerability and quick flights into "childlike delight or dismay," her stubborn obedience to "the voices of her fantasies," and her untouchability "beyond a certain point." Her costume of black silk sheath with a black tam o'shanter and a flame-colored scarf was "the uniform of her revolt" (declared Isherwood) as she became a sort of "bohemian Joan of Arc, battling to defend her way of life from the bourgeoisie" (Isherwood 1976: 52).

Harris repeated her performance (opposite a miscast Laurence Harvey) in a rather limp 1956 film version directed by Henry Cornelius, who had fled Berlin after the Nazi occupation and then gone on to movie fame in England on account of *Passport to Pimlico* (1949). Almost completely without a Berlin atmosphere of the period, the film opens with a book launch for Sally's *The Lady Goes on Hopping*, surprising not only Christopher

Julie Harris as Sally Bowles in the Broadway stage version of I Am a Camera *(1951)* *(Photofest)*

but the audience as well, for where in either Isherwood or the play is there any indication that Sally has literary talent? Laurence Harvey's handsome Christopher, who explicitly moves the story from the contemplative mood to an active one, appears to be asexual. We never see him make out with a man or a woman. Another flaw is the casting of Shelley Winters as Natalia, for the actress is clearly mismatched to the role, having neither submissive femininity nor Germanic physical attitudes. However, the portrait of Sally remains a vibrant one in the hands of Julie Harris, though English critics faulted her accent, feeling she was cast in a milieu that was quite alien to the real Sally. These critics seemed to approve more of Dorothy Tutin's performance in the London stage version in 1954, delighting in the young actress's husky voice that sounded (said one) like "curdled cooing" and predicting a glorious career for her, especially as she was able to be endearing, passionate, and capable of stirring pathos.

An interesting sidelight is that the play's and the film's portraits of Sally Bowles were considered to be too sensational for contemporary

Julie Harris and Laurence Harvey in the 1955 film version of I Am a Camera *(Distributors Corp. of America, Inc./Photofest)*

audiences. Hard to believe today, the film received an X certificate from the British Board of Censors. As Julie Harris commented later: "The trouble was that people would persist in seeing Sally Bowles as a scarlet woman. Of course, she is no such thing. She is sad, a child-like creature who behaves in an outrageous way because she wants to be noticed." In Britain, the play was considered to be outrageous—which seems ridiculous now. Dorothy Tutin recalls: "People were shocked by [Sally], and we used to get letters saying how disgusted and appalled they were by this blatant immorality on stage. It's a funny image of her. She just thought she was having a marvellous time" ("Bowles Players" 1974: 59).

HAROLD PRINCE

The seminal idea for adapting Isherwood's Berlin stories for the Broadway musical stage was not actually Harold Prince's idea. Sheldon Harnick was probably the first to have at least contemplated the idea for such a musical. Someone had said to him: "You know what would make a wonderful musical? The *Berlin Stories* by Christopher Isherwood." Harnick, the award-winning lyricist of such shows as *Fiorello!*, *She Loves Me*, and *Fiddler on the Roof*, read the book and thought: "It can't be done. Maybe you could make a play out of it, but not a musical" (Guernsey 1985: 135).

Years later—exactly how many is lost in the mists of time and the negligence of archivists—Harold Prince, sensitive to the acute need for a new type of Broadway musical, was eager for a fresh challenge. He knew that turning *I Am a Camera* into a musical had been the ambition of several librettists, but the drafts he had seen of their work appeared to have been motivated by the desire to produce a star vehicle for Gwen Verdon or Tammy Grimes, both considerably beloved by Broadway audiences. Prince was not drawn to these drafts, for he was not interested in the fact of Sally's racy nightclub act. It was only after he and his closest collaborators had found "a reason for telling the story parallel to contemporary problems" in the United States that the project interested him (Nadel 1969: 38).

Prince had long avoided any involvement with old-fashioned musicals or shows without some contemporary resonance. When David Merrick offered him *Hello, Dolly!* (first called *Dolly: A Damned Exasperating Woman*) on the basis of Prince's success with a New York State touring production of *The Matchmaker*, Prince turned him down. He explains in his memoir, *Contradictions* (1974: 99): "I didn't care for the score, particularly the song 'Hello, Dolly!' I couldn't for the life of me see why those waiters were singing how glad they were to have her back where she belonged, when she'd never been there in the first place."

It was abundantly clear that Prince did not fit into any old Broadway mold—neither as a producer nor as a director. His career was refreshingly distinctive: an apprenticeship under legendary director George Abbott, the first tentative efforts at producing (in partnership with Robert E. Griffith) and then directing, collaborations with Stephen Sondheim and Jerome Robbins, a sudden confidence, and a blossoming artistry—and all this with an eye on excitement, significance, innovation. The mediocre was anathema—as was any formula musical: the sort of stuff that bounced along on set-piece songs and dances that did not grow organically from a plot (whenever there was a real plot!) but which allowed for momentary razzle-dazzle and which lingered in short-term memory. No wonder he rejected Sandy Wilson's book, music, and lyrics for the Isherwood musical. David Black, a producer, had commissioned the show and sparked the interest of Julie Andrews, but the star's manager refused to allow Andrews, in high demand after *The Boy Friend* (written by Wilson in a twenties musical style) and *My Fair Lady*, to play such a part as Sally Bowles, and shortly thereafter she was lost anyway to Hollywood's version of *The Sound of Music*.

By November 1963, Wilson had completed about two-thirds of the score, but Black suggested revisions on the book and hired Hugh Wheeler for this purpose. There was also a problem with rights, for these were tied up in the estate of John van Druten. One evening, Wilson was invited to dinner by Prince and was astonished to learn that his host was also working on the same material and having the same problem with rights. Prince was confident that he would win the rights, and Wilson agreed. Prince informed him that he had engaged Joseph Masteroff, his librettist for *She Loves Me*, to do the book but had no one as yet for the music and lyrics. Would Wilson be prepared to play the score for him and Masteroff? Prince gave him complimentary tickets for a matinee of *She Loves Me*, after which Wilson went to an apartment to play his score. Masteroff declared quite candidly that the Wilson sound was far from his notion of what suited the characters of both Sally Bowles and pre–World War II Berlin. As Masteroff divulged in an interview almost two decades later, "there was really nothing wrong with the songs except they all sounded like *The Boy Friend*. The fact that it was 1920s Berlin had led Wilson to do the same thing as he had for 1920s Brighton (or wherever it was)." (Actually, it was the French Riviera.) He agreed with Prince that the show needed a radically different sound: something that evoked the Berlin of Kurt Weill and Lotte Lenya. That was that for Wilson. A few months later, Prince wrote to inform him that he had indeed secured the rights and was proceeding with the show. Black also was out—at least as sole producer—but was to receive a share of the property.

Harold Prince has never sought easy routes to easy hits. As Stephen Sondheim has remarked: "His career is all about forward motion. In fact, Hal doesn't think of what he does as a 'career' because he's always in the middle of it: he's too busy to be interested in an overview" (Hirsch 2005: xv). However, an overview is just what is needed here, if for no other reason than to show how his career is significantly linked to the development of the American musical, in both form and content. Many other Broadway luminaries have shown fertile imagination, extraordinary persistence and vision, courage, and high energy, but Prince surpasses all of them because his career is inseparable from the history of the American musical for the past four decades. That he has won more Tony Awards than any other person is of interest only to statisticians and trivia buffs; much more significant is the fact that his achievements (and missteps) are, according to Sheldon Harnick, notations of "the tremendous changes which have occurred in [a] widely popular but genuinely endangered art form." As we know from his productions of *Cabaret, The Phantom of the Opera, Sweeney Todd,* and *Kiss of the Spider Woman,* Prince has reveled in working on dangerous ground. Foster Hirsch (2005: 1) claims that Prince is "the architect of the 'dark' or 'anti-'musical,' and that he is "a true pioneer, the *auteur* of the modernist concept musical who has expanded a genre's thematic and theatrical possibilities."

Prior to the fifties, few people cared or needed to remember who had directed such shows as *Porgy and Bess, Lady, Be Good, George White's Scandals,* the original *Show Boat, Oh, Kay!, Funny Face, No, No, Nanette, Girl Crazy, Anything Goes* and the hundreds of others of that ilk. A director in the genre was merely someone skilled at directing traffic onstage, getting up the key songs and dances, and moving the plot (often terrible) along. According to Prince, "Joshua Logan led the way to the modern style in 1949, when he directed *South Pacific* without any breaks between scenes. He was the innovator of continuous action." Prince has evidently forgotten *Allegro* (1947), where Oscar Hammerstein II suggested that designer Jo Mielziner use a serpentine curtain allowing for continuous action, but the essential point is true: other directors (such as Rouben Mamoulian and George Abbott) did affect the look, texture, and pace of musicals, just as choreographers (such as George Balanchine and Agnes de Mille) turned stage dancing into stylized commentary on a show's characters and situations. But it was Logan who made it virtually primitive to do musicals without an organic structure. He made the idea of an "integrated musical" an exciting development in the genre. However, Logan was merely a precursor of Prince, who strengthened the notion of the "concept musical" and who, in the course of a long, rich career, has successfully managed to mediate between celebration and significance— that is, his productions never abandon the performance impulse even as they refuse to be superficial or to dilute the serious or disturbing elements that push the form into new thematic territory.

Harold Smith Prince was born in New York City on January 30, 1928, to (what he himself calls) "privileged, upper-middle lower rich-class" Jewish parents of German stock whose families had settled there soon after the Civil War. He was raised by his kind stepfather (because his own father, who lived to a ripe old age, rarely saw him). This stepfather was a Wall Street stockbroker, who possibly passed on his business acumen to him. Prince's mother, who was an avid theatergoer, probably fostered his enthusiasm for the stage. "Saturday matinees were part of a New York Jewish child's intellectual upbringing," Prince claimed in *Contradictions*, and he spent them in the orchestra with his parents or up in the top balcony by himself or with a school friend marveling at twenty-one-year-old Orson Welles in *Julius Caesar*, Burgess Meredith in *Winterset*, Tallulah Bankhead in *The Little Foxes* (before she became a camp icon), and Joseph Schildkraut and Eva Le Gallienne together in *Uncle Harry*. He wasn't as interested in musicals, and by the time he got to the University of Pennsylvania at age sixteen, he wasn't interested in them at all.

At university he formed a campus radio station and wrote weekly adaptations of plays, pirating everything from Eugene O'Neill, Clifford Odets, Maxwell Anderson, et cetera, and he would direct these and occasionally act in them as well. He was not a drama major simply because there was no such thing at the time, and, anyway, he didn't believe that college drama programs could provide practical experience for a professional career. He finished his liberal arts education at nineteen, avoiding summer stock because he did not believe in that apprenticeship system. Lazy about actively looking for work, he wrote plays that he thought would "make the rounds." One of his plays, *A Perfect Scream*, a murder mystery with dark comic overtones, reached the head of the script department at ABC-TV who then sent Prince for an interview with the George Abbott office.

Abbott was planning a small experimental TV unit, and Prince offered to work "on spec" for nothing. Two weeks later, however, he was put on the payroll at $25 a week, remaining at that salary for six months. Abbott proved to be a good luck charm because he recommended Prince as production stage manager to Robert Griffith on a revue called *Touch and Go* written by Jean and Walter Kerr, which opened on Broadway in October 1949 and ran for 176 performances. Things began to move quickly for Prince. He was hired as stage manager for *Tickets, Please* (1950), starring Paul and Grace Hartman. By the end of its run, the Hartmans optioned Prince's comedy-murder mystery, *A Perfect Scream*, written in collaboration with Ted Luce, though when their marriage fell apart, so did any chance of the play being produced. The Korean War interrupted Prince's showbiz career. He spent two years in Germany assigned to an antiaircraft artillery battalion, but after discharge he landed a job as stage manager of the musical *Wonderful Town* (1953), which brought him into contact with Betty Comden and Adolph Green as well as Leonard Bernstein and Jerome Robbins. A significant network of artistic relationships was thus established, but even more important was the fact that Prince had an invaluable opportunity to learn from George Abbott how a successful musical was created. As director, Abbott demanded precise timing and honest motivation for every action onstage. Prince once explained to Mark Steyn that Abbott did not think in terms of concept but in terms of the "arc" or "trajectory" of a show. Even when he directed farce, there was "never a dishonest moment on the stage" because characters were always consistent with their character. If someone slammed a door, it was always for a specific reason (Steyn 1997: 315). Prince recognized that Abbott never confused tempo with speed. His shows were honest and energetic— not in the phony manner of people running around wildly in circles. For Abbott, emotional reality was the basis of truth in the theater. Respectful of the artistry of all his collaborators, Abbott was nevertheless an autocrat who enjoyed taking total control of a play. Yet he was a benevolent auto-crat with a dry wit, spontaneous one-liners, and gnomic insights that were offered in swift, sturdy sentences—or what Prince calls the "Abbott shorthand."

This is not the place to repeat all of Prince's theater credits, but suf-fice it to say that prior to his success as director he triumphed as co-producer (with Griffith) and producer with such shows as *The Pajama Game* (1954), *Damn Yankees* (1955), *New Girl in Town* (1957), *West Side Story* (1957), *A Funny Thing Happened on the Way to the Forum* (1962), and *Fiddler on the Roof* (1964). Directed by Jerome Robbins, *Fiddler* marked a massive break from the Abbott musical tradition in leading Prince deeper into what has come to be known as the "concept" musical—that is, a show whose emphasis is on the pictorial and the theatrical and a musical that is governed by a central metaphor or statement rather than by the narra-tive itself. Of course, the term "concept musical" has been tossed around so carelessly and has been used so loosely that it has become a cliché. As Stephen Banfield (1993: 147) explains, it tends towards two mean-ings: "It has primarily to do with the idea of a director's theatre...and since director's theatre is a condition of our time it is little more than a truism as applied to modern productions, implying a kind of Wagnerian *Gesamtkunstwerk* with music, lyrics, book, set, choreography, lighting, costumes, and direction contributing to an integrated thematic whole whose elements are beholden to each other for style and content rather than to expectations based on their separate or corporate conventions." Bruce D. McClung (2007: 164) also finds two kinds of "concept musical": the first where "the director-author decides what the work is to be about and attempts to have it reflected in all aspects of the production" (as in *Fiddler On The Roof* where the concept is distilled in the figure of the fiddler on the roof); and the second where linear plot is abandoned "in favour of a series of vignettes unified by theme" (as in *Company* (1970) that is a sequence of snapshots, ideas, questions, and vignettes built around characters' isolation or disconnections from others and the world). Examples abound, especially in the work of Sondheim and Prince (*Company, Pacific Overtures, Assassins*), but there are ample other examples, such as *Hair, A Chorus Line, Cats, Chess*, though proper due should be paid to even earlier forerunners, such as Weill's *Love Life* and *Lady in the Dark*.

Fiddler on the Roof was the second show that Robbins directed for Prince, and its innovative movement, production concept, and musical acting style inspired Prince to do his own experiments, beginning with *Cabaret*. As he states in Foster Hirsch's book, Robbins taught him to look at musical theater in a different way, for the form was open to any influence, even to the point of borrowing from nonmusical theater. Not being a choreographer himself, Prince feared that by using dance more he would be less in control as a director, but Robbins showed him a new way of "integrating music as well as the possibility of attempting serious subject matter" (Hirsch 2005: 35).

Fiddler ran on Broadway for 3,242 performances—setting a record that was broken only many years later by *A Chorus Line*—and was sold to United Artists for $2 million, less than was paid for *My Fair Lady* or *Man of La Mancha* or *Mame*, though a twenty-five percent share of the distributor's gross after recouping costs more than compensated for this. Prince received many offers to direct musicals, but the projects—*Baker Street* (1965; director), *Flora, the Red Menace* (1965, producer), and *It's a Bird...It's a Plane...It's Superman* (1966, producer, director)—flopped at the box office. A quick look at the musicals staged in the early sixties shows a waning of an era in that the 1960–61 season was marked by a decrease in the number of new offerings (Richards 1976: ix). Large-scale musicals exploited various legends. *The Unsinkable Molly Brown* was lavishly mounted, with scenes about the ill-fated *Titanic*, as it romanticized a fascinating woman who became a legend in her own lifetime. Lerner and Loewe's *Camelot* drew on the Arthurian legend in a gorgeous mixture of realism and fantasy, and it exploited the charisma of both Richard Burton and Julie Andrews (who had become a star with *My Fair Lady*). Even *Do Re Mi* capitalized on legends—in this case, the great clowns Phil Silvers and Nancy Walker—but it did make a sustained attempt at dealing with greed and fraud (a jukebox scam) in the contemporary scene. In so doing, it was a precursor to what was to come the next season, when almost all the musicals "were steadfastly set in the present day; none looked back to the America of a half-century or so before" (Bordman 1978: 621). Romance and sentimentality were downplayed or presented with an unhappy edge—as in *Subways Are for Sleeping*, which portrayed two rocky love affairs. *How to Succeed in Business* typified the modern note of cynicism, being a satire (ironically charming) on double-dealing in the corporate world. The sole exception to the general trend was *A Funny Thing Happened on the Way to the Forum*, which harkened back to Plautus but by way of the Marx Brothers zaniness "without the Marx Brothers" (627).

The 1963–64 season was dominated by musical adaptations of popular plays. *110 in the Shade* came from *The Rainmaker*, with N. Richard Nash adapting his own play for lyricist Tom Jones and composer Harvey Schmidt. *The Girl Who Came to Supper* was a feeble musical version of Terence Rattigan's *The Sleeping Prince*, and it showed that Noël Coward was no help when it came to adapting someone else's stage play. Coward left his own *Blithe Spirit* alone but was delighted to find it turned into the critically acclaimed *High Spirits*, thanks to the stylishly inspired madness of Bea Lillie, who played Madame Arcati and who sent up the role as much as she did the curtain calls. The biggest hits that season were *Hello, Dolly!* and *Funny Girl*, the first being a colorful, exuberant adaptation of Thornton Wilder's *The Matchmaker*, the second a musical biography of stage legend Fanny Brice. Both productions consolidated their stars' legends as well—Carol Channing's in the first case and Barbra Streisand's in the second—glorifying the status of the diva musical as a popular form. Even the next season evidenced large debts to literature. *Fiddler on the Roof* grew out of Sholem Aleichem, *Golden Boy* was a descendant of Clifford Odets's 1938 hit play, and *Do I Hear a Waltz?* was a reworking by Arthur Laurents of his own successful play *The Time of the Cuckoo*. But by now the sociology of the era was having a huge impact on Broadway in general and the musical in particular.

As Carol Ilson (1989) reports, in the midsixties the Broadway musical appeared to be entering a period of "decreased creativity," caused in large measure by bloody international strife and turbulent national unrest. The Vietnam conflict kept escalating, and in the United States riots flared across cities and even on campuses. Economic instability did not help matters, as inflation kept rising and theater producers sought to cut costs by producing smaller shows with basic unit sets. Popular taste, of course, kept changing, especially because of new trends in music and film. It was an era of radical dissent, and popular culture reflected this metamorphosis. As Gerald Bordman writes in *American Musical Theatre*, "Beset by the collapse of so much order and decorum," the Broadway musical also "fell apart." Bordman paints a depressing picture of "aging playhouses" clustered together in "an area fast growing sleazy and occasionally dangerous." New York's Times Square was soiled by honky-tonk bars and pornography shops. Derelicts, prostitutes, and muggers "pestered and sometimes molested playgoers," and nightclubs dwindled, as did new musical work (Bordman 1978: 642). Occasional attempts at fresh, invigorating musical theater were ruined by unmelodic scores, scatalogical language, and a virtual formlessness; the total Broadway musical picture was one of exhaustion and waywardness.

The three most eagerly awaited new musicals prior to 1966 were *On a Clear Day You Can See Forever, Man of La Mancha*, and *Mame*. Alan Jay Lerner and Richard Rodgers collaborated on *Clear Day*, giving it literate dialogue, an imaginative story, and a theatrically effective score (courtesy of Burton Lane), but the libretto was a mess, and the theme of extrasensory perception was confusing to audiences who had to deal with a heroine who could predict the future as well as recall the past. Dipping into Cervantes, *Man of La Mancha* was, as Bordman (1978: 645) puts it, "a hard-driving, often rough-talking, frequently compassionate lyric drama" that "made few concessions to theatregoers, playing out its entire story in one basic set and without intermission." It certainly was more ambitious and less artistically compromising than Jerry Herman's *Mame*—a show that seemed derivative of Patrick Dennis's celebrated novel and the Hollywood film with Rosalind Russell but had Angela Lansbury and Bea Arthur as well as a colorful gaiety that appealed to audiences. *Mame* was another diva musical, but it showed, almost by default, that the role of the director was becoming increasingly important. Figures such as Tom O'Horgan, Gower Champion, and Bob Fosse realized that by assuming full creative control they could shape and save

many a musical. Conceptual musicals were already part of Broadway history, but they were still the exception rather than the rule, and the time
was ripe for assimilating every aspect of a work within an overall vision.
There would always be audiences who would never abandon conventional musicals, such as *Skyscraper, Mame,* or *I Do! I Do!,* and there would
always be those for whom the apex of innovation was found in such shows
as *The Apple Tree, Ilya Darling,* or *Hallelujah, Baby!* The parade of mediocrity was thereby safely functional, but afficionados hungered for new
works that, at least, mediated between the daring and the derivative.

Never one to curse misfortune or dwell long on failure, Harold Prince
was impatient to chart new courses as director of musicals. Sensitive to
the social, political, and cultural unrest of his time, he was not interested
in old-fashioned curios, even if these were replications of tried-and-true
formulae. He wanted new shapes, sounds, and textures—works that
would boldly assert their own forms while remaining rooted in a modern
sensibility. Unlike most of his colleagues, he was not obsessed with the
idea of creating hits; rather, he was charged by a vision of theater as a
world for nurturing talent. This accounted for his opposition to the star
system and for his experiments (as yet guarded) with expressionism
through mime, multisectioned sets, animated puppets, and mixed media.
True, his work was not consistent, caught as it was between a world of
intellect and one of spectacle and trivia, but it presaged the kind of artistry that might revolutionize American musical theater.

CHAPTER 2

PRINCE OF BROADWAY

THE DISTORTIONS OF THE STAGE AND FILM SALLY BOWLES DID NOT concern Harold Prince when he settled on Christopher Isherwood's material for a Broadway musical. Indeed, Sally was really of secondary importance to him, for what gripped his interest was the sociopolitical climate of Berlin in the thirties, the sort of degenerate ethos that provoked a challenging question to people of conscience. "What would you do?" the material seemed to ask. Prince wanted to exploit the intriguing interplay between reality and unreality (or hallucination) more than he wanted to fashion a musical about Sally or the introverted narrator. Even the politics of Germany would have to find a place within the plot without ever displacing the central theme about modes of survival in an evil, decadent society. Prince received Joe Masteroff's first draft of the libretto in the summer of 1963, when the struggle for civil rights for black Americans was heating up as a result of nonviolent but bold demonstrations being held in the Deep South.

As Masteroff recalls in *Broadway Song & Story,* "there were thousands of meetings," with "outline after outline" along the way and notes from Prince to him and vice versa as well as lyrics of songs long forgotten by everyone except John Kander, Fred Ebb, and him. "The show had a very, very gradual metamorphosis. Not a painful one, I think. But it certainly did change as we went along." Prince used meetings not to be officious, but because this was his mode of collaboration. As Kander put it, the abundance of meetings resulted in everyone "all doing the same show. It rarely happens with a Hal Prince show that you get out of town and the

Shown from left: Robert E. Griffith and Harold Prince (Photofest)

choreographer is doing one piece and the song writers are doing another and the playwright is doing another" (Guernsey 1985: 136).

Masteroff did a full first act and an outline of the second, but he found it difficult to complete a libretto without a firm sense of the sound for the show. Born in Philadelphia, on December 11, 1919, he had a degree in journalism from Temple University, where he had acted with the drama group, The Templayers, and had been editor of the student publication, *The Owl.* While at Temple he wrote *Brain Child,* which was performed in New York by a group called Six and Co. Next came a flurry of diverse experiences. Between 1942 and 1946 he served in the Air Force and was first stationed in Florida before being sent to England for two years. When he returned to Florida in 1947, he managed one of the chain movie theaters in Miami Beach. Eventually he served as assistant editor of *The Exhibitor,* a trade publication for motion picture exhibitors, and then in 1948 went to New York, where he wrote about a dozen plays and studied playwriting for two years (under the G.I. Bill) at the American Theatre Wing. His mentor was Robert Anderson, author of *Tea and Sympathy,* but Masteroff also worked as Howard Lindsay's assistant on *The*

Prescott Proposals, starring Katharine Cornell. In due course, he won a John Golden Fellowship and the New York Theatre Club citation as the most promising playwright of 1956–57. His next notable achievement was *The Warm Peninsula*, set in Florida, which was produced in 1958 and which toured nationally before opening on Broadway in 1959 with Julie Harris in the lead and with June Havoc, Farley Granger, and Larry Hagwood lending support. But it was not until he scripted the musical *She Loves Me*, his first collaboration with Prince, that his career really began to hit its stride, so it was natural that when Prince invited him to write a libretto for the show that was to become *Cabaret*, he eagerly accepted.

There were many obstacles. Like Prince, Masteroff thought van Druten's play was very thin: "I'm one of the few people old enough to have seen it when Julie Harris first did it on Broadway. She was incredible. She made the play work. But I don't think it would have been very much without her." The narrator, who was supposed to frame the plot somehow, was "a cipher" without real character. "When writing the musical, we felt we had to create some sort of a guy. I was more comfortable writing an American than an Englishman, so Christopher Isherwood was turned into an American named Clifford Bradshaw" (Guernsey 1985: 138).

Shown in rehearsal for The Warm Peninsula (1959), from left: actress Julie Harris, producer Manning Gurian, playwright Joe Masteroff (Photofest)

The first problem with that role was that it was passive. (Frank Marcus relates in *Plays & Players* of being told that one of the New York producers dismissed "Herr Issyvoo" with the remark: "We gotta put balls on the guy. If he shacks up with the girl, he's gotta sleep with her.") The second difficulty was that the role disguised Isherwood's homosexuality and so missed the homoeroticism of the young man. In van Druten's play, Christopher is heterosexual. In *Goodbye to Berlin* he is a disguised homosexual and "relatively sexless" (Garber 1995: 487), but in *Christopher and His Kind*, Isherwood drops the fictive mask and exposes his own literary and psychosexual subterfuge without seeking sympathy. It is not that Christopher leaves no clues in the earlier book; it is just that he is more reticent. As Marjorie Garber has pointed out, Isherwood (in a 1975 interview) acknowledged that he had created a problem for subsequent stage and screen adapters of his work. Christopher could not afford to display his homosexuality openly in that era because the topic would have overshadowed the other stories he was telling: "If I had made the 'I' a homosexual, especially in those days, I would have made him overly-remarkable, and he'd have gotten in the way of the other characters." Consequently, he downplayed some of the details of his relationship with Jean Ross: "how, at one time [when] I had no money, we actually shared our room and slept in the same bed, and, of course, the relations between my boy friends and her!" (Stoop 1975: 62). Jean knew of Christopher's "sexmates" but did not try to share them, though Christopher "wouldn't have really minded" (Isherwood 1976: 63). As Christopher tells it, he and Sally Bowles are a couple in *Goodbye to Berlin*—however "asexual" they are in his narrative. "Their lovers and pickups are interruptions—often welcome, highly courted interruptions, but interruptions nonetheless" (Garber 1995: 488–89).

There is a subtle irony in Christopher's disguised homosexuality because, as Marjorie Garber explains, Christopher is not sexually interested in Sally and, actually, is more her sexual competitor. When he notes her lack of success at the Lady Windermere in making advances toward an elderly gentleman who would obviously prefer the barman, Christopher is not "merely appreciative or amused by Sally's adventuring with men." He is "subtly competitive," though he himself is not angling for that gentleman's attention (Garber 1995: 489). It would take a long time for Christopher to come out in public, and even then, it would be on film and after a name change to Brian Roberts.

Of course in the sixties Broadway was hardly ready for such a candid sexual persona, and as Masteroff transformed the character into an

American, there was a different sensibility to be shaped and projected at audiences for whom "the gay life" was only the title of a droll turn-of-the-century American musical comedy set in Vienna and whose tolerance for sexuality was apparently limited to such material as *Tenderloin, Camelot, The Girl Who Came to Supper,* and *Pousse-Café.* Masteroff did not find an effective solution for these problems. Nor did he manage to create a Sally Bowles who was true to her real-life counterpart, Jean Ross, or to the demands of an interestingly full-fledged character who, to complicate matters, had to have a significant musical role even though she was not supposed to be genuinely talented musically. Masteroff knew that what drew Prince to Isherwood's Berlin was (in Prince's words) "the parallel between the spiritual bankruptcy of Germany in the 1920s and [the United States] in the 1960s." True, there was no real Nazi power in America in the sixties, but the country had the Ku Klux Klan, and where Germany had its gay bars and clubs where drugs and sex could be negotiated from table to table, each conveniently equipped with telephone, America discovered that cocaine, marijuana, and LSD were just around the corner and that free love was almost as prevalent as rock'n' roll. The Berlin of the twenties and thirties and the United States of the sixties were both riddled by the deepest social and political problems, often based on race and the arrogance of power. Berlin seethed with unemployment, malnutrition, stock market panic, hatred of the Versailles Treaty, and anti-Semitism. In the United States, Medgar Evers was murdered in 1963, and (as Scott Miller chronicles) "despite the civil rights bill that Congress passed in 1964, race riots were happening all over the country—in Harlem in July 1964, in Watts (Los Angeles) in August 1965, in Cleveland and Chicago in July 1966, as well as in Atlanta and other cities. Malcolm X was assassinated in February 1965. Martin Luther King Jr.'s first march from Selma to Montgomery, Alabama, took place in March 1965. Antiwar demonstrations began on the campus of the University of California–Berkeley in 1964, and continued throughout the sixties across the country" (Miller 1996: 30).

With such stirrings at home, there was little wonder that Prince went so far as to have one draft of the show end with film on the march on Selma and the riots at Central High in Little Rock, Arkansas. Of course, good moral and social intentions do not necessarily make for sound art, and Prince realized that the material was intrusive in this musical, its libretto scrupulously avoiding propaganda, though it never quite resolves its own schizophrenia caused by an uncertainty of how to fuse a core seriousness with musical formulae. The libretto evolved over many revisions and drafts. The Harold Prince Collection at The New York Public Library for the Performing Arts at Lincoln Center contains three typewritten versions of Masteroff's script: the second version (5/19/66), the rehearsal version (8/18/66), and the final version (11/20/66). Some of the differences are striking. The earliest of the three versions has three acts and makes explicit use of sociopolitical incidents and circumstances. For instance, act 2, scene 1 shows the Emcee appearing on the forestage with a group of less than prosperous Berliners, giving rise to the song "A Mark in Your Pocket," the moral of which is that money talks in every crucial situation in life. Four scenes later, the Emcee is in drag as one of two Chinese girls standing in front of a radio microphone of 1930 vintage sings "Herman, the German," a satiric song that celebrates a small, fat, ruddy-cheeked, healthy, and incredibly wealthy man. Ernst Ludwig's Nazi connection is brought sharply into focus in scene 7 of the second act when Cliff questions him about his swastika armband. Ernst replies that he kept silent about it because he did not want the American to know his politics. When Fräulein Schneider chimes in that she, too, did not know his politics, Ernst declares: "I am a German. We are both Germans. Someday, Fräulein—we will march side-by-side"—to which she shakes her head in disagreement. The party scene accordingly takes on a completely different mood. Herr Schultz falls asleep after "Meeskite," and Sally sings a ballad to Cliff that shows how their turbulent misunderstandings are unimportant in the final analysis because "It'll All blow over Soon!" The song then turns from her solo into a duet as Cliff responds and then into a trio as Fräulein Schneider adds her voice to the lyric. Fräulein Schneider's role is built up more in act 3, especially as she explains how she survived the war, then revolution, inflation, and maybe even the National Socialists, Communists, fire, and flood! Sally is also given a little more complexity when she sings "I Don't Care Much" and explains to Cliff that she has returned to the club for only one night as a favor to the manager who had begged her to do so after his regular singer fell ill. Cliff, knows she is lying, however, and Sally admits it, explaining that sometimes it is easier to lie a little about one's motives.

The rehearsal version (also in three acts) at first sketches a more charming picture of the Sally–Cliff relationship. In her first Kit Kat number, "Don't Tell Mama" (for which she is costumed like a schoolgirl),

Sally becomes aware of Cliff in the audience and sings to him as if he were the only one there. When Cliff speaks to her, she falls in love with his voice, and as they become roommates, she sings "My Room-mate," indicating that it will be his alibi to use if he is ever asked about their shared accommodations. When Cliff adds his own lyric to the song ("By simply telling adventures that she knows / She's got me writing / A better brand of prose"), their relationship is sealed, and the scene (act 1, scene 7) ends with the two of them quite entranced with each other, looking far more like lovers. The strain of events changes this relationship, especially with Sally's announcement of her pregnancy. Cliff asks Sally how she feels about her pregnancy, but when she turns the question back on him, he sings what sounds very much like an internal monologue: "I don't know myself. / That's right. / I don't know myself. / Not yet!" For her part, Sally discloses her unhappiness over what her parents would say, prompting Cliff to explain that people change. He proceeds to look at himself in a mirror and sing "See that man in the mirror?" Sally claims she can see him changing right before her eyes but that she remains "the same old Sally." She promises to change, too—only not yet! Sally seems satisfied to be divinely decadent, but at the end of the engagement party for Schultz and Fräulein Schneider, when Ernst elicits major frisson, Sally shows a rare recognition of the changing temper of the times when she sings "It's The End of the Party," the final two lines of which are: "What's the feeling I can't ignore? / The end of the party or something more?" This is an ominous rhetorical question. However, her newfound awareness dissolves in act 3, scene 4, where she claims that the Kit Kat Klub is the most unpolitical place in Berlin. Unable or unwilling to give up her career, she is impervious to Cliff's impassioned appeal that they leave the city and go to America. When his blistering honesty about her lack of talent does not affect her decision to stay in Berlin and perform at the club, Cliff knows he has lost her. But Sally is not triumphant. Her "Cabaret" solo is in counterpoint to her isolation. As she moves downstage, the light-curtain comes on behind her and the Kit Kat Klub disappears. Sally is shown standing alone onstage.

There is a downward trajectory for the Sally–Cliff relationship. Two scenes after her Kit Kat solo, Sally enters Cliff's room, exhausted and looking ill. She no longer has her beloved fur coat, and she's obviously given up their relationship. Schultz enters to bid his good-bye, for he is moving to the other side of the Nollendorfplatz in order to make it easier for Fräulein Schneider. After Schultz presents Sally with a bag of Seville oranges as his parting gift, Cliff gives her a ticket to Paris. Sally says she has always hated Paris, and puffing on a cigarette, she claims she will be fine without him but asks him to dedicate his book to her. Her brave front falls away as he leaves. She sits in a chair, looking fixedly at the door as the lights slowly fade. Her final appearance is in the kaleidoscopic finale, when the Emcee presents the main characters of the story as a sort of collage. Sally, in a convent-girl costume, bows to applause as the orchestra plays the introduction to "Don't Tell Mama." However, the song never really begins. It is nothing but an introduction, and the music grows increasingly frantic, and then there's only silence.

The final version reduces the libretto to two acts and a total of twenty scenes (thirteen for act 1). Gone are the Orators who, in the second act in the rehearsal version, appear as expressionist talking silhouettes presenting bald political commentary and burlesque comedy. Gone, too, is the Prostitute desperate for money—a sign of the economic collapse in the country. There are no more battling crowds and no cripple as in the rehearsal version, so the Emcee no longer has to leap into a wheelbarrow or do a frantic, rather insane dance to underline the point about desperate times or an intensifying political madness. Indeed, the libretto is more streamlined and closer to its final printed form. The three-act form—a defiance of the standard Broadway practice of two—was abandoned. Joe Masteroff liked the two-act version: "We thought there were a lot of different things about this show. But when we opened, it didn't work very well in three. It was quite easy to put it into two." Not everyone agreed that the change was for the better; Fred Ebb, for instance, preferred the longer version (Guernsey 1985: 143).

Fundamentally, Masteroff's play is about private worlds set jarringly in conflict against a larger political world bedeviled by social and moral vices. *Cabaret* really has two stories occurring during the rise of Nazism, as reflected in the smoky, noisy, garish cabaret: that of Sally and Cliff and the tragicomedy of Fräulein Schneider and Herr Schultz. Neither of these stories is deep enough to stand on its own, for the characters are largely superficial and the action is frequently telescoped in order to make pithy points about the soul-sickness overtaking Germany.

The year is 1929, and though storm clouds are accumulating outside the cabaret, the Kit Kat Klub pretends that all is beautiful and trouble-free. In this period Germany was experiencing massive unemployment and inflation. Germans felt a huge absence of confidence in the future—

rather like during the early, grim years of the Weimar Republic. Masteroff's libretto fails to expand this contrast between the cabaret world and the world outside, and it is only through external historical evidence that we are able to know the turbulence of German politics. After the elections of 1930, when the Nazis made great gains politically, they engaged in street violence and attacks on Communists, and in September 1931, on Rosh Hoshana, Jewish worshippers were beaten by Nazi youth in West Berlin. Such developments had a negative impact on many cabarets. Nowhere in Masteroff's opening is there any suggestion of the Nazi stronghold on the country, though the all-girl band, the leering Emcee, and the cabaret acts do vibrate with a crackling tension, an audible disquiet, and a simmering anticipation of trouble, not unlike the strange and ugly moods in Leipzig at the premiere of Brecht–Weill's *The Rise and Fall of the City of Mahagonny* or the temper of the times just a year before the Nazis won the second largest bloc of votes in the first presidential election in seven years.

In the second scene, young novelist Clifford Bradshaw enters Berlin by train, hoping to scratch a living by offering English lessons. Here the exposition is brief, almost perfunctory, though ripples of tension are created by the appearance of Ernst, a smuggler, who is saved by Cliff from customs detection. In gratitude, Ernst offers to become Cliff's first official pupil and recommends Fräulein Schneider's rooming house. This is a more personal or intimate welcome than the Emcee's vaudeville performance at the club, but the staging device (whereby the smuggler and the young novelist shake hands as the Emcee crosses downstage) pulls the brief ex-centric scene into the cabaret frame.

The libretto next yields up the bourgeois world of Fräulein Schneider's rooming house, where material comforts (such as cushions, towels, and hot water at least once a week) appeal to Cliff who manages to negotiate a satisfactory rent. Here the emphasis is on genteel comedy, as the various facets of Fräulein Schneider's personality are revealed: her illusion of quality, a touching nostalgia for vanished privilege, a bourgeois hostility to Fräulein Kost's sexual license, and a poignant responsiveness to Schultz's wooing. But just as the crisp sour notes of the background threaten to turn limp in this bourgeois mode, there is a surrealistic device that reabsorbs the plot within the cabaret. As Cliff sets his Remington typewriter on a table and contemplates it gloomily, a female voice and face from the club formulate themselves to the first strain of the "Telephone Song," and once again the show's naturalism dissolves into the cabaret milieu.

This scene, which introduces us to Sally Bowles and her jazz "babies," serves three functions. It reasserts the performatory nature of the show, propels the plot, and underlines the ambience. The scene marks the first direct encounter of the young romantic leads, although Masteroff's dialogue is somewhat stiff. Once again, the emphasis is on tempo and atmosphere rather than on deepening textures of characterization. Cliff has been in Berlin a mere three hours but is already at the club where he has met the capricious English flapper, ushered in the new year (1930), and tasted some of the flavor of German public mores. This is a scene of swift transitions, where caprices and sensations hold sway, for Sally sings jazzily of duplicity as she flirts with Cliff then deftly turns interlocutor before vanishing as the "Telephone Song" becomes the floor show. The number makes sexual dalliance appealing to those patrons who want such thrills. Sex is a commodity for barter, and Sally (who later reveals that she would willingly "sleep" her way to stardom) matches her eccentricity to the degenerate milieu.

The rest of act 1 is organized to lead to a chilling climax, as Sally battens on opportunity, Ernst reveals his Nazi connections, and Schneider and Schultz discover that the bubble of their amour has burst. The foreground is occupied by the two contrasting couples, but these romances link to a larger concern with centering the political evil. The two romances are played out within small rooms in the same house, whereas the larger subject (Nazi evil) is first reflected in the cabaret before growing to envelop other themes. This proliferation is amply marked by the multiplication of lies, character manipulation, plot machination, and emblematic configurations. Nobody remains untouched by mendacity. Even the sentimental Jewish widower and his gentile fiancée are contaminated by lies in the sense that both believe, against all odds, in the myth of love's ability to transcend any depth of despair. Their belief is both touching and ridiculous (especially in the Pineapple song, "It Couldn't Please Me More"), for it is circumscribed by an ugly reality that the two characters prefer not to acknowledge. Cliff's lie is the misinformation he sends home to his parents in Pennsylvania about his situation in Berlin. He badly needs their financial support, and when he allows Sally into his life, he becomes subject to even greater evil temptations. His ambivalence toward Berlin (he finds it tacky and terrible yet lovable) connotes his own moral dichotomy:

he is both artist as solitary figure and artist as compromiser, which probably accounts at this stage for his inability to be anything more than "promising" as a writer.

Sally and Ernst thrive on deception—she more blatantly than he. Sally celebrates the fact that her mother in England does not know her real profession and way of life. In scene 5 she talks her way into making Cliff accept her as a roommate, and in scene 9, after casually divulging that she's pregnant, she pressures him into becoming Ernst's secret agent in a dangerous smuggling operation—all in the name of her being "much too strange and extraordinary." Ernst remains shadowy, though in the final scene of the first act he emerges as a malignant Nazi who causes Fräulein Schneider to break off her engagement to Schultz. It is Ernst who pulls the other guests into a tight circle of ultranationalist fervor at the reprise of "Tomorrow Belongs to Me," as the two couples remain pointedly outside the circle.

With the ill-fated romance of Schneider and Schultz already decided in act 1, the only human suspense is reserved for the Sally–Cliff relationship, although Fräulein Schneider and her mousey Jewish suitor do make significant appearances in the foreshortened second half of the play. But in essence, act 2 does little more than confirm a pessimistic fate for the couple while expanding the significance of the cabaret-as-world metaphor.

There are really no new problems—merely the deepening and widening of old ones, for even though Fräulein Schneider tries as tenderly as she can to soften her breakup from Schultz with the excuse that her eyes are finally opened to a new reality, she capitulates to Nazi harassment. No longer able to share in the simple joy of her beau's gifts of fruit, she cannot even join him in the ballad ("Married") they had once sung in harmony, and she is obviously afraid when a brick comes crashing through a window in his shop. Unlike his middle-aged Juliet, Schultz does not open his eyes to the bare facts; he dismisses the incident as "nothing"—merely the work of "mischievous children" on their way to school (act 2, scene 2, Richards 1976: 450).

While such delusion is too obvious a means for evoking pity for a hapless character, the script develops the sense of growing unreality in Berlin. Sally, for instance, can see nothing beyond her own capricious needs. Though pregnant and in need of cash, she has not lost her yearning to be a star and fails to recognize the evil in the milieu that tantalizes her. She believes that "the Kit Kat Klub is the most *un*political place in Berlin," and she obviously misses what others (such as Cliff) acutely realize about the gathering evil. Even when Fräulein Schneider returns the engagement gift of a fruit bowl and asks "What would you do?" Sally disposes of political and moral ramifications in the whirlwind of her careerism. When Fräulein Schneider catalogs the travails she has so far survived—war, revolution, inflation—and professes regret for the way her life has turned out, Sally can do no more than offer clichés: "It will all work itself out." Then, refusing to heed Cliff's pressing admonition to "wake up!" because "the party in Berlin is *over*!" she refuses to forsake the Kit Kat Klub and accompany him back to America. Instead, she rushes out to the very thing that sums up the ugly reality of Germany and her own unreality as a self-centered, capricious woman totally dedicated to vain baubles (453–54).

In act 2, the drama of Cliff and Sally is sandwiched between cabaret scenes. There might be, as Cliff contends, vomiting in the streets of Berlin, but inside the club, the cabaret continues with ever-increasing political implications. The Emcee's "If You Could See Her" number (with a gorilla in a skirt) is cruelly mocking of the Jewish issue, and its gay waltz rhythm in the dance break exacerbates the contrast between tone and content. It is meant to entertain Kit Kat patrons, who think it's a wonderful parody of forbidden romance between Jews and Aryans, but to the theater audience it is an alarmingly contemptuous Nazi mockery and brings to the fore the limit of the German cabaret's ability to infuse spectacle with racial and political elements. The intimate size of the cabaret stage and the two performers on it accentuate a small-scale spoofing, but this is ironically misleading, for what the Emcee and his partner are really celebrating is unchallenged bigotry. The gorilla reduces the Jew to a disguised animal, in other words a target for Nazi ideology about racial purity. Another aspect of the number is the Emcee's power of seduction, for with his stage presence and innate authority, this *conférencier* is easily able to master his audience. And in this song, which is about perception, preconceptions, and prejudice, the Emcee makes the audience uncomfortable. It is well known that metaphors of sex and power abound in art, and what is especially chilling about "If You Could See Her" is the comic patina applied so casually to a fundamentally sinister exhibition. The number casts a spell on an audience that may be torn between admiration for its cleverness and disgust for its implication.

But it is precisely a spell that the play seeks to cast at the end, one that captivates Sally so thoroughly that she acts desperately gay, but her *carpe diem* tone is at once gaudy and self-defeating, for it cannot save her from the cabaret's power to reduce everything to illusion and delusion. As

Cliff attempts to make her bid good-bye to Berlin and the unreality of her dream of stardom, she battles back with her will to become the star attraction of the sleazy, smoky den of polymorphous seduction. As she runs off to prepare for her dazzling, full-out solo number, Cliff is left to resist the final temptations of Ernst and to pay a violent price for his courage. In the fight he precipitates by punching Ernst, he is beaten unconscious by two Nazi henchmen as the Kit Kat patrons watch in solemn silence. The Emcee laughs hysterically, "*as if the fight were part of the floor show*" (according to the script). The implication is irresistible: the patrons are becalmed by the violent spectacle, and the Emcee underlines the whole point of the world-as-cabaret metaphor (455).

Sally Bowles is the Emcee's trophy, for as the staging of the title song shows, she is left alone to belt out her relish for a cabaret world, asserting that life itself is a cabaret—only a cabaret—and that she loves a cabaret! (456–57). What she fails to realize is that the cabaret is a phantasmagoria; it has a sham reality. In her number, the stage disappears, the musicians vanish, and Sally is left in a solitary spotlight, singing of joyful escape while rooted only to a dream world. The title song is ironically a celebration of illusion. Not for this heroine the ordinary domestic routines of knitting, reading, and cleaning but, rather, of wine, music, and saturnalian revelry. Intimations of death or of death-in-life are unmistakable, for in the course of her shrill anthem Sally refers to both the brevity of life and the cost of hedonism. In the soaring finish, she is engulfed by a blackout that could also be emblematic of the story's nihilism.

Then Cliff and Schultz bid their respective good-byes, and Sally, who reveals that she has traded her fur coat for an abortion, sounds a portentous note ("I doubt you can stop *anything* happening. Any more than you can change people.") (458). The penultimate scene is marked by sentimentality, as Schultz genially but foolishly clings to his old optimism that the political madness will pass and as Sally reveals an unsuspected tenderness in her good-bye to Cliff while rejecting his offer of a ticket to Paris. But there are signs of disintegration in her determined bid to be her old self again and then, after Cliff exits, in her fading smile.

Prince insisted that atmosphere and sound were to be the defining elements of the show, but he had as yet only a vague idea of what he wanted. The form and metaphor of the show evolved gradually, and it took the recollection of an extraordinary experience abroad for the central metaphor to crystallize in his imagination. Being stationed in Stuttgart in 1951 had given Prince the opportunity to visit Maxim's, a nightclub situated in an old church basement where "a dwarf Emcee, hair parted in the middle, and lacquered down with brilliantine, his mouth made into a bright red cupid's bow,...wore heavy false eyelashes and sang, danced, goosed, tickled, and pawed four lumpen Valkyres waving diaphanous butterfly wings" (Prince 1974: 126). Prince's vivid recollections of this man and the nightclub show helped in the decision to make the Emcee and his cabaret the frame and central metaphor for the entire musical. The Emcee would perform various songs in styles evoking Lotte Lenya, Richard Tauber, Marlene Dietrich, et cetera. He was given rich material for his fifteen to thirty minutes in the spotlight, with his eight numbers scattered throughout the show "in an ascending curve energetically and descending curve morally" (27). As Prince saw it, the Emcee played to empty laughter in an empty house: "He'd lost the war, his self-respect. He carried his money around in bushel baskets. With National Socialism he found his strength, misdirected and despotic, feeding off his moral corruption." But neither Prince nor his collaborators knew how the show should look, and with only "half a concept" he felt he had no feasible option except to postpone the show. He wanted his musical to surprise audiences and not seem hackneyed or predictable. Stymied, he decided instead to do the musical comedy *It's a Bird, It's a Plane, It's Superman*, a comic strip show that opened in March 1966 but closed four months later, done in by Broadway's summer doldrums and its own pop art trends that at points seemed imitative of television's *Batman*.

CHAPTER 3

CURTAIN OF LIGHT, TILTED MIRROR

IN LATE SUMMER 1966, HAROLD PRINCE MADE A TRIP TO
Russia to escape both the *Superman* failure and "the insoluble problems
of *Cabaret*" (Prince 1974: 127). This resulted in an apocalyptic experience at Moscow's Taganka Theater, where *Ten Days That Shook the World*,
a political revue based on John Reed's book, was playing to packed
houses. Despite making "an awful scene" when his preordered tickets
were swallowed up by the Young Communists who had taken over the
theater, he had to enlist the help of the American Embassy in order to
ultimately receive two seats in the last row of the balcony. Luckily, it was a
small theater, and Prince experienced "a turning point" in his thinking
as a director. Although the text was "absurd," in his view, "the techniques,
the vitality, the imagination to make every minute surprising, involving,
yet consistent with a concept" were stamped with a genius bred in part by
cabaret and in part by the methods of actor–director Vsevolod Meyerhold
(1874–1940), who had begun with Constantin Stanislavsky (1863–1938)
at the Moscow Art Theater only to break away in protest against the repetition of extreme realism (127–28).

Prince was not a naïf. After all, he had been a fan of Joan Littlewood
and her revue-style productions with their nonlinear narratives. He had
also subscribed to ideas of Erwin Piscator (1893–1966), the great German
theatrical visionary who formulated a new aesthetic that took social
struggle from riot-torn streets of the Third Reich and placed it before the
footlights. Piscator revived classic works of world drama in a mode that
connected them with social revolutions that were intensifying in Europe,
particularly in Germany. Prince was not at all in step with Brecht's "epic

theatre" (that Piscator developed), for he considered alienation by definition to be alienating, but he was interested in Piscator's technical innovations that strengthened spectacle by the use of projections, music,
song, acrobatics, instant drawings, and short sketches. Piscator pushed
toward a new style of unambiguous, unsentimental acting to suit a new
sort of stage built of wood, canvas, and steel. Another element in this theater practice that especially appealed to Prince was the rejection of a star
system in favor of Piscator's idea of a company, right down to the smallest
bit player, totally dedicated to the dramatist's power.

But all this background hardly prepared Prince for the startling
epiphany at the Taganka. The theater itself was conventional in that it
had a stage, proscenium, orchestra pit, and auditorium. However, that
was where familiar convention ended and innovation began. As described
by Prince in *Contradictions*, an apron was built over the orchestra pit into
which searchlights were sunk to make "a curtain of light behind which
the scenery was changed." There was an entire range of expressionistic
devices, including paintings speaking from a wall, animated objects, and
disembodied limbs moving across the stage. Puppets and projections,
front and rear, were in the mix, and the sources and colors of light were
"always a surprise. All of it made possible by the use of black velours
drapes instead of painted canvas" (129).

The show "began in the lobby, spilled across the stage into the audience, shattering the fourth wall," while creating an emotional bond between actors and audience. Until this show, Prince had always believed
that the most important element of a musical was the libretto. Now he
wasn't so sure. The play was a trenchant but silly satire that exploited the
villainy of Alexander Kerensky and Woodrow Wilson, but this ultimately
did not matter much in the light of the startling theatrical techniques.
Prince did want a musical that was theatrically viable as a metaphor for
German society, so one of the first things he and Masteroff settled on was
the reduction of Christopher Isherwood's nightclub settings to a single
cabaret. In *Goodbye to Berlin*, Isherwood describes the Troika, Salome,
Alexander Casino, and the Lady Windermere (where Sally performs).
Van Druten used a boardinghouse as the single setting for his Broadway
play, though the weak film version of the same piece did have scenes at
the Lady Windermere. Prince and Masteroff replaced the Lady
Windermere with their Kit Kat Klub.

When Prince returned to New York, he called Jean Rosenthal, his
lighting designer, and describing what he had witnessed, asked her to

give him a curtain of light behind which to change scenery. An acknowledged lighting magician, Rosenthal informed him that there was no
equipment in the world powerful enough to accomplish what he wanted
in a Broadway theater because the throw from the source of light to the
back wall wouldn't be intense enough. Prince scrapped this idea, but he
conceived of dividing the stage into two sections: "an area to represent
the REAL WORLD, the vestibule in Sally's rooming house, her bedroom,
the train, the cabaret; and an area to represent the MIND." This second
area was called limbo. The Emcee's material was divided between "realistic numbers performed in the cabaret for an audience on stage and
metaphorical numbers illustrating changes in the German mind"
(130–31).

    Rosenthal turned Prince's idea into another of her miracles with light.
Her reputation was long celebrated. A native New Yorker, she had begun
her theater work at the Neighborhood Playhouse, where she attended to
stage details for Martha Graham. She had also worked in summer theater
and at the Federal Theater project in New York and had managed the
technical side for the Municipal Wagon Theater that played parks. She
observed closely as techniques of American stage lighting emerged during the Great Depression, when there was no money, no room, and little
scenery. Next she studied lighting in classes by Stanley McCandless at
Yale before moving on to the Parsons School of Design. She embarked
on a professional career in 1935, serving as stage manager, production
supervisor, and errand girl for the W.P.A. Theater Project. A year later,
when the man assigned to install lighting equipment for Leslie Howard's
Hamlet fell ill, she was pressed into his job. The next year she became an
all-around backstage participant at the Mercury Theater. For Orson
Welles's opening production of *Julius Caesar* she built platforms, shifted
scenery, gave cues during performances, and designed the lighting.
During World War II she interrupted her Broadway work to compile a
handbook on the electrical systems of cargo ships, and in 1940 she
founded Theater Production Service, Inc. (her answer to Sears Roebuck
catalogs and stores), manufacturer of kits containing makeup, costumes,
and portable scenic effects for G.I. theatricals overseas. In 1946 she took
over lighting for the Ballet Society (later to become the New York City
Ballet), designing for Gian Carlo Menotti's opera *The Medium* in 1947
and several Martha Graham dances, in the belief that ballet, being purely
visual, offered more leeway for imaginative lighting than did the theater.
In 1950, when the lighting cues for all productions in the New York City

Opera's repertoire somehow got mislaid, she was called in to rescue the situation, and in only six weeks she restored the lighting plans of fourteen operas. Where set designers painted with decor, she painted with light, her tools being batteries of spotlights, kliegs, scoops, and border lights. What one critic called her "poetical idea of voltage" epitomized lighting as an art. As she remarked in a 1955 *Sunday Mirror Magazine* feature, "Light on a stage should point up the effect of the music, the words, the scenery, the art of the performers, or whatever is on the stage."

A tiny, blue-eyed, curly-haired dynamic woman, she saw her work as a collaboration in which her role was an extraordinarily subtle one. For her, "everyone else—the actors, the directors, the producers, the writers"— were the stars. When no one in the audience knew where the lighting came from, and when no one noticed anything on the stage "except the actors, the sets, the costumes, and the words and music," then you knew that you had done your job the way it should be done.

Directors had been known to postpone Broadway openings in order to avail themselves of her skills. Actors and actresses trusted her implicitly, knowing that she would make them look flatteringly attractive. As Winthrop Sargeant wrote in a *New Yorker* profile, she was credited with carrying within her head an encyclopedic knowledge of the dimensions and lighting problems of every important theater in the United States and abroad: "Fellow-professionals talk admiringly, if somewhat cryptically, of her 'cyclorama blues' and 'color washes.' Instructors who teach her obscure craft in college drama schools have analyzed her methods in standard textbooks on the subject." Her genius was for *suggesting* light and shade when the stage actually contained no shadow at all. As celebrated for her stark, eerie mud-colored lighting of *The Medium* as for her "light-all-around" or wash effect, she was by her own description "a regular magpie" who would use anything that happened to come along.

Rosenthal was the first lighting designer with whom Prince had ever collaborated. Because of her design, *West Side Story* was Prince's first deftly lit show, in which the graceless beauty, tense horror, and aggressive energy of the musical drama were revealed without pretentiousness. Her lighting ranged from the naturalistic to the surrealistic, providing atmosphere—whether of early evening in an open street or a mere half hour later in an intimate space, whether a blackout and a quick flood of multicolored light or a nocturnal balcony scene suddenly melted by stars glowing through the dark wash of sky.

Following Prince's decision to use two specially demarcated areas in *Cabaret*, Rosenthal designed a light trough about six feet upstage of the apron edge. Prince described her design in *Contradictions*: "Covered with a wooden shield, it rose electronically and could be directed at an angle of forty-five degrees upstage to the rear wall (we danced a Tiller Chorus of lumpen Valkyries across the stage, lighting only their legs). Downstage at forty-five degrees we momentarily blinded the audience. And at ninety degrees straight up into the flies we made a curtain of dust" (Prince 1974: 131). The trough would serve as footlights for the devilish Emcee, and the lighting in general would enhance communication with the audience and define mood and meaning without requiring words or music.

Brilliant as it was, Rosenthal's lighting functioned integrally with the decor devised by Boris Aronson, which was far less naturalistic than was customary in Broadway musicals. Rosenthal's career had begun in the midthirties in New York; Aronson's, in the twenties in his native Russia. By comparison, Prince's career was still in adolescence. But Aronson, though broadly and deeply steeped in European design traditions, had never had such good fortune in working with a director who was able to challenge him to new heights. Aronson had worked with George Abbott, Harold Clurman, Max Reinhardt, Robert Lewis, George Balanchine, Lee Strasberg, Elia Kazan, Rouben Mamoulian, Clifford Odets, Jed Harris, Peter Hall, Michael Langham, and Jerome Robbins and had covered almost every style there was to explore on Broadway, winning plaudits and awards galore, but in Prince he finally found a director who could catalyze his fertile imagination as had never happened before.

One of ten children of the grand rabbi of Kiev, Aronson (born in 1900) trained at an art school before moving to Moscow. A radical impatience with old conventions was sharpened at a Kiev art school where instructors, who still slavishly adhered to French realism, disliked his work. It was only when he got to Moscow (where he was forced to sleep in the street on account of a civil restriction against Jews) that he saw firsthand some of the French modernist paintings he had admired in art magazines. Soon after the 1917 revolution, Kiev became the center of the Jewish avant-garde. Aronson thrived on the postrevolutionary cultural boom, and by 1920 he had helped organize a "Jewish Art Exhibition" featuring innovative work by him and several other artists. This impetus to discard old forms of expression dovetailed with a new preoccupation with sheer size and resulted in his commission to extend building facades artificially so that they could bear monumental slogans congruent with Marxist tenets.

Aronson shared Vsevolod Meyerhold's antipathy to Stanislavskian realism: "By the time I was fourteen, I was past crying over *The Cherry Orchard* and no longer cared whether the three sisters arrived safely in Moscow" (Rich 1987: 5). Influenced by Edward Gordon Craig (1872–1966) and Adolphe Appia (1862–1928), Meyerhold (1874–1940) imprinted his own strong style on a production. Trompe l'oeil effects were rejected in favor of plastic, three-dimensional settings, subtly lit, that stylized reality while revealing rather than camouflaging artifice. But Aronson was not sympathetic to Meyerhold's propagandistic "communal" theater. Instead he favored Alexander Tairov's credo of an "emancipated theater" that condemned not only naturalism (which gave "the false impression" of "the actual reality of life") but also the sort of stylized theater in which two-dimensional backdrops made "a marionette out of the actor." Tairov (1885–1950) emphasized the stage floor more than scenic background, and he felt that each play required its own "scenic solution" (5).

Tairov's principal designer was Aleksandra Exter (1882–1949), a pioneer of constructivism. Trained in Paris and well familiar with all the modernist currents in French art (impressionism, futurism, cubism), she created a Cubo-Futurist style that, as Frank Rich tells us, "adapted the modernism of Parisian and Italian painters to the stage." Aronson became one of her students, responding eagerly to her preference for working in various styles, often on the same day. A decade later, Aronson, in a New York newspaper interview, credited Exter with teaching him the primary purposes of a stage set: "It should...permit varied movement for the actor; present significant details characteristic of the mood of the play; dramatize the emotion of each scene; by its organic fusion of forms and color, be beautiful in its own right." No longer constrained by the demands of an exact copy of real life, a designer could choose to bring out "the inner essence of each dramatic work" (7).

Aronson left Russia permanently in 1922, settling briefly in Berlin, where he studied, painted, and published two books: one of them, a treatise on contemporary Jewish graphic art; the other, an early critical study of Marc Chagall, a Moscow friend who had designed sets for the Jewish Kamerny Theater and who synthesized "the Harlequinade of the Jewish theatre and the grotesqueries of the Jewish ghetto" (9). Unable to gain a foothold in Berlin theater, Aronson was luckily able, on the basis of his books, to gain a visa entry to the United States, where he arrived in November 1923, traveling to New York on the *Aquatania* (as he reported to Rich) with "some drawings, two books, a pair of socks, a membership in a union of German artists, paintbrushes, crowded emotions, little money, and less English." Then he was startled to find, as Rich comments, "that the American arts, especially the theatre, were often as backward as American urban civilization was advanced" (9). Where Aronson and other modernists had long been proponents of Meyerhold and Tairov, New Yorkers were still awaiting the importation of Stanislavskian experiments. Aronson found he was about thirty years ahead of the theater mainstream and, so, unfortunately, not confidently accepted by timid directors who did not fully understand or sympathize with his sophisticated ambitions.

Ironically, his first opportunity to design sets with full freedom came from experimental Yiddish theater, where most plays took place in either heaven or hell (Kanin interview March 1975), and his bold Russian avant-garde style caught the interest and patronage of the foremost Yiddish theater impresario, Maurice Schwartz, for whom Aronson worked regularly in the period 1925–29. Other influential individuals who lauded his work included Kenneth MacGowan (a close associate of Eugene O'Neill), John Mason Brown (critic of *Theatre Arts Monthly*), Brooks Atkinson, Sheldon Cheney, and designer Cleon Throckmorton. All of them knew that it was necessary for New York theater to catch up with Aronson. But Lee Simonson, an extraordinary designer in his own right, identified Aronson's dilemma in American theater: the Russian émigré's style was exotic because the commercial theater rarely needed it. Besides, how could Aronson use constructivism to abstract a landscape he hardly knew? Obviously, he would have to familiarize himself with New York, but this process took longer than expected, as Aronson moved from naturalism to expressionism and then to an abstract and economical ordering of space. His aim was always for heightened theatricality, though not necessarily through enlarging decor.

An association with the Group Theater begun in 1935 led to long-term relationships with Clurman, Kazan, and Odets, and then Aronson worked for Abbott, finding himself on what he called "the Broadway merry-go-round" (21). He made a strong impression in various productions. His set design for *Love Life* (1948), Kurt Weill's "concept musical" that prefigured Prince–Sondheim's *Company* (1970), employed a modular, cube motif. For *The Rose Tattoo* (1951), he painted (in Rich's words) "the deepest part of the set lightest in color, to give it an inner glow" (103). His sets for *The Master Builder* (1955) were (in Rich's words) "Nordic without being heavy and gloomy," for they used "a light plasticity and Paul Klee–like striations" (111). Quite capable of atmospheric realism (as he showed with the warm diner in the 1955 *Bus Stop* and, also that year, in the organized clutter and small compartments of *The Diary of Anne Frank*), he continued to favor abstract elements. However, according to Rich, Aronson's career was "in limbo" during much of the forties and fifties because his odd sense of geometry clashed notably with the prevailing style of American set design. While American theater became inordinately standardized, there was a time when virtually every production required a living room: "Aronson was more interested in epic plays requiring scenery that was not asymmetrical but full of obstacles, requiring the audience to look in several directions at once" (22). Nevertheless, while awaiting these epic plays, he was forced to accept pedestrian or mediocre projects or to work abroad with such respectable directors as Reinhardt, Hall, and Langham, for whom he indulged his urge to mix contrasting styles within the same production without losing either simplicity or strength.

The late fifties and early sixties were a breakthrough period in that Aronson was able to tackle "large themes in exotic, even fantastic environments" (129). There were startling experiments: a hieroglyphic Egyptian wall against a highly textured papyrus cyclorama in *The Firstborn* (1958), a desolate, cavernous circus tent for *J.B.* (1958), and an "ultracivilized" French vision of Assyrian barbarism in *Judith* (1962). Aronson became fashionable only with *Fiddler on the Roof* (1964), for which he used textures, colors, motifs, and a few props suggestive of Marc Chagall in the background while creating a homely and realistic poverty in the foreground. The drops demonstrated Aronson's distillation of fantasy as well as the seasonal flow of the story, while Tevye's house, superbly simple, opened up to reveal its interior. Prince believed that design was best when it approached the abstract—as, for example, late in act 1, when a tailor's shop was dissolved into an outdoor wedding scene as a Chagallian silver moon glowed in dark swirls of sky.

Fiddler converted Prince into an Aronson enthusiast. Although he felt that the designer had allowed himself to be excessively influenced by Chagall, he also recognized Aronson's "quirky and penetrating vision of people, time, and place." Aronson's analysis of news events or of conflicts invariably surprised him, and Prince always liked to be surprised by his collaborators. For his part, Aronson felt especially compatible with Prince because the director shared his strong belief in artistic collaboration. As Aronson told Garson Kanin in a March 1975 interview, the greatest achievement of a show is when all the artists share a common language by having the same approach. Prince discussed *Cabaret* with Aronson for three months, but the two rarely spoke of things visual. They talked mostly of the characters, and of motivation, behavioral peculiarities, and emotional expression as affected by ethnicity. Aronson had thousands of photographs to help his visual sense, but, as Prince comments in *Contradictions,* "he never observed the predictable: never the leg of a table, the shape of a lamp post, the ironwork on the hotel balcony rail." Instead, he was more interested in "the expression of the shoppers on the street," "the quality of light in a room," and "the emotional content in the architecture of a section of the city." And when Aronson spoke, Prince marveled at what he was hearing and seeing for the first time (Prince 1974: 132).

Aronson clearly had a unique approach to design. As he explained in the Kanin interview for the New York Public Library: "I design from inside of the people who inhabit the play, not architecturally.... Basically I'm more concerned with the nature of the script.... The tendency is to do beautiful sets. Some shows and their themes and characters don't call for this." In the course of their discussions, the two men studied silhouettes, reflections in windows, the calligraphy of street signs—details that, as Prince acknowledges in a foreword to *American Design,* "seemingly [had] nothing to do with a specific text" (Aronson 1993: vii). He and Aronson also looked at faces of people in the street or leaning out of windows. And, of course, they talked and talked about the quality of the libretto.

Just when he felt it was time for Aronson to stop talking and get to work, Prince was presented with a finished design that apparently had been developing throughout their frequent consultations. *Cabaret* was slower to develop than other Prince musicals. Problems with the early libretto, in which the cabaret sequences coalesced around an opening section, did not ease Aronson's task. The narrative scenes were conventionally written and staged, so Aronson felt compelled to use wagon sets that brought on and took off bedrooms and living rooms.

Once Prince and the designer had decided on the scale and relationship of the furniture, the shape of a roof, the adjustment of windows and doors, Aronson constructed a half-inch scale model for the scenic builders and stage managers. Minutely detailed right down to the texture of wallpaper and the pattern of a stained-glass window, it showed a slightly raked stage with three black velours drapes for the three walls. These drapes were rigged to fly up quickly so that scenery on winch-operated trucks or wagons could enter with parts of rooms. The black velours drapes were probably an idea taken from the Taganka Theater. Prince's imagination caught fire at observing the Taganka's practices of unorthodox stagecraft: searchlights sunk into the apron over the orchestra pit; wall paintings that seemed to speak; inanimate objects made animate; disembodied hands, feet, and faces washing across the stage; puppets and projections, front and rear; and surprising sources of light made possible by clever use of black velours drapes. Each of the ideas capitalized "on the special relationships of live actors and live observers" (Prince 1974: 129–30).

Prince recognized that these techniques were not necessarily new, but he also saw that they were superbly effective. He was not averse to stealing some of the techniques for *Cabaret*. As Carol Ilson (1989: 145) notes, "black velours were used to surround the rear and sides of the stage, and side panels could be flown quickly to enable the scenery to be rolled in on winch-operated trucks." The lighting equipment worked well against the black drops, making it possible for Rosenthal to design "subtle, realistic lighting for the book scenes and to give the cabaret and Limbo numbers the hard, sinister edge of spotlights" (Prince 1974: 133). Aronson introduced an iron staircase, enabling Prince to experiment for the first time with the use of observers onstage—something that has since become a staple of many metatheatrical productions. But the two greatest design inventions for the musical came from the designers themselves.

Rosenthal's curtain of light functioned in place of painted curtain. The abstract limbo area was defined by a huge iron spiral staircase stage left (suggestive of the type backstage of the usual cabaret), on which Prince could position onlookers serving as a "surrogate German population" who would silently and sullenly observe scenes occurring below. Further definition was supplied by streetlamps and expressionistically lit storefronts that, as Rich (1987: 190) describes, "converged toward a central vanishing point." In addition to this, a neon sign spelled out the word "Cabaret," letter by letter, culminating in the flashing of the entire sign.

But the real coup in Aronson's design (and one that was to be increasingly imitated by other designers) was a nightclub with its own stage and a large trapezoidal mirror "corresponding to the shape of the stage floor" that hung center stage and reflected the audience as they entered to take their seats. This was a total surprise to Prince but a masterstroke created by Aronson as a result of his very first discussion of the play with Prince, who wanted to stress the political similarities between events in Nazi Germany and those in the United States during the civil rights confrontations of Selma, Alabama, and Little Rock, Arkansas. Aronson decided on a stage metaphor that would reflect a society, and as he explained: "Tilted one way, [the mirror] would reflect the audience, saying, 'Look at yourselves.' It was a mirror of life—of a society." Tilted at another angle, it reflected the cabaret performers from a distorting perspective and emphasized "the intentionally grotesque quality of the cabaret numbers" (Rich 1987: 199).

The other important sets were relatively realistic interiors, ranging from a small train compartment and a grey-green fruit peddler's shop almost floating against the still-visible abstract limbo area to storefronts and the landlady's seedy room set off by drab, stained doors and a skeletal roof arch and containing decayed green wallpaper, a lumpy sofa, a washstand in a corner, and a small table with a Victrola. This bourgeois room, a simplified version of Aronson's memories of Berlin rooming houses and of the interior he had designed for *I Am a Camera* in 1951, suggested a mingling of genteel order and materialism, bourgeois cheer and

Scenic design painting by Boris Aronson for Cabaret *(1966) (Photofest)*

Set of the Kit Kat Klub for Cabaret *(1966). Directed by Harold Prince. (Photofest)*

pragmatic concealment. The sofa, one felt, could be pulled out and a door suddenly opened to discharge a lodger.

Aronson and Prince attempted a shadow-play sequence against an elaborate expressionistic projection of nightmarish Berlin, but this could never be staged to Prince's satisfaction. It looked too crudely forbidding, too excessively a projection of poverty and social horror, so it was cut from the text and design.

There was no question that the single greatest element in the design was the giant mirror. It provided a ceiling for the Kit Kat Klub, augmented the limbo area, and reinforced the cabaret's value as a political metaphor. And it was an image that sprang from the central meaning of the play. It forced members of the audience to be aware of themselves not only as voyeurs but also as participants in the cabaret, and thus it urged them to see a parallel between themselves and those Germans who tacitly observed Nazi horrors. "Look at yourselves and at the cabaret performers," it seemed to say. "Do you recognize yourselves in them? If you do, and if you were in their place, would you have behaved differently?"

CHAPTER 4

CABARET AMBIENCE

WITH THE SET DESIGN APPROVED, THE AMBIENCE AND SOUND OF THE show could now receive special attention. Prince did not expect a faithful, literal recreation of political or social *Kabarett*, such as had flourished in the early twenties and thirties, but an expression of the seediness, acrid smokiness, and Weimar decadence that swathed patrons. The politics of the period would have to be compressed and suggested obliquely by song, costume, brief snippets of dialogue, and flashes of incident. Ironically, this obliqueness ran counter to the tone and impulse of real cabaret, which, as Lisa Appignanesi (1984) shows in her chronicle of the form, were overtly didactic and aggressively avant-garde, even in their original French modes of the nineteenth century, when wine cellars or taverns served as sites for strolling players, balladeers, jugglers, and carnival performers.

In France, cabaret was a principal form of entertainment in cafés or bistros, where the chanson (love lyric or mood piece) was popularized and where patrons could voice their reactions to contemporary events. As bistros grew in size and stature toward the end of the nineteenth century, they became café-concerts (music-halls), often in the open air and with full-scale bands. But even as cabaret grew (along with the role of satire), it retained characteristic elements: a small stage and smallish audience, an atmosphere of smoke and conversation, and a relationship between performers and audiences that broke down the imaginary fourth wall of traditional theater and became warmly intimate or acidly hostile. The most famous cabaret was Le Chat Noir, founded by Rodolphe Salis, who satirized Émile Zola's cult of naturalism and launched a magazine of the same name. Here entertainment became a parody of middle-class culture, with Claude Debussy directing a choir, Erik Satie conducting improvisations, and Maurice MacNab delivering a few songs steeped in macabre gallows humor. Salis would preside as host, *compère* or *conférencier* (master of ceremonies), or emcee, dressed formally and welcoming guests in deliberately absurd academic fashion.

German *Kabarett* was born partly in imitation of the bohemian ambience of Montmartre and Paris, but there were other contributing factors. Wilhelmine Germany had a far more restrictive environment than that of Paris. The bourgeoisie was bored by the high tone of *Kultur*, and censorship was strict, even though sex ran coarsely through the private lives of the privileged. When Albert Langen returned to Munich from Paris, he and some partners (including playwright Frank Wedekind) launched the illustrated satirical weekly *Simplicissimus*, which attacked authority, kitsch, and hypocrisy. In 1900, in order to bring art to the people, poet Otto Julius Bierbaum published a version of chansons. *Deutsche Chansons* sold twenty thousand copies within one year and went through many editions. He also tried to raise the popular variety show, the *Tingeltangel* (the German name for variety spectacle), to the level of serious art, demonstrating in the process that serious cultural motives could lead to popular forms. Another individual who played an important role in the rise of German cabaret was the aristocrat and poet Ernest von Wolzogen, who rented a 650-seat theater where he served as *conférencier* (more as court fool than acid chorus) for a program containing satire, eroticism, and lyricism.

Cabaret became duly celebrated across Europe (particularly in Vienna, Moscow, Munich, and Berlin) as a vehicle for the artistic vanguard. It went through distinct phases, such as futurism (under the Italian Filippo Tommaso Marinetti's influence), expressionism (chiefly through Kurt Hiller, Jakob van Hoddis, and Eric Unger), and Dada (via Hans Arp and Tristan Tzara), but it always had a bitter or angry undertone. In Berlin, which, according to Lisa Appignanesi (1984: 94), emerged as "Germany's first truly cosmopolitan centre," the common aim of cabaret satirists was to oppose the nation's militarism and glorification of war. Among the many outstanding performers who came to prominence were singer-monologist Paul Grätz, a master of improvisation; the gangly, rubber-faced Munich comic Karl Valentin, whose art fell somewhere between music hall and literary theater; red-haired, flaming-eyed, furrow-faced Rosa Valetti, a large *diseuse* who belted out her songs; Trude Hesterberg, a singer who could be whimsical or harsh; Valeska Gert, who invented "social-critical dance pantomime" that was sometimes frenziedly expressionistic; elegantly vampish Gussy Holl; and Blandine Ebinger, a slender, expressive singer of tragicomic songs in a street dialect.

Post–World War I *Kabarett* used jazz, pornography, song, sport, and stinging satire—all recorded in Josef von Sternberg's classic 1930 film *Der blaue Engel* (*The Blue Angel*), starring Marlene Dietrich and Emil Jannings. "Gaiety bordering on hysteria was the keynote of the day," as Appignanesi asserts, and Berlin briefly welcomed "expressionist artists and comintern agents, nudist dancers and sexologists, embezzlers and black marketeers, drug addicts, transvestites, pimps, courtesans, homosexuals, prophets vegetarian, magical and apocalyptic." The city harbored hordes of refugees from eastern and southeastern Europe: various ethnic groups from the Balkans, Hungarians, Viennese, Poles, Russians (fleeing the Communist revolution), and pogrom-escaping Ukrainian Jews. Major social problems were soon to surface and smoulder, and left-wing critics chose the cabaret stage (in addition to newspapers and journals) as a medium for exposing and satirizing the storm and stress of German society. These performances transformed cabaret into "an outpost of dissent, a finely tuned instrument for illuminating and battling contemporary ills" (Appignanesi 1984: 94). Such serious artists as Kurt Tucholsky, Walter Mehring, Erich Kästner, George Grösz, and Bertolt Brecht succeeded in closing the gap between high, elitist art and mass market entertainment by offering chansons, aphorisms, fairy tales, parodies, babbling monologues, earthy repartee, crude dialects, humorous verse, slogans, and posters.

Serious artists learned from cabaret even as they developed it into an art form. Using a pseudonym, Wedekind performed as a satirist to mock establishment authority, thereby earning himself the reputation of a revolutionary. His onstage character was electrifying as he would walk on casually, look contemptuously at his audience, and sharply sing his satiric songs in "a raw, jarring, high-pitched, slightly nasal voice" (44) His harshly ironic, brittle, abrasive tone influenced Brecht, who imitated and popularized it as a German cabaret song style. Many of his actors came from the cabaret stage. Cabaret also helped Brecht formulate his theater practice and theory of *Verfremdungseffekt* (alienation effect). The small cabaret stage and smoky, sexy atmosphere produced an intimacy and immediacy for performers and audiences. The performers played directly to the audience rather than to fellow performers, thereby breaking down the imaginary fourth wall. In fact, there was no wall onstage—only, usually, a curtain of glittering foil strips—so any feedback from the audience was incorporated into a spectacle that included them both. "The actors constantly 'send up' the illusion that reality lies in the on-stage fiction and that they are the characters they are portraying." This deliberate distancing of performers from their roles prompted the audience into "an awareness of its own role as an audience." Brecht's use of "a 'poor' stage almost bare of props and effects, reinforces this break down of illusion." In other words, the actors insist that they are playing roles and so urge the audience into an awareness of its own role as audience (130–31).

In the early twenties, Brecht spoke of an "epic smoke theatre" or a place that people might visit casually, speak without hushed tones, and sit, smoke, and think while laughing or grimacing at the performances. Sentimental and satiric cabaret songs became models for Brecht's ballads in collaboration with Kurt Weill—most outstandingly in *The Threepenny Opera*—and the short sketches of cabaret, often only loosely linked, left their mark on Brecht's work—as in *The Resistible Rise of Arturo Ui*. Weill and Brecht were both influenced by *Neue Sachlichkeit* (often translated as "New Objectivity" but which should have been called "New Matter-of-Factness"). As Weill's biographer Ronald Sanders (1980: 82–83) points out, this movement, "which had arisen in the mid-twenties as a reaction against the unworldly excesses of expressionism," aimed for "a relationship with ordinary people that had been largely lost amid the artistic Brahminism of the late nineteenth and early twentieth centuries" Art had become less elitist and more democratic, and such artists as Brecht and Paul Hindemith came to think of the new art as somehow utilitarian or pragmatic. The democratic thrust was sharpened by the jazz craze in which the public enjoyed "bare bones" music that evoked direct emotional response.

So thoroughly immersed was Brecht in the cabaret world that when he was taken by Ira Gershwin to a rehearsal of *Porgy and Bess* he was filled with wonderment. "To his ear, the insolent jazz sounds of the twenties were taking on new meanings in this music and yielding to a lyricism worthy of the finest elements in the European operatic tradition. And yet it all remained so fresh, so American" (219). Brecht opened his own cabaret, the Red Grape (*Die Rote Zibebe*), in 1922, several nights after the Munich premiere of his *Drums in the Night*, which featured a tavern called the Red Grape. Unfortunately, his real-life cabaret did not last long because the police closed it down after Brecht fell into government disfavor for his pronounced criticism of war "heroism."

It was unfortunate that neither Prince nor his composers, John Kander and Fred Ebb, sought to exploit more explicitly the political and social wit of German cabaret or the scope of the form to create a melting pot of fringe theater, satire, music hall, spectacle, eroticism, and journalism. The American producers did reproduce the role of the cabaret *conférencier*, representing it as a complex, manifold one. In the Broadway musical, the Emcee, like his real-life model, draws the audience into the spectacle inside the club, engages in repartee, improvises, and mocks certain social and political subjects by specific numbers or by his comments. However, the Kit Kat Klub is far less literary or purposefully didactic than its historical antecedents. Although it does not forsake sleaziness or spasms of viciousness, the Kit Kat Klub has a clientele that is not fully into fierce fun, and its stage could welcome, without blush, German equivalents of Jerome Kern or Irving Berlin. Broadway commercialism had something to do with the limits imposed on Prince's Kit Kat Klub. After all, if audiences were not considered ready for an explicitly homosexual male lead, they certainly were not ripe for exposure to the full flavor of Weimar cabaret, where the master of ceremonies often ran afoul of authority, with many such *conférenciers* paying a brutal price at the hands of the Nazis. The irony was that although Weimar Germany allowed cabaret freedom of opinion and expression, the authorities eventually exacted drastic penalties from the left-wing satirists who had mocked and denounced them. Tucholsky, a little fat Berliner, created four personae to voice his parodies, chansons, aphorisms, fairy tales, and babbling monologues, but he was eventually silenced by the Nazis, who burned his books, forcing him into silence and then suicide. Paul Nikolaus, who had been acidly satirical in his commentary on contemporary reality, was so hounded by the Nazis that in 1933 he fled to Zurich, where he committed suicide shortly after. Nazi retaliation was not confined to Germans. Viennese Fritz Grünbaum, for instance, was tortured during his internment at Dachau, resulting in his death.

In the United States of the sixties, sharp social and political satire seemed to be limited to stand-up comics, such as Mort Sahl, Shelley Berman, Mike Nichols and Elaine May, and, most notoriously, Lenny Bruce. Their performance attitude was "half intimate, half hostile, for like the original cabretists [*sic*] they were breaking down the mystique of the stage and simultaneously provoking or insulting their audience into reaction or participation" (Appignanesi 1984: 174). In breaking down long-existing taboos, they became targets of all those to whom moral outrage came as easily as graft, sexual exploitation, and double-talk as practiced by politicians, evangelists, and corporate executives. Presidential power quickly aligned with the FBI to spy on and harass some of the most devastating satirists, and eventually Sahl, Berman, and Bruce disappeared from broad public view. Although great art is always ahead of its audience, no art can flourish without audience acceptance, and so Prince had to compromise to a certain extent with his audiences' tastes. Consequently, for *Cabaret* he sought suggestive ambience rather than literal reproduction, and this approach extended to all areas of the production, including the look of the show that was completed by costume designer Patricia Zipprodt.

This was the second time that Zipprodt had collaborated with Aronson, the first being *The Rope Dancers* (1957), a sentimental drama about "a shiftless husband, his wife, and their deformed daughter in a turn-of-the-century New York tenement" (Rich 1987: 120). Aronson had made Zipprodt visit his painting studio, where he was orchestrating the whole design and where he taught her (as she said) "the difference between warm and cool colors, the relativity of values" (Rich 1987: 120). A native of Illinois, she stood five feet, eight inches, had a mop of reddish curls and a low, husky voice. She had run the gamut of work experiences before her first Broadway show, having tried social work, puppetry, painting, and teaching horseback riding. There were early signs of an interest in design, for during her Chicago girlhood she kept a large paper doll collection. She told journalist Laurel Graeber in May 1986: "I had not only designed clothes for the dolls, but stories—I'd clip the interiors of yachts, great houses, offices where they went to jobs. My 'cast' went to all these places I dressed them for." But she did not settle into her costume designing career until the fifties, when she moved to New York, excited by "a lot of dreams to be a painter and live in a garret, and starve and be happy. But I found that didn't work at all." Her bohemian life was supported by painting at the Art Students League and by waiting on tables at Schrafft's. One night, however, she saw the New York City Ballet's *La Valse*, which had costumes by Madame Karinska: "And I saw them as a pure painting with fabric. It was layer upon layer with tulle, with colours. It wasn't like I was seeing yellow and green and red. It was very layered, colour upon colour, air and light filtering through it. I had never seen anyone using colour that way—net upon net upon net in those lovely dancing dresses. It just swept me away."

A second epiphany came as she was walking one afternoon past the windows of Lord & Taylor, where some of Charles James's camel-hair coats were on display. Fascinated by James's "sense of architecture," she wrote him letters, phoned incessantly, and finally sat directly outside his door, refusing to budge until he relented and thundered that she should come in the next morning. After a year-and-a-half apprenticeship with James, she got her first theater break when a friend advised her to present her costume portfolio to the production team of *The Potting Shed*, a play by Graham Greene. She had to cool her heels for five to six hours while they examined her portfolio, but she got her chance and went from there to *A Visit to a Small Planet, The Rope Dancers, Back to Methuselah,* and *Miss Lonelyhearts,* earning an unprecedented costume designer's accolade in the form of an entire paragraph in a Brooks Atkinson review, all over a tenement doctor's suit she actually purchased for $2 in a Lower East Side thrift shop. "I almost fainted," she laughed. "I haven't got a paragraph since" (Graeber 1986).

Her costumes for a notable Off-Broadway production of Jean Genet's *The Blacks* in 1962 brought her to the attention of Jerome Robbins, who hired her to design his directorial debut, *Oh Dad, Poor Dad, Mamma's Hung You in the Closet and I'm Feelin' so Sad,* by Arthur Kopit at the Phoenix Theater. Robbins next commissioned her to do the costumes for *Fiddler on the Roof,* where she enjoyed her second collaboration with Aronson. On that production she established her approach to design

Patricia Zipprodt, 1972
(Photofest)

by beginning with color selection because, as she claims, "it's the beginning of inner sight." The intriguing feature about her Jewish peasant costumes was the "aged" look she achieved by clever craft. She had the "non-dancing" clothes sewn in raw silks and tweeds (fabrics that "get old fast"), then dyed and hand-painted in a "pointillistic effect" so that patches seemed to shine from wear. She then took vegetable graters to the knees and afterward returned the garments to shocked tailors to be repaired and patched. She remembers their disbelief: "They had immigrated from impoverished areas of Italy, and they wanted to do gloriously beautiful ballet costumes. Instead, their fine, carefully and lovingly made outfits came back from the 'aging loft' in shreds and stains—for them to repair and patch! Two or three of them actually went down on their knees and started to pray" (Graeber 1986). But her startling method paid off, and she won her first Tony Award.

Not wanting to be typecast for what she terms "raggy clothes," she rejected an offer to costume Emlyn Williams's *The Corn Is Green*, set in a small Welsh mining community. "Too much of any one thing is too much," she insists. *Cabaret* was a refreshing challenge, for it offered her a most unusual world with a range of extraordinary tones and garish colors. Christopher Isherwood's stories were not particularly helpful for her design concepts because color is hardly one of the key features in his Berlin stories, despite occasional flashes of it in Sally Bowles. Instead she and Aronson scrutinized films by G. W. Pabst and Josef von Sternberg (those with Dietrich) as well as drawings and cartoons by Grösz. In a letter to me (May 26, 1994) she remarked that she was "put onto them by members of the Berlin Jewish intelligentsia in exile in New York who had remained in New York and who had worked with Pabst." As a matter of fact, she spent "several afternoons at the Museum of Modern Art's film archives (with Lisa Aronson, Boris's wife) gluing together old Pabst films and organizing them on reels so that we could run them."

Often evoking what Kenneth Tynan called "a moral coolness" that assumed "neither the existence of sin nor the necessity for retribution," Pabst used Art Deco in *Pandora's Box*, his version of the second of Wedekind's Lulu plays, in order to project romantic agony beneath starkly, stylized patterns. But just as deftly, he also used sub-Dostoevskian settings and a clever change in Louise Brooks's coiffure in order to enhance Lulu's self-defaced iconography. Zipprodt also found Dietrich useful in her mode as a composed blonde Venus with an insolently carnal mouth and eyes that looked impassive even as they preyed upon her sexual victims. In *The Blue Angel*, the film that first brought her notoriety in America, Dietrich showed off more skin and angular eroticism than expected as she sang in her smoky nightclub and seduced the puritanically tyrannous schoolteacher. But both Pabst and Dietrich were levels above the low imagery of Grösz, who reveled in deliberate grotesqueness, especially of murderous gangsters or corpulently lascivious lovers. His cartoons showed heavy men and women with swollen flesh around the eyes and cheeks. His erotica exposed thick penises and bulbous breasts protruding through filmy trousers and bodices. Aristocrats in their tuxedos or cocktail dresses oozed lust, with depraved desire showing in a facial grimace or tense finger clenching or skin that was mottled and flushed. One particularly remarkable study entitled *Lovesick* shows a bony male sitting semirigidly in a bistro chair. He is dressed in a dark suit with a wing tip collar and thin cravat; he holds a cane with a metal head, and a revolver shows like an X-ray image through his jacket. But what is unforgettable is his profile: painted in chalky white, it looks like that of a puppet, only bald puppet with darkly shadowed eyes, an insignia tattooed on one temple, and high cheekbones, long earlobes, and a mouth that is almost a gash in the chalky facial mask. Many of *Cabaret*'s design ideas were fertilized by these images.

Zipprodt's costumes, like Aronson's sets, fell into two general categories: the cabaret world and the realistic one. But even these had subdivisions: for instance, the band, chorus, waiters, and patrons were distinguished from the Emcee. Zipprodt fused styles for the Kit Kat Klub, using a mixture of German expressionism and trashy glitz, based in part on her research of Pabst and on conversations with Dolly Haas, a Berlin cabaret singer–entertainer of the period and the wife of famed caricaturist Al Hirschfeld. The expressionism entered through the textures and silhouettes of the four-piece, all-girl band. Each band member wore the same basic, bare-backed costume that accentuated the breasts and hips and that had a tight-fitting top and short, gold metallic–net, leg ruffles cut above the knee and flouncing from the leg-line area. The breasts were framed in triangle patterns; the abdomen, in a large diamond shape. The triangular motif was extended by large drop earrings in the same shape. Flesh showed amply, particularly in the neck, shoulder, thighs, and arms that had gloves extending from the wrist to above the elbow. These gloves were like grotesque gauntlets, pleated and flared in the upper part, which gave an angular though distorted look to the arms. Although this basic costume had homogeneity, distinctions were made among the four instrumentalists through their short hairstyles, hats, accessories, and shoes. The pianist had ringlets tucked under a sailor hat and wore a choker as well as a pendant. Her boots boasted spats. The saxophonist nestled frizzy hair under a derby and wore knee-high, lace-up boots. The trombone player wore a panama, rolled-up stockings, and single-strap shoes, while the drummer wore a drummer's hat, carried her drum over her left hip, and wore a garter and strap shoes. The quartet wore crude, garish makeup and looked boldly unfashionable, as if in rebellion against good taste. The lack of uniformity in the hairstyles, hats, and footwear created a dual effect: on the one hand, it turned boldness into a cachet; on the other hand, it emphasized the crude chunkiness and daunting, masculine force of the performers. The costumes were deliberately cut to effect a bad or uncomfortably tight fit, and their androgynous look was quite congruent with the ambience of sexual experimentation. The band were complemented by a pair of men in mated, dressy suits and by the dancers in the Kick number wearing beaded vests, belts at the waist, and hats with spray. Further complementarities came in other novelty numbers in which kitsch came to the fore in the form of limbo area dancers with a feline look. The novelty acts were tinged with cynicism, as in "The Money Song," sung by seminude girls each representing a specific nationality and wearing a distinctive headdress and accessories. Miss America, with sparkler in one hand, bore an almost overpoweringly large eagle on her head. She had spangles on gossamer fabric draped over her lower arms and wore fringed half drums over her breasts, a triangle over her groin gleaming with rows of metal coins, and a drum suspended by halter straps on her bare back. But she was only marginally more in bad taste than the high-booted Miss Russia (who glistened like a peacock with her feathery, tasseled look, crowned with a peacock fan headpiece) or the almost nude Miss Germany (a Valkyrie whose pulchritude showed clearly under Viking helmet, long braids, shield, and an oversized German mark hanging from her neck and falling all the way to her crotch). In these instances and in those of Miss Japan (a sort of undressed Madame Butterfly) and Miss France (with an absurd silver Eiffel Tower on her head and a fleur-de-lis over each breast) Broadway playfulness combined with the seminal impulse to be daringly superficial, exaggerated, and in bad taste.

"The Money Song" incarnated the idea of kitsch, providing a carnal spectacle of fun, excitement, energy, and over-the-top "beauty" that could be interpreted ironically rather than literally. After all, "The Money

Costume sketches by Patricia Zipprodt for the original Broadway production (1966) (Photofest)

Costume sketches from
the Broadway production

Song" (just like the Kick number) was hardly spontaneous, harmonious, or truly aesthetic. The design effectively satirized the German desire to negate or evade purely realistic, slice-of-life quotidian banality and to seek fascination by what was strong, dynamic, and freakishly compelling. The appeal of such novelty acts was a simple, figurative, or emotional one but certainly not an intellectually demanding one. In the abundance of naked flesh, the erotic titillation, the suggestions of sexual adventurism lay the "sexy" aspect of Nazi society. It was a sort of theatricality that was not available to the ordinary masses, a magnificently exclusive experience to camouflage a rehearsal of enslavement. "The Money Song" and the Kick number showed sex not simply as an activity but also as a general taste for seduction and ecstasy.

In "If You Could See Her" in act 2, the Emcee entered, hand-in-hand with a handbag-toting gorilla that wore a chic little chiffon skirt, bra, and necklace. Had this number not grown out of one of Fred Ebb's dreams, it might have come from a photo of Ilse Bois performing in a skit at the Kabarett der Komiker in which she hugged a real baby gorilla to her girlish bosom. Zipprodt's costume was quite in key with the note of devilish glee that undercut the surface frivolity.

Expressionism reached its apogee in the Emcee's costume, for in that sleekly attired, groomed figure in dancing shoes lay the metaphor of a rotten country. Made up to look like a grotesquely smiling death's head, the Emcee embodied the soul of a sick nation. His hair shining with pomade, his mouth perverted into a bright red cupid bow, his eyes glittering with feral intensity, the Emcee showed the monster under a facade. His tails and red bow raised him above the folk comedian, but his costume changes (chiefly of a hat or vest, except for a single complete change in the New Year's Eve sequence in which he first came on as Father Time and then as a diapered Baby New Year with bonnet and cigar) emphasized that he should always be seen as a mask for the character in particular and for the show in general. As such, he made the perfect statement for a treacherous environment in which well-dressed patrons sat, talked, danced, drank, and smoked as if cocooned from the reality outdoors.

The cabaret world was one of camp, reflecting as it did a sensibility alive to a double sense of spectacle. Zipprodt's costumes for this world showed characters as pure artifice as well as representatives of the social context. The ugly flamboyance or relish of exaggeration (particularly of the sexual) seemed to put everything in quotation marks, as if the extremes of artifice sponsored a playfulness that was an extension of the metaphor of life as theater.

In vivid contrast was the costuming for the noncabaret world, which was realistic rather than mannerist—except in the case of Sally Bowles—and not generally attempting the extraordinary or glamorous. Zipprodt's costumes for the protagonists, except Sally, were down-to-earth, warm, and sometimes homely. Sally, the show-offy flapper, was allowed to be outrageous, as exemplified by her green fingernails, but her offstage costume suggested the schizoid split in her personality, as the demimonde pretense was contradicted at times by a rather childlike plainness. Fräulein Schneider, appearing at first as rather dowdy, wearing a flowered dressing gown and carpet slippers, later was transformed into a touching spinster in a flounced pink blouse and shimmering deep green, skirted jumper layered with ruffles. Her suitor, the grocer Herr Schultz, remained conservative in his dull brown suit with old-fashioned high stiff collar. This humdrum reality was interspersed with moments of scrubbed loveliness, such as when the waiters became Hitler youths or when Fräulein Kost dressed provocatively for her sailors. But in general, the costuming for the noncabaret narrative emphasized the banal and the old-fashioned.

All in all, then, the costuming was divided into the presentational and the metaphorical, on the one hand, and the realistic and mundane, on the other hand. This split personality imparted a deliberate anomaly for a show in which culpability was disguised, depravity masqueraded as jollity, and the sounds of goose-stepping fascism were muffled by the raucous cabaret music in the Kit Kat Klub.

CHAPTER 5

KANDER AND EBB

JOHN KANDER AND FRED EBB HAD NOT YET RISEN TO THE TOP OF musical theater when they were commissioned to work on *Cabaret*. To that point they had had relatively brief Broadway careers, *Flora, the Red Menace* (1965), with its voguish thirties sound, being their first Broadway collaboration of note. Actually, the duo had worked together in 1964 on *Golden Gate*, but that show was never produced, and *Flora* flopped. *Cabaret* was, in effect, their third Broadway collaboration, and their first winner. Because their musicals have not generated the same level of debate or notice as those by Stephen Sondheim and Andrew Lloyd Webber, Kander and Ebb are unfairly omitted from the top of the list of Broadway composers, and to date only one complete book (James Leve's thorough study published in 2009) has been devoted to them. However, in terms of musical theater, as Michael Frank (1995: 205) has remarked, they are "able to blend their musical vocabulary to a formidable variety of periods and places."

Kander (born in Kansas City, Missouri, on March 18, 1927) fell in love with the piano at about age four. Everyone in his family loved music or making music. "Nobody was professional and some of them were tone-deaf, but there was a lot of enthusiasm," he later recalled (Bryer and Davison 2008: 96). In second grade, he startled his teacher by claiming to be writing a Christmas carol during math class. "I only found out years later that she had called my parents, very perturbed because we were a Jewish family, and asked if it was all right for me to be writing Christmas carols." Precocious about music, he was interested in both classical and "show" music. His bureau bore a picture of Gertrude Lawrence at one end and a picture of Lotte Lehmann at the other. "I knew that if I ever ran away from home I would run away to one of those two women!" he joked (97). Kander eventually received classical training in counterpoint, orchestration, and form (his master's degree, from Columbia, was awarded in 1954), ostensibly as preparation for a career in concert music and opera. At one time, he was undecided between art music or pop music. Opera and Broadway musicals held his interest equally, not only because of their technical sophistication but also for their stirring passion. Kander has always wanted to be remembered as "an emotional stirrer," someone whose music contains "emotions that have impact, feelings that don't just wash over you and do nothing" (Kasha and Hirschhorn 1987: 205).

Ebb (whose date of birth remains a mystery, though it was possibly 1932) was a native New Yorker with a literary pedigree, receiving a B.A. from New York University and an M.A. in English literature from Columbia. Despite his academic training, Ebb claimed in *People* magazine (September 17, 1979) that he got the majority of his ideas for lyrics from the working class: waiters, cab drivers, grocers—and, most of all, his own mother. Unlike Kander's childhood, which Ebb said resembled a Norman Rockwell painting (Leve 2009: 14), his lacked an exposure to concerts and theater. Early in his career he dabbled in limericks and light verse and peddled song lyrics to record companies. Phil Springer taught him the mechanics of songwriting, tutoring him on structure and rhyme. Their first collaboration, "I Never Loved Him Anyhow," was recorded by Carmen McRae, but Ebb did not create theater music until he teamed up with composer Paul Klein in 1951. The pair composed three full-length musicals that were never produced (*It Gives Me Great Pleasure, Simon Says,* and *Morning Son*). Meanwhile, Kander was earning his living by coaching singers, playing piano at auditions, and conducting summer stock productions. Kander's big break came when he met Jerome Robbins, who hired him to accompany auditions for *Gypsy* and later to write the dance music. Then David Merrick signed him to write dance music for *Irma la Douce.*

Kander and Ebb were introduced by Tommy Valando, a publisher friend, and within an hour of their first meeting they had produced "Perfect Strangers." Ebb claimed: "It was a case of instant communication and instant song. Our neuroses complimented each other, and because we worked in the same room at the same time, I didn't have to finish a lyric, then hand it over to John to compose it" (Leve 2009: 16).

Their first ballad, "My Colouring Book," became an instant hit, earning Sandy Stewart a Grammy nomination for her recording of it. They came to enjoy "the longest composer–lyricist collaboration in the history of musical theatre," a partnership that ended only with Ebb's death from a heart attack on September 11, 2004 (1). At the time of Ebb's death, the two were working on several projects, including a revision of *Over and Over* (a musical version of Thornton Wilder's *The Skin of Our Teeth*) and the murder–mystery musical *Curtains*, which Kander saw to completion on Broadway. Their career credits include more than twenty musicals (twelve of which opened on Broadway), Hollywood film music, a wide range of special musical material (including television specials for Shirley MacLaine and Liza Minnelli), and numerous honors and awards, including the Tony, the Oscar, the Emmy, and the Kennedy Center Award for Lifetime Achievement in the Performing Arts.

As James Leve has shown, Kander and Ebb found their distinctive voice just as the Broadway musical was starting to move in an increasingly serious direction. The team of Richard Rodgers and Oscar Hammerstein II was no longer the prevailing model, due in large measure to the nervous uncertainty created by the Cold War and the Vietnam War. Moreover, rock 'n' roll was quickly becoming common currency on Broadway, and librettos were moving away from linear narratives toward "more fragmented structures." Also, with the consolidation of concept musicals, the focus was shifting from the celebration of community (as in *Oklahoma!*) to the Self (as in *Company* and *A Chorus Line*). Kander and Ebb took to the new developments eagerly, especially with *Cabaret*, which dealt with disenfranchised members of society confronting "existential challenges within a hostile, cynical, and nihilistic world" (4). Their work on *Cabaret* showed them as provocateurs and subversive practitioners of the concept musical, at least in the Kit Kat Klub portions of the show that obviously owe debts to Brecht—the chief being an aesthetic disjunction between song and narrative. As many critics have noted, the cabaret songs comment on the book scenes. However, as Leve has pointed out, the songs "are more than commentary; they are the mood of the piece," with their primary purpose being a point of view. "Collectively, the cabaret songs reflect the moral decline in Germany: they start out as risqué diversions but gradually become racist political propaganda" (41). Added to this was their unique sense of irony, particularly in the manner in which they used show business as a symbol for life in the implicit belief that musical theater could reflect human nature. *Chicago* (1975) used vaudeville as a metaphor for a corrupt legal system that rewarded only the most dazzling courtroom performances; *Kiss of the Spider Woman* (1993) used the Hollywood musical as a form of mental escape from oppression; and *Steel Pier* (1997) turned the dance marathon into a promise of a better life. These musicals, like *Cabaret*, drew attention to theatrical artifice.

This artifice (incorporating camp) is expressive of their gay sensibilities, especially when attention is drawn to the nature and scope of camp. An understanding of camp derives, of course, from the idea of gay sensibility—"a creative energy reflecting a consciousness that is different from the mainstream, a heightened awareness of certain human complications of feeling that spring from the fact of social oppression; in short, a perception of the world which is colored, shaped, directed, and defined by the fact of one's gayness" (Bergman 1993: 19). It is interesting that Christopher Isherwood's novel *The World in the Evening* has "perhaps the earliest discussion of the subject" (Bergman 1993: 4). Isherwood divides camp into two categories: low (such as "a swishy little boy with peroxided hair, dressed in a picture hat and a feather boa, pretending to be Marlene Dietrich") and high (subjects with "an underlying seriousness") (4). For Isherwood, camp was only possible about something you had to take seriously: "You're expressing what's basically serious to you in terms of fun and artifice and elegance." In her groundbreaking essay "Notes on 'Camp'" Susan Sontag (1966: 279) claimed that camp was "a certain form of aestheticism," which elevated objects "not in terms of Beauty, but in terms of degree of artifice, of stylization." For Sontag, Camp was "esoteric—something of a private code, a badge of identity," and its essence was "its love of the unnatural: of artifice and exaggeration" (277). Jack Babuscio's seminal essay on the subject, "Camp and the Gay Sensibility," asserts that implicit in the very nature of camp is the idea that life is theater where various roles are played by persons and where reality and appearance are often in conflict or in uneasy alliance. By focusing on the outward appearance of roles, camp implies that these roles are superficial or a matter of style. Hence, life itself is a matter of role-playing or impersonation (Bergman 1993: 19–38). There is general agreement in some areas of the topic, as summarized by David Bergman: camp is "a style" that favors "exaggeration," "artifice," and "extremity." It exists "in tension with popular culture, commercial culture, or consumerist culture." Anyone who can recognize camp or who can camp "is a person outside the cultural mainstream." And "camp is affiliated with homosexual culture, or at least with a self-conscious eroticism" (4–5). According to Babuscio, "Camp is never a thing or person per se, but, rather, a relationship between activities, individuals, situations, *and* gayness," but people who exhibit camp need not be gay. Four elements are basic to camp: irony, aestheticism, theatricality, and humor (20).

Kander and Ebb apply these ideas in their musicals, and their material thereby acquires an edgy quality (Leve 2009: 21–22). Sally Bowles and the Emcee are the most obvious figures of camp in *Cabaret*: Sally because she deliberately acts as a bad girl who embraces sin right from her opening number ("Don't Tell Mama"), which mocks respectability and her judgmental mother; the Emcee because of his cross-dressing, sexual deviance, and ironic, self-conscious humor. The Kit Kat Klub scenes push the limits of perversion by offering patrons an escape from the dreariness of their mundane existence. The patrons, for their part, derive pleasure from the mockery, sexual byplay, and parody, but they see the cabaret entertainment "within a bigger framework, one that encompasses Berlin, its inhabitants, and its politics" (45). The cabaret numbers are lewd camp ("Two Ladies" in act 1; the kick line dance at the top of act 2, with the Emcee in drag and high heels; and "If You Could See Her through My Eyes"), provoking mirth or discomfort at either the ambiguity inherent in a number or its sinister intent. Just as Hitler and his Nazis depended on mixed theatricality and hysteria to cast a spell on their audiences at rallies, the musical draws attention to the role of artifice, fantasy, and spectacle during the creeping fascism of the period. "Tomorrow Belongs to Me," first in a book scene and then (at least in the Sam Mendes version) in the cabaret, and the kick line goose-stepping of the cabaret girls in the next scene show that Nazism has begun its encroachment upon German culture. So, *Cabaret* is theatrical in its evocation of Berlin sociology, German politics, and the myth of Sally Bowles. Its music "evokes the decadence and foursquare jazz playing of Berlin nightclubs in the thirties" (22), thereby creating a patina of verisimilitude, but its various textures of sound also brilliantly push into larger areas of culture and symbolism.

When Kander and Ebb were composing their score and lyrics for the show, they knew that German jazz had a rigidity that could not compete with the economy, dynamism, and freedom of American jazz. American popular music (especially by George Gershwin and Louis Armstrong) had (with the exception of some German classical musicians) been ardently welcomed across Europe in the midtwenties. In Berlin, the trend had been to listen to music of the past (Beethoven, Bach, Mozart, in particular), but a growing number of people were receptive to "the free tonality of Schoenberg and his disciples, and to an American import called jazz that seemed excitingly exotic to many Germans only recently liberated from a prolonged cultural exile" (Hirsch 2002: 17–18). Paul Whiteman and Gershwin were thrilling audiences, and Kurt Weill, for instance, was especially fascinated by *Rhapsody in Blue*. Hans Heinsheimer (publisher and promoter of classical and contemporary music) explained some of the allure: "We went to nightclubs where some American jazz bands—negroes, colored people—played something we had never heard; it was like somebody in America hearing a tune from the Eskimos" (18). The jazz that Berliners were commonly exposed to was not, however, the real thing. Whiteman's sound was more commercial than the New Orleans original, and Berlin cabarets played "an even more corrupted version"—not that it mattered, for jazz's simplicity and directness were appealing, and jazz became a hot new style as well as "an emblem of the openness and modernity of Weimar culture." Soon jazz began to infiltrate musical performances in revues, cabaret, the concert hall, and opera house. "As such jazz-based elements as syncopation, improvisation, a greater use of wind instruments, and a driving percussive beat mixed with native expressionist and atonal idioms, a fusion was born that was to prepare the way for Kurt Weill's music-theatre hybrids" (18).

Because he was very young during the thirties, Kander had few firm memories of that period—except for the sounds. *Cabaret*, of course, required German sounds, so he listened to German jazz of the twenties. As Leve (2009: 49) asserts, Kander discovered the "sound" of Berlin in the "stylized piano playing of Pater Kreuger and the incongruous harmonies and rhythms of Friderick Hollaender's cabaret songs." Hollaender had composed music for *The Blue Angel*, which was released in 1930, "the second year of Isherwood's stay in Berlin and the year in which *Cabaret* takes place." Characteristically, his cabaret songs mixed sentimentality and sarcasm. In *Notes on Broadway* Kander is quoted as remarking, "The Germans took American black jazz and turned it into something altogether different. So I listened and listened and then put it away and forgot about it. That sort of seeps into your consciousness" (Kasha and Hirschhorn 1987: 195). But there was a particular kind of sound that he always remembered consciously. German cabaret had boasted a number of remarkable female singers, such as Trude Hesterberg, Rosa Valetti, Gussy Holl, Blandine Ebinger, Margo Lion, Claire Waldoff, and (through the movies) Marlene Dietrich, but perhaps the most haunting performances were those by Weill's wife, Lotte Lenya, who had a high but murky voice and a facade of tough courage streaked with hints of vulnerability. Her lack of pretense somehow added to the drama of her renditions, and Kander was hooked by her style, as he recalled in Donald Spoto's biography of the actress–singer: "I had Lenya and the sound of her voice in my head the entire time I was composing" (Spoto 1989: 255).

Of course it helped that Lenya was the first to be signed for the cast. "We never thought of anyone but Lenya for Fräulein Schneider," Joe Masteroff revealed in an interview, "and had she chosen not to play the role it would have been a great blow. Both Lenya's role and that of Jack Gilford [as the Jewish grocer Herr Schultz] were written with the expectation that they would do them." Lenya had become a "living symbol" for the time and place used in *Cabaret*, but composing a score for a story set in Weimar Berlin with Weill's widow as its star worried Kander and Ebb. Acknowledging Weill's influence, they did not want to do a mere imitation. Besides, they preferred the Weill who created new works in America (*Lady in the Dark* and *Street Scene*) to the Weill who had started in Germany (*The Threepenny Opera* and *The Rise and Fall of the City of Mahagonny*). While working on the musical, Kander refused to listen to Weill's German music, electing to concentrate instead on Berlin cabaret music and the popular music of the period that had influenced Weill. Kander and Ebb recognized the genius of Weill, but they also knew that the important thing was to present their own individual voice (Hirsch 2002: 338). The pair received the comforting approval of Weill's widow, Lenya, who was sympathetic when Kander was criticized in some quarters for writing "watered-down Kurt Weill." She remarked: "No, no, darling. It is not Weill. It is not Kurt. When I walk out on stage and sing those songs, it is *Berlin*" (Guernsey 1985: 145). Remarks such as these could only help publicity for the show, especially when she told a reporter: "For me, it's just as if I left the Kit Kat Klub in Berlin last night. It's so authentic, it's frightening" (Morris 2004: 146).

Ebb had more trouble composing than Kander did because German jazz and cabaret recordings of the twenties did not come with any lyrics either in German or in English. He did scan some histories of the period, but his chief sources of information were the records that Kander played for him. As he recalls in *Broadway Song & Story*: "That gave me sort of a feeling. I remember one of them was during a live performance of something and it was getting *screams*!" It was frustrating for him not to understand the content, though he could guess that the songs were "impudent and irreverent and were often sexual." He knew he should "probably go for some good sex jokes" (Guernsey 1985: 146). Kander and Ebb both wanted an entertaining piece as well as one with emotional power. They didn't have the idea of a concept musical in mind when they were composing the score and lyrics. As Ebb revealed, the songs were "made to order. Hal would say, 'Maybe we should have a number here for this moment.'...I don't think that I appreciated the portentousness of the subject we were treating with a cabaret in Hitler's Berlin, or the seriousness of it, until that was pointed out to me" (Kander and Ebb 2003: 60). However, as Kander recognized, Prince often used a conceptual mode "with actors observing and songs that comment on the action," so his concept in this sense influenced them (60).

Kander and Ebb both recalled how they would sit in a room with Prince and Masteroff and play a game that Kander would call What If? The group would invent incidents that were to be part of the story. "What if such and such happens? What if somebody throws a brick through the window?" Ebb divulged that out of such meetings came the

John Kander and Fred Ebb,
1966 (Photofest)

Emcee as well as many of the theatrical devices that worked to the show's advantage, and both composers swear that *Cabaret* was the "best collaborative process" they ever had (60–62).

Kander and Ebb originally composed about forty-seven songs for the show, but only about fifteen were ultimately used. According to Ebb: "The narrative kept shifting, and there were many more scenes that were seriously considered that never were done. Also, characters were being added" (Guernsey 1985: 139). Actually (as Scott Miller has shown), the composers wrote two scores (one dealing with the book scenes, and the other with cabaret numbers), although there were quotations from one number in another, or echoes from the cabaret score in the book score. For example, the introduction of "Don't Tell Mama" echoes the introduction of "Willkommen," connecting the two cabaret numbers, just as the introduction of "Perfectly Marvelous" is an instrumental reprise of "Don't Tell Mama," showing us that while Sally is actually performing for Cliff, she is suggesting that living with him would meet with her mother's disapproval just as her cabaret singing does. The introduction of "Tomorrow Belongs To Me" quotes "It Couldn't Please Me More," making it clear that the anthem is commenting on the wholesomeness of the Fräulein Schneider–Herr Schultz relationship, and subtly foreshadowing how the happiness of this couple will morph into horror. Additionally, the introduction of "Why Should I Wake Up?" shows that Cliff has subscribed to Sally's worldview and that, as a result, she distracts him from his literary purpose and the course of politics in Weimar Berlin. The marvel is that while there are joyous songs and melancholy ones, sexy ditties and Eastern European Jewish tones, there is an astonishing overarching quality that is not jarring. As Thomas Hischak (2008: 113) has remarked: "Because of their chilly, distanced tone, all the numbers are of a whole."

When (upon the advice of George Abbott) Prince and Masteroff changed three acts to two, they sacrificed "Good Time Charlie" sung by Sally and Cliff on their way to Fräulein Schneider, a filthy number for the Emcee called "Song of Love," and "The End of the Party" that ended the first act. A song called "Roommates" was replaced by "Perfectly Marvelous," sung by Sally to Cliff to coax him into letting her move in with him. An early draft of the three-act libretto had "I Don't Care Much," staged as a production number in which the Emcee was backed up by girls in men's suits. Prince cut the song, though he reinserted it for his 1987 Broadway revival, and years later, Sam Mendes's version would have

Alan Cumming's Emcee sing it while using heroin (Leve 2009: 43). Masteroff recognized that the composers had written cabaret songs that did not seem to relate to anything in particular. However, they sounded like "what you might have heard in a night club in Germany in 1930." These were not book songs, but more songs of atmosphere, and they were inserted in between the book scenes. In the early scripts, they were just "higgledy-piggledy." Masteroff never discussed his script ahead of time with Kander and Ebb. He would simply write scenes, and then the two composers would pluck the songs out of them by intuition and genius. For instance, the pineapple exchange between Fräulein Schneider and Herr Schultz first existed as a dialogue scene, but Kander and Ebb quickly turned it into a comically romantic number ("It Couldn't Please Me More").

True to their customary working method, Kander and Ebb started with the show's first song. "I don't think it's necessarily the most important song," says Kander in *Notes on Broadway*, "but the opening of a show tells you something about what you're going to do. I can't say it more clearly than that. It gives you some sense of the language and style you'll be working in." There was no overture, for the stage had to be dark for the Emcee's dramatic entrance, and the overhanging mirror had to make the first important statement visually. The casual sounds of the club band tuning up, with stray notes from brass or piano or drums, would create a softly slurred, jangled net of sound to catch an audience's interest in a deliberately skewed orchestration. A seven-second drumroll and weak clashing cymbals precede the opening of "Willkommen." First a pause, and then the vamp begins—"arguably the most familiar two measures in musical theater" (Leve 2009: 53). The number mixes various modes—song, speech, choral upsurge—and the instrumentation has brassy honky-tonk passages wherein an out-of-tune piano creates tinkling embellishments to the accompaniment of a coarse trumpet. As Leve points out, the vamp "recurs throughout the opening scene, underscoring the emcee's salacious remarks to the audience," coupling with his lurid punch lines to capture "the menacing artifice of German culture during this period" and foreshadowing "Sally's, as well as Germany's, downward spiral" (53). Leve identifies this vamp at the end of "Don't Tell Mama" and "a tightly wound version of it in the minor key at the opening of 'Cabaret' as an allusion to the ultimately sad outcome of Sally's decision to have an abortion." The music allows for the entrance of a vulgar chorus line of worldly girls, pretending to be innocent virgins, as the vamping in the background acquires a brisk, lively rhythm. Then the instrumentation blossoms into a glistening nightclub pitch as the coarse texture is smoothed for the dancing chorus. A whispery passage modulates into foot stamping and then into carnival gaiety before the chorus swells to a crescendo with typical Broadway flourish.

In one sense, this ending is a disappointment, for it casts the number into an American mode that is all-too-obviously presentational. In another sense, however, the number's "show biz" style confirms Kander and Ebb's love of the American musical form, for as Ethan Mordden (1997) remarks, "at the center of their art lies a love of the talent-take-all wonder of entertainment." *Cabaret* is like other Kander and Ebb musicals (*Flora, Chicago, Zorba, Kiss of the Spider Woman*) that, whether set in Germany, the United States, Greece, or South America, flirt with chaos and death without ever losing their sense of delight for strutting, show-offy musical numbers. In sum, then, the polyglot lyric, mixed instrumentation, and tonal modulations, as well as the sheer integration of song, music, choreography, and costuming, stamp "Willkommen" as a signature piece that creates a specific ambience while conjuring up a metaphor for the show as a whole.

However, "Willkommen," just like the cabaret metaphor, evolved gradually. Wanting to establish the show's atmosphere from the start—even before the first draft of the script—Prince asked Kander and Ebb for a mixture of songs that would express what was happening in Berlin during the period. The composers accordingly wrote several. Fred Ebb's papers contain a list for a possible running order: "Angel of Love," "Two Ladies," "I Don't Care Much," "Tomorrow Belongs to Me," "Herman, My German," "A Mark in Your Pocket," "Yodelin," "Liebchen," "Policeman," and "Bücher." Sketches exist for all except "Yodelin," "Policeman," and "Bücher." There are also sketches for other Berlin songs—"Berlin, Berlin, Berlin," "A Little Geld" (alternatively titled "Good Neighbor Cohen," which later supplied the melody for the "Money Song" in Bob Fosse's film), "Haven't They Ever," "Welcome to Berlin," and "This Life" (Leve 2009: 319). These songs—exploring such topics as economic hardship, prostitution, and sexual adventure—were to be sung by various characters: a fat man, an aging operatic tenor, a streetwalker, a group of college boys, et cetera (41). The songs also appropriated popular German musical forms: the male choir and folk song, lascivious cabaret numbers, and drinking songs (56). What

Kit Kat Klub Band in
Cabaret *(1966) (Photofest)*

was to become "Willkommen" (though the first number created for the musical) included five short eclectic songs. One was about a German named Herman; another was set in a radio station; and a third was a Chinese song about decadence delivered by a Chinese girl. The informing idea was that the central story of Sally and Cliff would begin at the end of the five songs and that this story would have its own particular score (Ilson 1989: 139–40).

The prologue did not retain its original structure. Kander and Ebb inserted the five songs "between the book scenes in random fashion instead of at the beginning of the show" but soon realized that the songs intruded on the book scenes. Consequently, only "Willkommen" was retained for the Emcee, who became "the thread for the entire musical" by reflecting his nation and serving as a metaphor for the "mindless gaiety" as well as the menace of Nazi Berlin (140).

The Emcee's opening is an apparently innocent greeting in German, French, and English ("Willkommen, bienvenue, welcome"), but it radiates disconcerting signals in the next four lines. The gesture of welcome is paradoxically distancing, for the club's clientele is addressed as strangers, which is precisely what they are. Estranged, perhaps, from one another, they are certainly distanced from the limbo area that the Emcee inhabits. They are inside the cabaret to escape the sordid and morbid tensions of the real world. *Enchanté* is a deceptive word, denoting pleasure while connoting a charm. The Emcee is charming even as he weaves a spell over his audience, cocooning its members, as it were, within the trashy glamour of his number. "Leave your troubles outside," he urges, downplaying the rank disillusionment of a generation in the phrase "So—life is disappointing? Forget it!" The invocation to forgetfulness is virtually demonic, for the "beauty" and "innocence" of the cabaret girls are obviously parodies of those ideals, as the Emcee reveals by his lewdly mocking, titillating tone. His brief falsetto eruption (it occurs only once and late in the number) is not simply camp; it is an emblem of his nation's and his own unreality. The lyric signals the false cosmopolitanism of Berlin. The subtle clues of danger (in the words *stranger, enchanté, forget*; the interplay of appearance and reality; the symbolism of the host; the falsetto; the chorus line, which momentarily suggests a sinister goose-step) are all embedded in the kitsch of the presentation. So, taken as a whole, "Willkommen" is brilliantly multifaceted, not only serving as exposition of a time, place, and atmosphere but also emitting an ambiguous radiance of the damned.

The Emcee's song is set in a limbo area, where it functions as an ironic signpost. Indeed, all of his songs, as Foster Hirsch (2005: 61) comments, frame and pointedly disrupt book scenes, and his routines, "like the songs in *The Threepenny Opera*, use musical interludes in a self-conscious way to isolate and to enlarge the show's themes. As they fulfil the entertainment imperative of musical theatre the comment songs also create intellectual detachment."

The cabaret world makes an indelibly strong impression in the first act, though the twelve songs of this portion are evenly distributed between the Kit Kat Klub and the private worlds of the main characters. Following the long-established convention of musical theater, each scene has a song that completes its character. The six noncabaret songs include a solo for Fräulein Schneider, a duet for Sally and Cliff, two duets for Schneider and Schultz, and a solo apiece for Sally and Cliff. All of these numbers establish character and situation while appealing mainly to comic feeling. The cabaret numbers, by contrast, have more of an ensemble quality, despite the key role played by the Emcee in three of them.

Kander's interest in creating a musical ambience to support Masteroff's story and its time and place was helped by orchestrator Don Walker, who had been music writer and arranger for Fred Waring and Benny Goodman's radio orchestra before he scored the Romberg–Hammerstein *May Wine* (1935) and *Best Foot Forward* (1941). Walker had become a popular leading orchestrator on Broadway, with such major credits as *Ziegfeld Follies* (1936 and 1943), *On the Town* (1944), *Carousel* (1945), *Finian's Rainbow* (1947), *Gentlemen Prefer Blondes* (1949), *Call Me Madam* (1950), *Wonderful Town* (1953), *The Pajama Game* (1954), *Damn Yankees* (1955), *The Music Man* (1957), and *Fiddler on the Roof* (1964). In fact, Walker had so much Broadway work that he did not have time to be employed in other media. He started the trend of smaller orchestras and deployed unorthodox devices (such as nothing but resonant celli in string sections) in a quest for strange, exotic colors of sound. Walker had a crusty demeanor and a grim presence, but his artistic brilliance more than compensated for his personality. For *Cabaret* Walker used two orchestras: one that played "standard music for interpersonal songs, and an orchestra for the presentation numbers that took place in the cabaret" (Suskin 2009: 110–11). He made room for exciting piano writing, something that had not been given a major role in the so-called golden age of Broadway musicals. Instead of relegating the pianist to playing chords, offbeats, and fills, Walker left space for the frisky Kit Kat Klub Band numbers that created genuine excitement in the cabaret. It is estimated that he provided about 85 percent or more of the orchestration, all written in his own hand (117). When the show was revived in 1987, Walker was responsible for everything apart from the "Married Reprise," prelude act 1, prelude act 2, "Kick Line I," "Kick Line II," utilities ("Married," "Pineapple/Couldn't Please Me More"), and he revised four- or eight-bar introductions to "So What?" "Telephone Song," and "Tomorrow Belongs to Me." His contribution led Kander to send him a written note on opening night (which Walker could not attend because of illness): "Your wonderful work sounds even more impressive after twenty-one years. You will always be an important part of *Cabaret*" (350).

Kander and Ebb wisely avoid striking an audience on its collective head with clanging symbols. They refrain from presenting Nazis overtly onstage because they prefer to trace a dramatic trajectory that will not give the play's provocative statement away from the start. They preserve momentum and tension by structure and style, for each of the cabaret numbers is a different revelation of a city and nation on the edge of nightmare. Introduced by the Emcee with a drumroll and cymbal, and with bars from "Willkommen" sneaking in and out and actually framing the ballad, Sally's "Don't Tell Mama" has a brassy, racy sound. At first, the piano arpeggio and trills suggest a cocktail lounge production, but Sally creates a husky rawness in the release, and the drums add jazz accents to what is predominantly a character song, aided and abetted by the cabaret girls. A Charleston rhythm does insinuate itself to fortify the gaiety, and this also reinforces the image of Sally as a flapper who hides her "secret" from her mother. Sally's number begins as ironic speech, then pretends to be plaintive before breaking into gusty self-assertion. There is a tone of naughty deceit, for Sally allows her mother no inkling of her work in the nightclub "In a pair of lacy pants." The cabaret chorus underlines the deception in typical jazz babies style, and the dainty or pedestrian rhymes ("pickle"/"nickel"; "fine"/"line"; "grim"/"him") impart a very English or American flavor to the number. But "Don't Tell Mama" is obviously a song very much in Sally's performance character while also linking her deceitfulness to the general falsity of Berlin life, where evil is often disguised by perverse jollity. As "Willkommen" pulses intermittently under Sally's lyric, Kander and Ebb make the point that Sally is part of the same moral sickness that infects Berlin. Her bubbly mischief is a gleaming bubble that will burst once the grim reality of fascism envelops the nation.

"Telephone Song" and "Two Ladies" fall into the novelty category. The first has a very brisk tempo that is the essence of a showbiz tune. Designed in a three-part form, it obtains its dynamism from the quick sexual assignations negotiated by aggressive women who know how to target lonely males. Although it is meant to have a tonal harmony, it uses rapid-fire conversation sparingly before breaking into pure instrumentation for dancing and then building to a virtual medley of voices. Alcohol, music, and sex are the catalysts for its bursts of hectic tempo, and although the song is less effective on its own than as choreographed onstage, it does convey the mood of sexual yearning that beset many young Berliners in the period. Each of the three parts has a modifying tempo and quality. The first is characterized by swirls of music; the second, by a strong use of strings; the third, by a hard jazz edge created by drums and brass. The sexual pairings also have their own configurations, as the first sequence involves a single pair, while both the second and third sequences double the pairing. This adds to the cumulative speed and volume and amplifies the sense of frothy gaiety that covers the new barbarism. The apparently light-hearted, whirring fun of nightlife is a respite from the general discord and political terror that George Grösz and other artists of the period depicted in their caricatures.

"Two Ladies" and "Money Song" put the Emcee's devilish glee back at the center of the cabaret world. The suggestive sexual antics of the Emcee and the two "ladies" with whom he cavorts bawdily underline the celebration of a ménage à trois. The out-of-tune piano, Swiss accordion, and brass carry the melody, raising the pitch on the nonsense syllables "beedle dee dee dee dee" as the novelty act verges on soft porn. Tacky and smutty, the number revels in kitsch and is an effective expression of the impulses toward perversion that were shamelessly satisfied by hordes of young people who considered it a disgrace to be suspected of virginity or chastity. Successful even out of context, the number cleverly extends a theme already developed by the preceding duet with Sally and Cliff, "Perfectly Marvelous"(originally called "Roommates"), in which Sally craftily persuades the shy, introverted young writer to become her live-in boyfriend.

"Money Song" does nothing to really further the plot, but its perversely lewd, smug tone, set to a rollicking beat with banjo and brass, has a Las Vegas quality in at least one passage, and the song does extend the vile character of both the Emcee and the cabaret. It had an early incarnation as "A Mark in Your Pocket," "a rather mild commentary about economic deprivation during the Depression" (Leve 2009: 58). A second incarnation was as "Sitting Pretty," a vitriolic attack on capitalism and, therefore, a progression in tone from the first incarnation. Now, as "Money Song," there was "a new, implicitly anti-Semitic" tone (60). A rowdy, gaudy act (in which chorus girls represent the currency of miscellaneous nations), this song has a vulgar thrust. The rapid patter lyric is performed almost totally by the Emcee and amounts to a flaunting of his financial fortune at the expense of his own family's sheer economic misfortune. The blaring opening, forced rhyme, and unnaturally quick tempi of some sections suggest the amoral freakishness of the man. The finale (where the chorus girls join in lewd byplay with him) soars with trumpet and horn rather than with banjo and piano, sealing the number's stridency.

As the bulk of the score up to this point shows, *Cabaret* uses standard musical comedy conventions (the comic romantic couple formula), though there is more than one curve in this pattern. The comedy is sometimes sour, often bawdily flamboyant, and occasionally tender, but it is always an interesting bridge between the slender plotlines and the significant interior tone that, despite the satiric elements, is sober and ironic. The cabaret world carries impertinent and often grotesque sound, but as the solos and duets of the protagonists show, there is another world of human dimension with characters bearing real faces and vulnerabilities.

There are two comedies within the plot boundaries: one about Sally Bowles, the breezy mediocrity and silly heroine; the other about Fräulein Schneider, the landlady who puts a bright face on caustic failure and who, in tandem with the unfortunate Schultz, accounts for some of the most sentimental moments. Where the Emcee and his cohorts are the heady, horrible metaphor of a nation, and where Sally and Cliff are eavesdroppers on an era, Schneider and Schultz are middle-aged Germans who blossom in gentle love before becoming victims to the storm and stress of putrid nationalism.

Sally has the most exhibitionistic songs of the quartet of protagonists. Appropriately, she has a rooming house duet with Cliff in addition to her cabaret piece, but even in its domestic milieu, "Perfectly Marvelous" is a show-offy number. In it Sally deploys wit, charm, and audacity. The irregular rhyme scheme (with only two sets of rhyming or off-rhyme words) is a clever indicator of Sally's eccentricity and capricious flight of fancy. The most repeated word in the unequal duet is "girl," and it is clearly Sally who initiates and develops the adverbial–adjectival matrix, adding to her own lustrous self-image: "I met this perfectly marvellous girl / In this perfectly wonderful place / As I lifted a glass to the start of a marvellous year." She is clearly putting words into Cliff's ear in the hope that he will then repeat them and, thereby, bring to reality her wish-fulfillment fantasy. Cliff's own vocal part is subordinate to Sally's, probably because, as Leve (2009: 68) claims, of his "sexual ambiguity," which made it difficult for the writers to find a musical voice for him. In other words, Cliff could not express himself musically "as either a heterosexual or homosexual." Another possible reason could be his function as voyeur or camera: he records rather than creates. When he does set about creating, it is only at the end when he is leaving Berlin, so in terms of the Sally Bowles story, his role is to be charmed by this clever siren. Cliff's capitulation is borne out by his duplication of her rhythm, tempo, and verbal pattern and, finally, by his harmonizing the final line and crescendo with her. Initially,

Cliff was given eighteen songs, most of them duets with Sally (a complete list can be found in James Leve's book on Kander and Ebb), of which only two were solos: "Maybe Down That Street" and the hauntingly romantic "Never in Paris" (rather reminiscent of Vernon Duke and E. Y. Harburg's "April in Paris," though Cliff explains why he came to Berlin rather than stay in Paris). By the time the show premiered on Broadway, he was left only with "Why Should I Wake Up?" Using her flair and "divine decadence" to full advantage, Sally is very much in control of Cliff at this stage, and his solo ballad demonstrates this in more than one way. Tonally, it is almost sickeningly sentimental (even in the instrumentation, which relies on lush strings), as Cliff ardently sings of being lost in a dream of Sally. His diction is that of a charmed victim, with such words as "dream," "enchanted," "spell," and "euphoric" making it clear that he is happy to be Sally's captive. The soaring notes of the ballad, especially on the title line and the couplet at the end of each release, reveal a character who is incongruous with the one projected in either Isherwood or van Druten, for gone is the shy, reticent, but sharply intelligent witness to life, and in his place is a Broadway romantic who is quite gratified in being under a woman's spell. Both the tone and the scoring of the ballad compromise the character of Cliff and that of the show in general, though in one sense this song does extend the deep-rooted interplay between reality and unreality.

This ballad and the lovers' duet contrast with the cabaret numbers. For a brief while, at least, Sally and Cliff need not worry about anything other than their own intimate relationship or about making the most of a tight situation in a cheap rooming house. Their private and public lives are kept distinct. Fräulein Schneider has two songs that define her character and introduce warm glints of optimism into Berlin's spreading gloom. Her first song is in her ugly flat in scene 3, when she and Cliff, newly arrived in Berlin, discuss his rent. The polite haggling prompts her to express her resignation, yet she demonstrates her innate toughness bred from experience and a worldly wisdom that allows her to settle for what she can get.

"So What?" has an accordion accompaniment with an underlying piano texture and select accents from brass and strings. But it is very characteristic of the spoken-songs that *chanteuses* and *diseuses* performed in European cabarets. It begins as expository speech that summarizes the situation, then alters deftly with spoken song ("When you're as old as I") as Fräulein Schneider settles into a lyrically philosophical mode before

opening up as full-blown song. The slow polka rhythm, with strings pluck-
ing in undertone, preserves the melody, but the tonal texture is reminiscent of that in chansons sung by Edith Piaf and other boulevard or café
artistes. Adroit in its long end-stopped lines ("When I was a girl my
summers were spent by the sea, so what? / And I had a maid doing all of
the housework, not me, so what?"), it recapitulates the spinster's vanished privileges and asserts her determination to survive and transcend
the pinched meanness of her current straits. Her physique has deterio-
rated along with her opportunities for romance and wealth, but as surely
as the sun rises and the moon waxes, she goes on, learning to shrug off
the cares that would oppress most others. What makes the lyric so alluring
is its clever pragmatic tone. The release or refrain is the philosophical
core, and it is the most melodious and concise portion of the ballad,
whereas the longer passages (some lines carrying ten or more syllables
each) are excursions into the Fräulein's past. Banjo, brass, winds, and
out-of-tune piano combine to create a peculiarly slanted tonality perfectly in key with the attitude of unflinching resignation. The gesture of
the song is, of course, a brave shrug, and the tonality conveys this gesture
effectively, as the strings increase their sweep and surge and the ballad
grows climactically dizzying in tempo and pitch.

The giddy upbeat ending adds to the comic moments of the first act,
as does "It Couldn't Please Me More," a duet performed by Fräulein
Schneider and her suitor, the shy Jewish grocer. In this ballad, his
Jewishness is not overtly of any significance, though an audience senses
that his Jewishness will eventually become a problem in the plot. With this
tension foreshadowed lightly, the song proceeds as if the two characters
were quite oblivious to any dangerous portents. The melody (that breaks
into a slow waltz tempo) and the instrumentation are genteel, but the
lyric inverts convention. Instead of young lovers, we have a middle-aged
couple that shares a mildly vulgar humor (Schultz jokes about a fart at
one point) as they exaggerate courtesy and passion. He has brought her
not wine or flowers or chocolates, but a pineapple, and his exotic gift
appeals to her sense of romance. There is a motive for middle-aged ecstasy,
as Schultz, buoyed by her gratitude and elation, responds with slightly
breathless excitement. As the pair hum in romantic unison, the situation
grows increasingly comic and touching, for (according to the stage directions) Schneider becomes giddily overwhelmed; Schultz, "all a-tingle."

This poignant interlude dissolves in a blackout, and with the next
number, the score returns to the chilling reality of German politics.

"Tomorrow Belongs to Me," sung by the cabaret waiters in a crystal-clear chorus, is, perhaps, the only number close to Nazi musical taste that, as musicologists and historians inform us, ran primarily toward rousing marches and café tunes. According to Robert Everett-Green (1993), "The party line on music was variously defined by propaganda minister Joseph Goebbels, racial theorist Alfred Rosenberg and critic Fritz Stege. Generally, they rejected music that challenged traditional principles of harmony, and anything by 'non-Aryans.'" *Cabaret*'s score doesn't fit the category of Nazi music: its jazz and blues elements would have been branded as "Jewish-nigger filth," and its mixture of English and American melodic lines lacks High German seriousness. But it is important to remember that in the play, the Nazis have not yet come fully to power, and the show's mixture of lowbrow and middlebrow music captures something that was in vogue in Brecht's and Weill's day. Moreover, "Tomorrow" sounds an ominous tocsin, for it signals the ascendancy of something ultimately terrifying in its power, sweep, and aim. However, Kander and Ebb use guile in making it sound wholesome and musically appealing.

Beautiful voices harmonize in a stirring anthem to racial supremacy and manifest destiny, though the song sounds like the type of waltz one would hear at a German Beirgarten. The anthem gains particular power by its structure, in which a beautiful tenor voice is first heard before the chorus unites with it. The imagery of the first two lines is gloriously pastoral with the reference to sunny meadow and running stag, but the third line breaks this bright mood with its reference to an impending storm. The dominant tone is still one of optimistic confidence, for the singer urges others to "gather together to *greet* the storm" rather than fight it. As the chorus joins the soloist, the imagery becomes apocalyptic, with the Rhine giving "its gold to the sea" while "somewhere a glory awaits unseen." The line about the invisible "glory" stretches out its vowels in eerie fashion, and the chilling effect is increased when the Emcee adds his voice to the chorus on the blatantly provocative line: "Oh, Fatherland, Fatherland, show us the sign." The musical qualities are well described by Scott Miller (1996: 37), who notes that the song begins with "an a cappella tenor solo about the natural beauty of Germany" as "a humming counterpoint" is used "against the main melody." The second verse breaks into "beautiful, hymnlike four-part harmony. As the lyric becomes less pastoral and more nationalistic, the orchestra joins in, the French horn and guitar prominent, adding a rustic, bucolic sound."

The song was so plausibly performed in actual performance that it was denounced as a grossly offensive Nazi anthem. Ebb was infuriated by such accusations, mired as they were in utter ignorance. One man had the audacity to tell him that he had known this song as a child. A rabbi wrote to Ebb claiming he had absolute proof that it was a Nazi song, quite oblivious to the fact that it was composed by a Jew in the midsixties for a Broadway musical (Steyn 1997: 86). Although beguilingly innocent in sound, "Tomorrow Belongs to Me" obviously completes the dramatic trajectory of act 1, encompassing the cabaret world and the rooming house within a circle of deception and incipient evil. By his participation in this song, the Emcee completes the impression of an evil host. His cabaret is now a mirror reflection of a nation on the cusp of fascism.

And yet, the musical comedy arc is not stopped. Act 1 does end with a frightening reprise of the chilling anthem but only after two comic ballads, consisting of a gentle duet in a slow waltz tempo and a Yiddish fable. Both have obvious charm, and both depend on force of personality rather than vocal technique or instrumental sophistication for their peak effects. "Married" (sung by Schneider and Schultz from different stage areas after she has retired to her room to consider his marriage proposal) begins as a male solo but eventually becomes a braided duet in which the wonder of marriage is magnified by the two lovers. Her soprano takes over the direction and shape of the ballad. "Meeskite," on the other hand, is a frank entertainment, an impromptu anecdotal song by Schultz in his fruit shop. Ebb attributes it to his mother's story about two very unattractive people she had known who had a beautiful child. In the show, the purpose was to expose Schultz as a Jew at his own engagement party. Surprisingly, it contains the longest lyric of the musical, and it is made appealing by its humor and optimism. Sheldon Harnick regards it as "an absolutely perfect lyric" because of its expert development and expression of its idea (Guernsey 1985: 140). However, as Leve (2009: 24) notes, it has "an uncomfortable ring of irony because it reinforces [Schultz's] outsider status, the opposite of his drunken intentions." After Jack Gilford, the original Broadway Schultz, left the show, the song became less effective, and many contemporary productions of *Cabaret* omit it. Ebb approved of this measure, claiming that "Meeskite" slowed down the action (Leve 2009: 317).

The song has three parts: the first is an exposition about two ugly young people ("meeskite" is the Yiddish word for "ugly") who get married; the second is a turnaround or reversal, for it celebrates in two symmetrical, rhymed quatrains the unexpectedly beautiful child produced by this union; and the third is the moral ("Anyone responsible for loveliness, large or small, / Is not a *meeskite*/ At all!"), which is couched melodically and in key words that recapitulate the story. The tug at our heartstrings is palpable but well earned by the grocer, whose Jewishness, once revealed, prompts the Nazi Ernst Ludwig to fracture the celebratory mood by informing the landlady that her marriage is "not advisable." Then, in an even more chilling sequence, Fräulein Kost, the slut who is always accompanied by a sailor or two, tries to resume the festivities by reprising "Tomorrow Belongs to Me." This jolts the story and serves a reminder that this is a show where horror is masked by a gaiety that is grotesque.

The score and lyrics express the show's trajectory vividly, partly because the songs, in most instances, grow directly out of the dialogue. As Masteroff reveals in *Broadway Song & Story*, he wrote scenes from which Kander and Ebb plucked songs. There was no advance consultation: "They just took the scenes and found what turned them on." The clearest example is the pineapple exchange that became the basis for "It Couldn't Please Me More." Kander and Ebb admit to having stolen it from the librettist's own text, but Masteroff generously compliments them: "… with these gentlemen, the really terrific songs in the show are always the ones in which they have gone beyond what I have written—beyond the book scene—and into their own imaginations" (Guernsey 1985: 140).

The trajectory of act 1 reveals a dramatically rich subject made significant by the period's decadence and the foibles of the main characters. The stylization of the cabaret numbers rubs against the relative realism of the two couples, but both modes of presentation are meant to trace the rise of fascism through the dissolute cabaret world and the effects of this on four human beings. Act 2, however, compromises the show, despite an extension of the cabaret floorshows and a thickening of Nazi horrors. Having set up the contrasting romantic pairs, the text and score seem unable to develop the dramatic situations into anything that might elicit more than stock pity when the romances come to grief.

After an "Entr'acte" that reindulges the raucous, off-key jam session quality of cabaret—brisk reprises of motifs from "Willkommen," "Two Ladies," and a rapid run-through of the "Cabaret" title song—the show settles into a reprise of "Married" followed by three new numbers, one performed by the Emcee, another by Fräulein Schneider, and the third by Sally and the Kit Kat girls. The "Finale" encloses the play within the cabaret metaphor and leaves a haunting echo, but the lack of adequate development of both romances and the indecisive mixture of naturalism and stylization dilute the score and lyrics.

Taken as a cluster, the last two songs of act 1 and the first two of act 2 coalesce around the Schneider–Schultz subplot. There are instrumental and melodic connections, as well, for all four numbers contain a predominance of wind and string instruments, and three of the four are set to waltz or some other dance tempo. "If You Could See Her" is a vocal solo for the Emcee, though he performs it with a gorilla dressed like a lady. The Emcee apparently reads our minds, for he anticipates our bemusement at this incongruous partnership. Why choose a gorilla for his beloved? Is the gorilla just a gorilla or a representation of something else, as suggested by the lines: "If you knew her like I do, / It would change your point of view"? The song really represents an oblique form of anti-Semitism, with the Emcee obviously mimicking a love match that is *verboten* in Nazi Germany. (An earlier version of the song ended the following way: "She's tall, you can tell / And she's Jewish as well / But if you could see her through my eyes / You'd know why I'm madly in Love!") (Leve 2009: 320). This version is far softer and less controversial than the one that came to be used. Played to a soft-shoe rhythm, the song blossoms into a full-blown waltz passage of ironic gaiety, for it is followed by the concluding quatrain with its clincher, through which, despite every objection and problem, the singer defies other peoples' biases: "But if you could see her through my eyes, / She wouldn't look Jewish at all." The last line is meant to be a solar plexus punch delivered by the surrogate Hitler, but it proved too upsetting to overly sensitive Jews. During the musical's Boston tryout, a rabbi complained to the composers in writing that the ghosts of six million Jews were begging them not to use that last line. Jewish patrons were considering canceling their tickets. "It was the first show where we had a crack at success—not just John and me, but Hal Prince, too—and we were all more frightened than we might be today," Ebb later recalled (Steyn 1997: 86). Because of the pressure, which continued after the show had moved to New York, he changed the punch line to "she isn't a *meeskite* at all!" A weak line, by his own admission.

As Ebb confesses in *Broadway Song & Story*, this number evolved out of a baroque dream he had had of Joel Grey coming out on a runway with a gorilla in a tutu: "That's the truth. No words, no music, but that was the image. And then I told Hal I had dreamed it." Kander and Ebb had to produce a song to go with the dream image and which would serve to show how anti-Semitism was creeping into Berlin. In Fosse's 1972 film version, the last line ("She wouldn't look Jewish at all") is spoken with no accompaniment at all. Joel Grey merely whispers the line. Ebb explained the reason for the absence of music: if Fosse got any flak from people he could bring back his musicians and rerecord the line (Guernsey 1985: 142). By the 1987 Broadway revival, however, Prince, Kander, and Ebb could afford to be more courageous, offering a moment of pure musical theater. As the Emcee sings the final line, we are tempted to laugh, but the laugh dies instantly, as we realize we are laughing at a brutal mockery and not an amiable joke. Those who can see themselves in the tilted mirror shrink into embarrassed silence. All the components of musical theater have fused to make a point that normally would require pages of dialogue in a straight play.

The song is an effective transitional link to Fräulein Schneider's "What Would You Do?" (the most Weill-like song in the show), which is motivated by her dilemma of having to choose between marrying a Jew and becoming the object of vile Nazi persecution or of renouncing that forbidden love and living the rest of her life alone. It is a poignant song that has a dark, reedy quality made all the stronger by flute and strings, particularly in the plaintive passages. Every repetition of her question ("What would you do?") is so underlined by the wind and string instruments as to become a hauntingly traumatic shadow cast over her soul.

There appears to be no self-evident trauma, however, for Sally Bowles, who willingly settles for the hedonistic lures of the cabaret rather than the quiet life with Cliff in America. Having gone through an abortion and witnessed assorted Nazi horrors, she refuses to renounce her capricious, superficial life as a nightclub performer. Her final song, a powerfully building anthem of hedonism, determinedly renounces anything that would inhibit her quest after sensual pleasure—at any rate, this is how the number is usually performed in production. Yet another dimension is possible, for as actress Jane Horrocks showed, at director Sam Mendes's instigation in a 1993 small-scale chamber version in London, Sally's lyric can be essentially ironic—an admission of defeat rather than a defiant or exultant anthem. In that production, the song was delivered as a moment of mental breakdown, an interpretation, however, whose shape must be supported by earlier shifts in focus and tone for the role. But the words and music do support a darker emphasis.

"Cabaret," the title song, is technically adroit. The thrust is in the two quatrains that form a refrain, but the song also has an anecdotal section ("I used to have a girlfriend known as Elsie…") and an intense climax that repeats the main motif ("Life is a cabaret, old chum"). It is Sally's great star turn, and its placement in the score indicates an irony. Sally believes she has distanced herself from humdrum cares and doomsday prophecies, but her implicit *carpe diem* creed is a self-betrayal, for as trumpets and saxophones embellish her accelerated crescendo, she is shown to have capitulated to the cabaret and the growing unreality of German politics. She fails to see that she has abandoned her true self as much as the general population has succumbed to a hallucination of Aryan power.

The "Finale" emphasizes the hallucination through a vocal and musical kaleidoscope that ends with an eerie *envoi*. Its structure enables it to function as a plot device, narrative and melodic summary, and a metatheatrical emblem of life as cabaret. It begins with Cliff's solo reprise of "Willkommen" as he relives the start of his Berlin memoir while his train pulls out of the station. But the past is reincarnated as the harlequin Emcee materializes, taking over the number and repeating motifs: "Where are your troubles now? Forgotten? I told you so! We have no troubles here. Here life is beautiful—the girls are beautiful—even the orchestra is beautiful." The mood, though, is different. The off-key dissonance of "Willkommen" grows as snippets of other numbers slide in and out of the finale, forming a dynamic kaleidoscope by which to recall significant characters and moments of the story. Sally's "Cabaret" refrain grows, then recedes as the Emcee pronounces the *envoi*, bidding farewell to the patrons. His last line is followed by a drumroll and clashing cymbals, just as in the prelude to "Willkommen." What was erected at the start of the story is now deconstructed. And the final silence is tense, for in its stillness there are unanswered questions that grow out of the show: Who are we in relation to the Emcee and the cabaret? What would we have done in that time, when the world was growing alarmingly dissolute and terrifying?

CHAPTER 6

CASTING

WHEN FRÄULEIN SCHNEIDER'S SONGS WERE COMPLETED, KANDER AND Ebb met with Prince, Masteroff, and Helen Harvey of the William Morris Agency, which represented the legendary Lotte Lenya. There was no question that Lenya (Kurt Weill's widow who was popularly known by her surname to fans, friends, lovers, husbands, and critics) should play the rooming house lady because, as Donald Spoto (1989: 6) puts it in his biography of Lenya, her songs in the show were "eerily accurate stencils of her life story." She was the "living symbol of the Germany depicted onstage in *Cabaret*" (3). Although her voice was never truly a musical instrument in terms of euphony and pure tones—she herself described it as "an octave below laryngitis" (3)—it was full of character and energy, a voice that could communicate the personality of a particular song, as it did so well in Weill's *The Threepenny Opera*, in which she performed "Pirate Jenny" and "Surabaya Johnny." Prince knew, of course, that though Lenya was Viennese by birth, hers was the voice of Germany. A small, thin woman (just over five feet tall) with flaming red hair and angular features, she had been a performer and recording star in Berlin in the 1920s. The unrivaled interpreter of Weill's music, she personified the spirit of the European artiste of the 1920s and 1930s, and her boldly defiant life force carried her from Europe to America, where she achieved mythic status in her own lifetime.

The role of Fräulein Schneider was built around exploiting Lenya's renown as Weill's widow and a survivor of the Weimar Republic. Kander had her husky vibrato in his head the entire time he was composing Fräulein Schneider's songs (255). As Fräulein Schneider, owner of the rooming house where struggling young American novelist Clifford Bradshaw rents a room, she was to provide some light comic and romantic relief—particularly in her scenes with Herr Schultz. However, the role also had a tougher side. She would need to perform four songs (two of them duets with Schultz) that would collectively sum up her insouciant, inviting character, with elements of melancholy courage, grainy humor, and tough resilience. "Well, Lenya, do you want to do it?" Prince asked after she had listened to the music. The actress responded immediately, "Of course, I do it!" Her agent interrupted, "Lenya, don't be so quick!" But Lenya, having heard "So What?" which she felt had the tone and texture of a Brecht–Weill song, promptly accepted, though she refused Prince's offer to sign a contract for a year. "Mr. Prince, I don't want to sign that because, you see, if I like the show, then I stay forever. If I want to get out of the contract, I can get out of it. You know that. So, just believe me. I love it, and I will do it" (Farneth 1998: 187). Then she proceeded to make coffee for all present. "This is a woman's job," she insisted.

The third child and second daughter of a carriage driver and a laundress, Lenya was born on October 18, 1898, and christened Karoline Wilhelmine Charlotte Blamauer, memorializing by her Christian name her sister, who had died of a fever just before turning three. Karoline, however, was nicknamed Linerl by Johanna, her gay, stalwart, intrepid mother, and by Franz, her dashingly handsome alcoholic father, who frequently abused her physically and emotionally. He would force her to sing and dance in imitation of her deceased sister, and this childhood humiliation taught her how to barter for affection. Family poverty also led her into becoming a street prostitute at age twelve. Eventually, in 1920, she found her way to Berlin and changed her name to Lenja (later anglicized to Lenya). Amid the prolific cultural activity, she attempted to live as a true Bohemian.

The theater was advancing rapidly under the influences of Erwin Piscator and Max Reinhardt, and German film triumphantly used expressionism in works by Fritz Lang, F. W. Murnau, Ernst Lubitsch, Robert Wiene, and Josef von Sternberg. The country was also excited by old and new American cultural influences, such as jazz, the films of Charlie Chaplin, the poetry of Walt Whitman and Carl Sandburg, and the novels of James Fenimore Cooper, Edgar Allan Poe, Herman Melville, Mark Twain, and Upton Sinclair. Germany felt young, vigorous, and daring, and the flourishing literary cabaret attracted Lenya. Berlin was the site of the polymorphously perverse: bare-breasted prostitutes, nude dancers, cocaine addicts, and exotic cabaret performers. Crime, unemployment, and chronic shortages of food and housing multiplied; and everywhere were noise, rumors, and political slogans.

In 1923 Lenya joined a theater troupe run by Otto Kirchner. She was limited to playing only small parts, and her paper earnings were of virtually no value in the country's highly inflated economy, but this was her entrée to a more significant art world, for it was through the troupe that she met Georg Kaiser, the leading playwright of the day, and through him, the young composer who was destined to be her first and most important husband, Kurt Weill. Then experimenting with jazz, Weill later became Bertholt Brecht's greatest collaborator, in particular for his scores to *The Rise and Fall of the City of Mahagonny, Mahagonny Songspiel,* and *The Threepenny Opera*). Lenya, with her unpretentious smoky voice and psychological vulnerability, eventually discovered her true artistic niche as the foremost interpreter of the Brecht–Weill repertoire. Ned Rorem once described Weill's music as "dew" shed onto Brecht's "sour books" (Spoto 1989: 74), and Lenya's voice—slightly frantic, sometimes scrappily vivacious, and mostly full of romance or regret—added an inner glow to that dew. Alfred Kerr, generally regarded as the preeminent theater critic in Berlin, claimed in the *Berliner Tageblatt* that she made a whole world visible by a simple movement, and he predicted that she would reach the forefront of German theater. Even Brecht thought highly of her talent. Once in response to her request to clarify his epic theory, he patted her cheek and said: "Lenya, dear, whatever you do is epic enough for me."

A measure of her quality is evident in G. W. Pabst's film version of *The Threepenny Opera*, shot in 1930 after many legal complications over creative control and eventually condemned by the Nazis. The 112-minute black-and-white film is a truncated and radically rearranged version of a masterpiece that almost manages to turn an opera into an unmusical expressionistic story with strong allegorical nuances about tyranny. Indeed, Tiger Brown and Macheath's final ballad about soldiers and their ruthlessness could well be taken as a portent of Nazi atrocities. Certainly Reinhold Schuenzel's Tiger Brown looks and acts like a well-groomed but still feral machinator. Pabst's film depends heavily on silent movie techniques (particularly in the close-ups of grimacing faces), and there are significant omissions, not the least of which are the "Tango Ballad," some of Mackie's songs, and the role of Lucy. Several numbers are reassigned, principally because Lenya is in the cast and her Jenny is given scenes normally played by Lucy and Polly. Her performance, claims Spoto, "is the memorable highlight of Pabst's film" because it is "soiled and dangerous…pathetic and tart." Her physique is slim and bony, her face angular, and her voice high and thin. Whether smiling or whining, flicking a wrist boldly or turning a hip in a mocking insult, she is dramatically effective and almost cancels out both Carola Neher as Polly and Valeska Gert as Mrs. Peachum. Lenya's biggest moment (when she finally sings "Pirate Jenny" in the bordello) summarizes her genius, for in a remarkable display of casual ambiguity, as she leans against a windowsill and delivers the song like a dramatic monologue, she becomes weary, rueful, pessimistic, and sexually alert, though her dark eyes look dead and her body turns virtually still. The only movement, apart from her mouth, is a slow semaphore of her right hand. As Spoto remarks, "Had we no other facts about her life before and after, we could infer from this coolly detached but passionately involved actress that there were reservoirs of personal history that matched all the heat and anger, the pride and resentment, the despair spiced with hope" (88).

As the country hurtled toward an unprecedented nightmare of fascism, Weill and Lenya (as well as many other artists) knew that only self-exile would rescue them from the barbarism about to engulf Germany. They moved to Prague and then to other safer European cities before moving in 1935 to New York, where Weill had plans to stage *The Eternal Road*, a Jewish musical epic with text by Franz Werfel. Though legally divorced at the time, they registered as husband and wife at the Saint Moritz Hotel, overlooking Central Park. They had already memorized the city's famous skyline from American movies and quickly set about trying to adapt to a new way of life, though neither could as yet speak English without difficulty. In fact, while buying a sweater at Saks Fifth Avenue, Lenya once startled a salesman by requesting: "Rape it, please, in a gift box" (108).

They had arrived in America when *Porgy and Bess* was making theater history. Weill was impressed and felt that he, too, could create a score that would fuse lyric, action, setting, and music into an integrated whole. He and Lenya forged many artistic friendships, and his career expanded his reputation as a musician whose insolent jazz sounds could acquire new meanings while yielding to a lyricism worthy of some of the finest elements of the European operatic tradition. *Johnny Johnson* (1936), *Knickerbocker Holiday* (1938), *Lady in the Dark* (1941), *Street Scene* (1947), and *Lost in the Stars* (1949) sealed his reputation on Broadway, while Lenya (who remarried him) had to be content with lesser fame as a supporting player to Helen Hayes in Maxwell Anderson's *Candle in the Wind* (1941), almost stealing the unworthy play from the star in her portrayal of a Viennese maid with horrid German memories. After another play flopped, in which she was miscast as a duchess, she began her ascent as a performer who specialized in Brecht–Weill songs. Concerts and recordings boosted her celebrity, but she gained her greatest plaudits only after Weill's untimely death in 1950, though they came for a work that he had stamped with his own genius. In Marc Blitzstein's version of *The Threepenny Opera* staged by Theatre de Lys in Greenwich Village in 1954, she shone in the role of Jenny, the same part she had essayed for Pabst's film. Her half-singing, half-speaking was, as Spoto believes, "perfect for a character shorn of pity" because "the merest crack in her voice" suggested "not so much the age of the singer as the effects on the character of too many brutal years." In the "Tango Ballad," her tone changed with the character's bittersweet memories, and her voice cracked with a regret that was (in Spoto's words) "half anger, half shame" (187).

Other successes followed: recordings of *The Seven Deadly Sins* and *The Rise and Fall of the City of Mahagonny*; a concert version of the *Mahagonny Songspiel*; a revue called *Brecht on Brecht*; movie roles in *The Roman Spring of Mrs. Stone* (opposite Vivien Leigh and Warren Beatty) and in *From Russia with Love* (opposite Sean Connery). Her private life was far less happy, with anxiety-ridden marriages to two self-destructive homosexuals, which led her into semiretirement while she attempted to heal herself. But with *Cabaret* in 1966 came her renaissance. The irony was that her role as Fräulein Schneider was by no means a large part, though she had one more song than did Sally Bowles and appeared in seven scenes (discounting the musical "Finale"). Her smoky voice, her furrowed and lined face, her enigmatic, insouciant manner, her flashing white teeth and red gash of a mouth made her the perfect actress for the role.

Her stage partner was also perfect for his role, even though he was ten years her junior. The middle of three sons born to Jewish parents, Jack Gilford (born Jacob Gellman) grew up on Manhattan's Lower East Side and, like Lenya, knew economic hardship and domestic struggle from childhood. When his parents separated and his father was unable to support the family any longer, his bootlegging mother (a Romanian immigrant) moved with her three boys to the Williamsburg neighborhood of Brooklyn, which Gilford later recalled as "a better class of slum"

Lotte Lenya and Jack Gilford in Cabaret *(1966) (Photofest)*

in *170 Years of Show Business* (1978). Young Jacob's skill in mimicking Rudy Vallee, Laurel and Hardy, Al Jolson, Calvin Coolidge, Jimmy Walker, and Georgie Jessel impressed Milton Berle, who hired him as a sidekick in his vaudeville routine. But Berle insisted that Gilford change his very Jewish name—a handicap in show business at the time—into something Anglo-Saxon. After proposing such names as "Black," "Brown," and "Green," to the young man's obvious disapproval, Berle suggested "Guilford." This didn't meet with any enthusiasm, so Berle said, "Okay, kid, forget it." Sensing that an opportunity of a lifetime was slipping away, the young comic reluctantly agreed to the proposed name change: "Okay, I'll be Jack Guilford. But without the 'u.' "

Jack Gilford and Milton Berle (with Sadie Berle as chaperone) played four shows a day (five on weekends) in movie houses and three a night in clubs across the country. After he and Berle parted company, Gilford performed solo in clubs and vaudeville, touring the Borscht Circuit for four years. When he played a benefit for the Theater Arts Committee to aid Spain and China, his routine caught the attention of a representative from the Shubert organization who invited him to audition for *Hellzapoppin*. After a failed audition, Gilford went to work at Café Society, at the invitation of Barney Josephson, the owner of this socially rare nightclub where blacks and whites mingled as both entertainers and patrons. Meade "Lux" Lewis, Albert Ammons, Pete Johnson, Joe Turner, Lena Horne, and Billie Holiday were some of the jazz artists who worked there, and the club drew everyone from Eleanor Roosevelt to Bob Hope. In addition to offering jazz, it presented satirical humor in an atmosphere that was later duplicated by the Hungry i in San Francisco and by Second City in Chicago. Gilford, who was only a teenager, loved the ambience and developed skits, including one about a man who can't stay awake on a subway. Then he made his debut in a revue at the Music Box, and the next year (1940) he opened on Broadway in *Meet the People*, although his theatrical career was still insecure and supported by moonlighting in nightclubs.

During the war, he toured with the U.S.O. in the Pacific, and after the war he married Madeline Lee Fein, a writer, actress, and producer. He was cast on Phil Silvers's *Arrow Show* for NBC, but by 1950 his career had plunged almost to oblivion after he was blacklisted during the height of the Red Scare. The legitimate stage and opera offered momentary relief. He enjoyed the comic, nonsinging part as Frosch, the drunken jailer, in the Met's *Die Fledermaus* (a role he reprised several times later in his career), and his first dramatic role came in 1953 when in *The World of Sholom Aleichem* he portrayed an impoverished, long-suffering man who has one line. Told in heaven that he can ask for anything, the chronically silent character finally says: "In that case, if it's true, could I have, please, every day, a hot roll with butter?" His malleable face and poignant tone stunned audiences, who were to be further impressed by his performances in *The Diary of Anne Frank, Romanoff and Juliet, Once Upon a Mattress*, and *The Tenth Man*. Still, blacklisting seriously affected his career and kept him from enjoying the fame and success that was his due. Nevertheless, when he was called before the House Un-American Activities Committee in 1956 and asked: "Do you believe in the overthrow of the United States government by force and violence?" he responded: "No, just gently" (Mostel and Gilford 1978: 115).

His performing signature was a mixture of buoyancy and jitteriness, of resignation and courage, of exquisitely timed improvisation and acutely observed detail. Directors and fellow actors appreciated his ability to play both comedy and drama. Alfred Lunt thought that Gilford's Frosch was the best ever, as he wrote in a letter to Garson Kanin, who directed the performance: "I've seen Grock, the Fratellinis and Slivers [*sic*] and all the best, but none could touch him. How he manages to dissolve, vanish completely, while manacled to the terror, is I think, the greatest feat of acting I ever saw." Besides sending audiences into laughing hysteria, Gilford could wring sympathy in certain roles, as he showed with his performance of the fussy, frightened dentist, Mr. Dussel, in *Anne Frank*.

He went on to his greatest Broadway success in *A Funny Thing Happened on the Way to the Forum*, opposite his friend Zero Mostel. His versatility in both comedy and drama helped Masteroff, Kander, and Ebb when they were creating a foil for Lenya's Schneider. With these two performers on board, *Cabaret* had a solid acting base, and the roles of Schneider and Schultz were completed for the libretto once Lenya and Gilford were contracted.

Joel Grey also had his part scripted to suit his stage personality. Because Prince knew from the start how he wanted the Emcee played, he insisted on casting Grey, who, at a very trim five feet four inches, was short enough to incarnate Prince's memory of the little *conférencier* in Stuttgart. At his audition, Grey immediately registered the character's courage, self-delusion, fear, and sadness without bothering with the German accent or personality. Given the actor's background and training, the role was a stretch, for Grey (the son of Mickey Katz, a Yiddish comedian and bandleader whose popular recordings in the 1940s included "The Little White Knish That Cried") was virtually born into vaudeville and the Borscht Belt. Grey made his debut at the age of nine at the Cleveland Playhouse. One reviewer remarked: "I can only say that the boy is phenomenal. He is as completely at home on the stage without being in the slightest degree precocious as any child I have ever seen." After he graduated from high school in Los Angeles, Grey was allowed to appear on weekends in his father's revues (one of which was *The Borscht Capades*) and then in nightclubs. At nineteen he was performing at New York's Copacabana and London's Palladium. He was also featured in Eddie Cantor's *Colgate Comedy Hour* on television. In a 1987 interview with Diana Solway, he confessed: "I was at war with myself. I should have just called it to a halt but I couldn't because it was succeeding." Finally he did quit and moved to New York to study acting with Sanford Meisner at the Neighborhood Playhouse. This paid off with parts on television playing everything from psychopathic killers and juvenile delinquents to western bandits and rock'n' roll singers in such shows as *Maverick* and *December Bride*. After winning national attention in a starring role in NBC's musical special *Jack and the Beanstalk*, he appeared in three films (*About Face, Calypso Heat Wave, Come September*), and was seen Off-Broadway with Tammy Grimes in Phoenix Theatre's *Littlest Revue*. His career passed into what he called his "replacement era," for he took over for Warren Berlinger (*Come Blow Your Horn*), Anthony Newley (*Stop the World—I Want to Get Off!*), and Tommy Steele (*Half a Sixpence*). Additional credits came in the form of a part opposite Dustin Hoffman in Ronald Ribman's *Harry, Noon and Night* at the American Place Theatre, summer stock roles in *West Side Story, Finian's Rainbow*, and *Tom Sawyer*. He yearned for a role that would put him over the top, and the next summer he appeared in *Mardi Gras* at the Jones Beach Marine Theatre. Then came the call from Prince, and Joel Grey found the role of his lifetime.

Prince and his collaborators had problems finding the right Cliff (a surrogate Isherwood) and Sally Bowles. More than two hundred girls auditioned for Sally. One was Liza Minnelli. Kander and Ebb thought she would be excellent, but their view was not shared by Masteroff and Prince, both of whom believed she was too American and too strong a singer to play a mediocre British flapper. As Masteroff remarked later: "Liza is phenomenally talented and was the same then. But she was extremely young at the time, and somehow she could not be a British girl" (Guernsey 1985: 145). The writers could have turned her into an American (as in the later movie version), but that solution did not occur to them. Even if the idea had come to them, it would have been too late to make such a major change in the libretto. The team just couldn't envisage Liza Minnelli playing a girl who was neither overtly talented nor merely untalented. As Masteroff has said: "The average audience isn't sophisticated enough to know that someone who can really sing is singing badly on purpose. If Sally can't sing, you have no show" (Hirsch 2005: 67).

Once Minnelli was rejected, the search for the proper Sally was wide open. Jill Haworth, the young actress who seemed to have most of the requisites for the role, was a beautiful blue-eyed, five-foot-two blonde. Born in 1945 in Sussex, she had a most unusual upbringing. The initials of her baptismal names (Valerie Jill) were in honor of her birth on VJ Day. Her wealthy father raced cars and yachts and invented the fiberglass shirt. Her mother had been a ballet dancer before rheumatic fever cut this short. As a child, Haworth had not played with dolls, but with boxing gloves and toy guns. Yet she displayed a most attractive grace, having attended the Sadler's Wells Ballet School after her parents' separation in 1963 and then the Corona Stage School. Her film experience began early, when she appeared as one of seven children in the sci-fi thriller *Village of the Damned*, then in *Carry On, Teacher, Brides of Dracula*, and *Idle on Parade*. Television commercials also came her way before Otto Preminger gave her her first big movie break in *Exodus* (1960). Accompanied by a chaperone, Haworth (then fifteen) went to the Shaftesbury Theatre in London to audition for the role of Karen, a Jewish girl found by an American nurse in a British detention center on Cyprus. Her closest competition was another beautiful teenager, German actress Christine Kaufman, but Haworth got the part. The director further rewarded her with a trip to New York, which she was allowed to make in the company of her mother and stepfather. The first thing she asked to see was the Bronx because her prospective screen lover, Sal Mineo, was born there and had told her about it. Her film role encompassed romance and drama, for Karen was to fall in love with Dov Landau (Mineo, which led to an off-screen romance) and then be killed by marauding Arabs. She took the extravagant publicity in stride and easily handled Preminger's famous rages. She amazed many in Hollywood by her precocious composure, defusing Preminger's screaming fits by gently asking him what was wrong. Preminger's Prussian tyranny bent under this cool poise, and he ensured that she would become his protégée by having her attend meetings in his palatial Fifth Avenue office as well as official dinners as his emissary, forbidding her to live in Hollywood, and rewarding her lavishly for her publicity tours in Israel, Hawaii, Europe, and the Far East. He wanted her to preserve a virginal public image, though in private he had designs to seduce her. At first she was only too willing to comply with his wishes, even agreeing to attend Rhodes School on 53rd Street, chosen by her mentor, who signed her to a seven-year contract. Haworth's film career did not turn her into a star, however, for she played only small roles in *The Cardinal, In Harm's Way*, and *The Greatest Story Ever Told*. Her association with Preminger petered out when in 1964 she asked that her contract be canceled because no movie roles were forthcoming in any of his productions. She subsequently returned to England.

Accounts vary as to how she met Harold Prince, but some say it was at a party or through an agent. What is certain is that Prince made two trips abroad to catch up with her and then offered to fly her back to New York for a one-day audition, even though she had never sung professionally and hadn't planned any song for the test. When he first asked her to sing, she refused bluntly, saying she'd never even hummed. Prince and his colleagues coaxed her: "You must know some song." So she finally tried

"Happy Birthday" and "Someone to Watch over Me" (of which she knew only the first line). She had to repeat "Happy Birthday" over a dozen times, as Prince prowled about and finally said: "Go back to London and take singing lessons." Not catching his meaning, she protested: "Oh, look, I'm busy as it is." When he explained that she was going to play Sally, she burst into tears and kissed everybody in the room. Then Prince played her the theme song from the show and she cried again.

This piece of casting was to prove highly controversial, but Prince, who always liked to gamble on newcomers, was impressed by her desire to succeed and by her loud, clear, untrained voice, which was suited to Sally's brassy, unsentimental performing style. Both he and Haworth knew that she had a lot of work to do in preparation, but her modest though eager talent was just right for the role of a rather mediocre but brave overreacher.

Her counterpart signed on a few months later. Bert Convy was known to Fred Ebb because the actor had appeared in *Morning Sun*, which Ebb had written with Paul Klein. Convy was twelve years older than Haworth and had much more singing and stage-acting experience. A native of

Jill Haworth as Sally Bowles in Cabaret *(1966) (Photofest)*

St. Louis who had gone to school in California, he once aspired to have a professional career in baseball. Indeed, he had played two seasons in the Philadelphia Phillies' farm system a year before a rookie named Mickey Mantle joined the same club. But he gave up his baseball dream to return to California and major in theater arts at UCLA. He and two friends formed a rock'n' roll band called The Cheers, and as he told James Bacon in 1961: "We were just lousy enough to become a hit as rock'n' rollers. My cut of the act was $1,000 a week, and here I was barely old enough to vote." The group's first recording, "I Need Your Lovin'," became a nationwide hit, selling over half a million copies, and Convy enjoyed his new celebrity, especially when Maurice Chevalier caught his act. The group's "Black Denim Trousers and Motorcycle Boots" sold over a million copies, and the band received bookings at the Copa, the Brooklyn Paramount, and Chicago's Chez Paree and also went on tour with Danny Kaye. This good fortune was fleeting, however, for as Convy related to Bacon: "Then along came Bobby Darin, Fabian, Frankie Avalon, the Haircuts, the Crewcuts, and a dozen other favorites the kids idolized. Suddenly, we had outgrown our fans." His group disbanded, and a year later, practically broke and a "has-been" at twenty-three, Convy ushered at CBS Television City for $32 a week.

Then fortune changed again. One day, after writing a song, he cornered Muzzy Marcellino, Art Linkletter's music director, who found him a job as a singer for the *Oscar Levant Show*. From there Convy moved to the *Billy Barnes Revue* in Los Angeles and New York and to the Off-Broadway company of *The Fantasticks*. His first New York musical was *Nowhere to Go but Up*, which he acidly renamed *Nowhere to Throw but Up*. Starring Martin Balsam, Tom Bosley, and Dorothy Loudon, with Convy and Mary Ann Mobley as the juveniles, the production was directed by Sidney Lumet, but a month's previews in Philadelphia brought devastating reviews. Lumet quit and was replaced by Mel Brooks, who rewrote the entire first act but apparently not well enough to save the show. It played only a week on Broadway in November 1962.

Convy survived on television commercials, talk and game shows, and parts in such shows as *Perry Mason, The Untouchables, 77 Sunset Strip, Alfred Hitchcock Presents*, et cetera. His Broadway career suddenly perked up in 1964 when he landed the part of Perchik, the radical Jewish intellectual in *Fiddler on the Roof*, before sagging again a year later when he appeared in *The Impossible Years*. Prince obviously remembered him from *Fiddler* and knew that although Convy was a lightweight musical comedy

Jill Haworth (Sally Bowles) and Bert Convy (Cliff) in Cabaret *(1966) (Photofest)*

performer, the actor could probably cope with the role of Cliff, which, as scripted by Masteroff, required a pleasant-looking, wide-eyed American innocent. After all, Cliff had a song called "Why Should I Wake Up?" which Foster Hirsch (2005: 66) calls "a salute to an American ostrich, oblivious to history, and which in context [is] startlingly superficial."

With the five leading roles cast, Prince had no trouble filling the rest of his company. In retrospect, however, the original billing is a little surprising, for Joel Grey, who became the overnight sensation, received only fifth billing. This was partly out of deference to Lenya and Gilford and partly out of recognition of the fact that the Emcee's role has limited stage time—fifteen minutes, according to Masteroff, but actually just over thirty-three minutes (64). Moreover, as conceived by Masteroff and Prince, *Cabaret* was not meant to single out a lone character; it was more a story about a particularly vicious atmosphere than a tale of foiled lovers and dreamers.

CHAPTER 7

REHEARSALS AND BOSTON

BECAUSE OF PRINCE'S REMARKABLE RECORD ON BROADWAY, THERE WAS no need to run backers' auditions to raise the $500,000 production budget. On July 11, 1966, Prince sent out circulars for General Partners (who would receive 15 percent of net profits), special Limited Partners (who would receive 35 percent), and Limited Partners (who would make a $10,000 contribution for which they would receive 1 percent of net profits). Prince himself was assured of 50 percent of net profits. The projected budget was raised before very long, and he set aside $7,500 as scenic design fee, $2,500 for electrical design, $7,500 for costume design, $5,000 for the author's advance, $3,500 for the choreography, and $5,000 for his own director's fee. Advertising was to cost $38,500, while $56,000 was reserved for rehearsal expenses. An arrangement was made with Columbia Records for the original cast album, by which Prince would receive a basic royalty of 12 percent of the suggested retail price of the first 200,000 albums sold and 15 percent of anything more thereafter.

With budget and backing in place, Prince poured his energy into rehearsing the show at the George Abbott Theatre. After the cast had been shown the set and costume designs, he offered them another visual stimulus by showing them a centerfold from the August 19, 1966, issue of *Life* magazine featuring a group of blond males in their late teens, who (in his words) were "stripped to the waist, wearing religious medals, snarling at the camera like a pack of hounds" (Prince 1974: 125). When he asked the cast to identify the time and place of the photo, they incorrectly assumed it had come from Munich of 1928 or thereabouts. In fact, it was a photo not of Hitler youth, but of a group of students in Little Rock, Arkansas, in 1957 violently resisting the desegregation of a high school. The irony was now obvious: human nature does not change, despite the lessons of history.

Prince emphasized that he wanted the show to shake up facile assumptions about fascism and guilt. Act 1, he maintained, should indicate characters having a good time, and these should not be turned into melodramatic grotesques just because many of them would later become Nazis. Ernst Ludwig was to be friendly and likable; Fräulein Kost, fun-loving and brazen, much in love with money and clothes; Fräulein Schneider, full of vitality, interested in everything immediately around her, and apparently indestructible. Prince's aim was to reveal that today's fun loving, apparently apolitical people could easily yield to external forces and become tyrannous, but he wanted this process to develop organically, from characters that were dimensional and rounded. So Edward Winters's Ernst, for instance, should not give the show away by being sinister from the outset. He should downplay the anger by beginning casually and by showing an attraction to Cliff. Sally's first entrance in Fräulein Schneider's flat should be an upbeat surprise, with an undertone of hysteria, because she has just been thrown out by Max (a lover), but she's a survivor. She should be fully narcissistic, absorbed in her own bubbly, antic activities, even to the point of showing off her green fingernails and disregarding Cliff as she concocts prairie oysters, her favorite drink.

Prince wanted a symbolic edge to make the show more than a simple musical. Certainly, *Cabaret* had strong elements of generic Broadway musicals in its love plots and some show numbers, but its dark aspects expanded the genre's possibilities. The director pushed his cast away from superficiality, and this created problems at times for those, such as Joel Grey, who had to present verve and spectacle while also expressing, however obliquely, the malaise of a country. Grey's role was both concrete and abstract, being a real character as well as an emblem. The actor spent hours before a mirror looking for the character from the inside and the outside, trying to concoct a look that would be absolutely right for the part. As he revealed to Richard Alleman in 1987: "Eventually I came to see him as a sort of marionette, and I saw his eyelashes moving all in one piece—not feminine or fluttery—but like a ventriloquist's dummy. Then I found this greasepaint called 'Juvenile Pink,' and I thought to myself, 'this creep, he would want to look young, and this is what he would use.' "

Grey fleshed out the creep by calling on his own memories of every second-rate music hall entertainer he had ever seen. "I tried to cram all that terrible stuff—the stuff that I hated on those guys—into this one man." He thought of the Emcee as "a central figure in a Günter Grass novel rather than as a device in a musical." He claimed that he needed to do that because, otherwise, there was no continuous connection, merely several musical numbers. So he created a rather complex offstage life that he continued with the girls in the club, "sometimes to their delight and sometimes to their terror." His Emcee was played "on the edge. The edge of darkness and of danger," for Grey thought that the audience "should feel that."

Everyone in the cast worked hard, especially Jill Haworth, who had to find a voice and manner that went against her type, but none worked harder than veteran Lotte Lenya. "She was so unlike many other players," according to Fred Ebb, "those who ask for rewrites of lyrics one on top of another. She requested only one change in a line of one song, as a favour to rescue her embarrassment." As recounted by Donald Spoto, she was disturbed by the phrase "the abundance of me" in the song "So What?" She whispered to Ebb, "Darling, look!" as she opened her blouse. "I can't sing about the 'abundance of me.' *What* abundance? Please, dear, to rewrite the verse, yes?" Ebb felt no compunction about altering the phrase to read "the uncorseted me" and so won her gratitude (Spoto 1989: 256–57).

At the time of rehearsals that summer, Lenya was sixty-eight, and yet she had a vitality and candor that thrived on straight talk. "You never had to be diplomatic or fancy-talking with her," said Prince, "and as a director I never had to soften any comments. In fact if you weren't straight with her you got into trouble. She was exceedingly receptive to my notes, which I gave her as I gave other members of the cast. She was impatient only with herself, when she went wrong" (257). All forewarnings from certain sources that she would be difficult to work with proved false. Joe Masteroff remembers: "We told her, 'If anything on that stage isn't right, tell us, you're the expert, you were there.' She loved the role, which allowed her a range from broad comedy in Act I to tragedy in Act II; it was her one great success without Weill."

John Kander supports the praise: "During rehearsals she was terrifically cooperative, great fun and very encouraging to everyone. Any suggestions she had about the details of authenticity for Berlin 1930 were made just as suggestions, with no trace of Grande Dame attitude at all"

(258). In fact, even though she knew that the cabaret scenes were not authentic re-creations of what were staged in Berlin, she was impressed by the way the designers and director had caught the atmosphere of that era in the telephones at the tables, the chorus girls, the kick line, the monkey number, the Nazi presence, and the frightening inflation. "I was just like Fraulein Schneider in the play," she remarked to Richard Gilman of *Newsweek*: "I had a suitcase full of money. At 2 it was worth 3 million marks. At 2.30 it was worth nothing." When Kander told her he suspected that he might be criticized for having written "watered-down Kurt Weill," she took his face in her hands and comforted: "No, no, darling. It is not Weill. It is not Kurt. When I walk out on stage and sing those songs, it is *Berlin*" (Guernsey 1985: 145). Of course, she modestly neglected to say that if the music evoked Berlin, it was principally because of her particular temperament and style. She exuded joy during rehearsals, especially when she performed "It Couldn't Please Me More" with Jack Gilford and when she danced with him and the sailors at the engagement party. *From Russia with Love* had appeared in cinemas, and suddenly she was rediscovered by audiences. She was not merely a distant legend. As Prince summed up: "It was hard for her to spend so many years walking around on this earth representing a period, representing Weill and Brecht, always and forever. What sort of lunacy is that?" (Spoto 1989: 257).

Prince wanted the show to break down the usual barriers between stylized musical theater and realistic drama. When the characters performed songs, they had to treat the music as a continuation of the realistic action. He wanted the singing to be more intimate and casual, especially in the duets "Perfectly Marvelous" and "It Couldn't Please Me More." In the first instance he bound the song to the scene by giving both Cliff and Sally a series of actions that would register Cliff's surprise at the fact of Sally's having hooked him so soon. In the second song, a duet for Fräulein Schneider and Herr Schultz, Prince wanted a fusion of contradictions in Lenya: a grainy humor made genteel, courage and independence with a streak of insecurity, and a need for love.

As a director, he was wont to offer line readings, replete with gestures, emphases, and timing, but instead of intimidating his actors, he amused them with his "hammy" panache. As Foster Hirsch (2005: 45) observed directly during rehearsals for the 1987 revival of the show, Prince built up "a reserve of good will" because he never told actors what to do when work on a scene began: "his orders [seemed] to issue from spontaneous problem-solving as he literally [thought] on his feet. As he [moved] through the actions of a scene, standing in for each of the actors, handling props, exploring the space, he [seemed] to receive cues from his body."

He never had a predetermined mise-en-scène but knew the general shape and texture he wanted in scenes. He approached each scene fresh, referring to the prompt book marked by long-time associate Ruth Mitchell when he wanted to clear up a difficulty with a prop or blocking, and always urging his actors to dig into subtext to find unspoken tensions. He loathed displays of cheap sentimentality and pathos and actually walked through scenes onstage with the actors in order to feel their physical responses to one another. Every line reading had to have accents properly placed, and all stage business, even silent crowd moments, had to look convincing and suggestive of an intrinsic drama. Prince encouraged rigorous textual analysis in order to examine motives, and contradictions between words and feelings, between actions and intentions. But (as described by Hirsch) his working method was never abstract or intellectual, for it was always rooted in practical matters, such as the shape and color of a prop, the beats and tempi of speech and song, the spatial relationships between decor and actors, the total stage picture. His eye for detail and attention to subtext showed most clearly in two intense moments in act 2. In the first, Fräulein Schneider had to demonstrate the beginning of her surrender to fear when she visited Herr Schultz's fruit shop in order to break off their engagement. Prince wanted his Schneider to show crusty irony and his Schultz to feel that he could dissuade her from ending their relationship. While shaping the center stage action, Prince framed upstage action in the shop window, using a deep focus for the first time in the show in order to reveal how the Nazi menace was now directly invading the characters' lives. The script called for a brick suddenly to be hurled through the window, and Prince plotted the stage business in a way that never seemed contrived. He wanted intensity from everyone onstage, urging the brick-throwing boys to be jolly in their delinquency, Schultz to be oblivious to the real threat at hand, and Fräulein Schneider to be wracked by guilt as she distanced herself from her Jewish suitor.

In the second scene, involving Sally, Cliff, and Schneider, the key moment is the landlady's song, "What Would You Do?" which is sung after she returns the fruit bowl given to her as an engagement gift. Prince directed the scene in a way that would register all the relationships in the room. Schneider had to divide focus between her innermost self and the young couple, while Sally had to be uncomprehending and Cliff provoked into some understanding of the landlady's capitulation to hysterical nationalist propaganda. But rather than aiming for pathos, Prince aimed for clarity and strength in the moment, demanding that the landlady not sound apologetic or weak about her decision. Once again, the director's emphasis was on the character's inner life, and his advice helped Lenya create an emotional contradiction between the landlady's outer strength and inner defeat.

And yet for all his belief in truth as the basis of situation and character, Prince had a trick up his sleeve—one that Hirsch describes as "a concept that in a stroke overturns the Broadway formula and sentimentality underlying Masteroff's well-written book." This was the limbo world presided over by the sinister Emcee. According to the director, this character "metaphorically represents the Depression. He starts out as a pathetic, self-deluded entertainer who gradually turns into an emblem of the Nazi mentality." His songs, as Hirsch (2005: 60–61) phrases it, "comment critically on the characters, linking their unconventional sexuality, money problems, and political cowardice to Berlin's general moral collapse."

Slipping into metatheater, Prince underlined the intellectual detachment of the limbo area by using onstage observers, a device that was to be much imitated by other directors and which has since become part of Prince's signature. As with many theatrical innovations, the device started by accident, for, as Masteroff recalls, it was developed in order to time a scene change: "Two girls from the cabaret lingered as they went up the spiral staircase stage left while the scenery changed, and Hal liked the way it looked and decided to keep it. It wasn't something that we had thought of before we put the show on stage" (61).

While Prince was busy with his actors, Ron Field, the choreographer, was developing the show's dance numbers about twelve blocks away in the ballroom of the Diplomat Hotel. The work of director and choreographer did not overlap at this stage because Field was hired only after a script and score had been finished. In fact, he had gone into his *Cabaret* assignment under a cloud because just after he had created a successful nightclub act for Liza Minnelli—which convinced Prince to sign him on—he was involved in a terrible Lincoln Center production of *Show Boat*, and Prince had had serious second thoughts. Prince asked a couple of bright young choreographers from the New York City Ballet to tackle the show, but neither agreed to take it on. So, deciding to be fair to Field, he met with him, aware that Kander and Ebb were in favor of the choreographer, who had compiled impressive credits ever since debuting on Broadway as a dancer at the age of eight in *Lady in the Dark*. In May, Prince told Richard Seff, Field's agent, that the choreographer would have to drop everything else until rehearsals the following September. "I want him to spend the summer researching the period and working in a studio with the score." The problem was that Field already had a commitment to Howard Hoyt to stage an Industrial Show in July. He didn't want to miss out on *Cabaret*, but he was not going to let down Hoyt, who had helped him during some lean years. With heart in mouth, Seff called Prince to tell him about the complication. Prince was amazed: "I don't believe this. He's turning down Hal Prince for an Industrial Show?" There was a long pause, but Prince then said: "I like that. Okay, he can have *Cabaret*, but he'd better deliver come September!" (Seff 2006: 148).

A native New Yorker, born in 1934, Field had been the first male dancer enrolled at the High School of Performing Arts. He had caught the performing bug after his first glimpse of vaudeville in Atlantic City, where for twelve seasons his father ran an ice cream stand. An aunt who

Ron Field, ca. 1970
(Photofest)

worked as a Broadway wardrobe mistress had wangled him his first stage role, and another aunt, Stella Fields, who taught dancing in Washington Heights, was his main influence, as he became her pride and joy. At seventeen, he danced in the congruently named *Seventeen* in Boston and afterward entered his "gypsy" decade on Broadway, television, and in nightclubs extending from Hollywood and Miami to Paris and Beirut. His Broadway hoofing included assignments in *Gentlemen Prefer Blondes* and *Kismet*, but he also ventured into choreography in summer stock and staged dance programs at the 92nd Street YMHA. Lawrence Kasha, former stage manager who had just become a Broadway producer, caught one of these shows and led Field's cheering section. By age twenty-four, Field had worked for Jerome Robbins, Jack Cole, and Agnes de Mille, and at twenty-seven he got his opportunity to choreograph his first Broadway show, the disastrous *Nowhere to Go* (1962), the same debacle that almost crippled Bert Convy's career, but miraculously Field escaped with his reputation unscathed. He was the only one on the show to receive critical approval because his choreography caught the shoddy flavor of the prohibition era and matched the slapstick pace of the show.

That same year, Kasha hired him to choreograph an Off-Broadway revival of *Anything Goes*, for which Field won notices that sent him into euphoria. *Theatre Arts* reported: "Mr. Field did something better than were footling recreation or bootless parody of dated choreography. He painstakingly compiled every conceivable dance platitude of the Thirties, giving us a kind of commonplace book or museum showcase or, better yet—by conceiving of these dances as an ethnic phenomenon—a sociological documentary" (Simon 1962: 59). The *New Yorker* agreed: "While the dancing—the strenuous, eyes-front hoofing and the ballroom swooping of the nineteen-thirties—is funny and ingenious, Ronald Field, the choreographer, never allows parody to get out of hand" (Oliver 1962: 93). And to top this off, *Dance Magazine* added: "Just about everybody in *Anything Goes* dances, and everybody in it or watching it would want to dance what Ronald Field has recreated from what was popular on stage, screen, and dance floors thirty years ago. It is all precisely the way Ginger Rogers and Fred Astaire, Eleanor Powell and Ruby Keeler did it" (Lerman 1962: 26). The reference was to skirt twirlings, nightclub finishes and stunts, tap routines, supernal postures, and plastique posings. In other words, Fields accurately reconstructed the style of the period.

Just three years later, Field was the toast of television, supper clubs, and nightclubs around the country, doing work for the *Ed Sullivan Show* and *The*

Hollywood Palace (where he created dances for the legendary Astaire) and staging club acts for Chita Rivera, Shari Lewis, and Liza Minnelli in addition to devising elaborate revues for New York's Latin Quarter and Miami Beach's Carillon Hotel, the famous Casino de Paris, and the Casino du Liban in Beirut. Now it was his turn to become a mentor or teacher to other aspiring choreographers, and Michael Bennett was to become one of his assistants.

But on *Cabaret*, Field did not have full autonomy, for he had to serve Prince's concept. He spent a summer with Prince, off and on, discussing the show, but the idea of the cabaret as the central metaphor was Prince's, just as the cabaret music and lyrics were other artists' material he had to enhance. But by imagining himself as a choreographer in Berlin in 1930 working in a second-rate nightclub, Field realized that Germans would have turned to American films for inspiration. As he explained in *Broadway Song & Story:* "I had worked so much in Europe and I understood the European choreographers. They were always ten years behind us. 'Le jazz hot' and all that. The genesis was always on this side of the ocean" (Guernsey 1985: 146). American influences became increasingly apparent in the vaudeville trappings for Joel Grey and the Kit Kat girls, as (in Hirsch's words) the "insignia of American show business [were] transformed into social and political satire: Al Jolson [became] Brecht" (Hirsch 2005: 64). Accordingly, everything became "harder and more Germanic. The time-steps weren't Fred Astaire–like. They were Brunnhilde-like. Fred [Ebb] would sing the songs to me, and, with that orientation in mind, I'd go ahead. And I hired girls with sort of heavy thighs and had the costumes cut in sort of the wrong places."

But the elaborate evolutions of choreography and story had disconcerting effects. Joel Grey was unhappy because he felt that his role had nothing to do with the book and because he hadn't seen much of Prince. He complained to Field: "I don't like this at all. I feel I have no connection with the show." But the choreographer placated him: "I have this sneaky suspicion that this is the part people would dream to have. The part of the decade."

Field's instinct was to prove correct, and the choreographer went about his business, transcending his sense of alienation, meeting Prince only at run-throughs, and patiently allowing the concept of the show to sink into his imagination. He never presumed to offer his notions for songs, and nobody thought of soliciting his opinions. However, despite Prince's occasionally intimidating authority, Field played a significant part in ensuring that the title song came to be used as such. He was amazed at the way Kander and Ebb would defer meekly to the director, accepting even withering scorn at times. As recalled in *Broadway Song & Story*, the two musicians would sing song after song, and Prince would just eye them and say, "For *this* production?" as if the two men were gross novices. The next day they would be back with another song, usually better than the ones they had tried out the previous day, and Field would be awestruck by their versatility and quick inventiveness. In admiration of their equanimity, Field remarked: "I don't believe how good-natured you are. You sell a song to Hal, and he says: 'What high school production would you like that to be in?'" Ebb turned to Kander: "Well, let's show him." And the duo showed him a stack of music that had been rejected by Prince. They played three of the songs, and one of these began, "What good is sitting alone in your room?" Field stuttered: "But that's wonderful! Why isn't that in the show?" Ebb replied: "Hal says he doesn't want two title songs." "What's the other one?" "'Wilkommen.'" Prince figured that "Wilkommen" should be the title song, and he didn't want another song with the word "cabaret" in it in the second act. "Oh, my Lord!" gasped Field. "That is *so* wonderful" (Guernsey 1985: 147). When Kander and Ebb asked him to use his diplomatic suasion at the next meeting with Prince, Field agreed. He was nervous, of course, at the meeting in George Abbott's office, but he put in his oar: "Hal, I heard a song yesterday that I think is wonderful." Prince asked to hear it again, and after Kander and Ebb had played it, the director realized that Field was correct, and "Cabaret" was confirmed as the title song.

In rehearsal, Kander and Ebb found that they had to be flexible in the way they distributed arrangements or taught the singers. "What you give the singer depends on whether the singer can read music or not," explains Kander. "My process is to write out a piano-vocal version of the song. It gets printed and distributed to those who can use it" (Guernsey 1985: 147). But *Cabaret* was rehearsed before cassettes were extensively used, so most of the time if somebody could not read music, Kander or the rehearsal pianist would repeat the tune for the individual.

The score underwent substantial changes. There was a number called "I Don't Care Much," which had been written when Kander and Ebb were dining with a couple of friends. The composers were showing off about how quickly they could create a song, and when challenged to a demonstration by their dinner companions, they boasted that they would write one between dessert and coffee. The table was cleared, and as the composers moved to a piano, Ebb asked, "What will we write about?"

which immediately prompted his partner's response: "I don't care much." In this nonchalant mood, Kander began playing a waltz rhythm while Ebb tried out a lyric to match, and in fifteen minutes a song was born. Prince liked the number, and for a while there was talk about making it one of the ambience songs because it seemed to conjure up the image of a singer in a trench coat leaning against a lamppost. However, when "I Don't Care Much" was used in place of "Cabaret" in the second act with the title song moved up to the first act, the rearrangement misfired and the new song was dropped.

At the final technical rehearsal, Prince scrutinized the cabaret scenes, sharpening them so that they would become an integral part of the action rather than a divertissement. His critical faculties were alert and sharp as he picked up on orchestral overamplitude, lighting miscues, slow set changes, inappropriate costume effects, and inaudible lyrics. Doors that had to open and close in exact counterpoint were worked as hard as the lighting crew who had to provide blackouts after a certain number of beats and make the singers disappear into total darkness.

The show was scheduled to open at the Shubert Theater in Boston on October 10, 1966, but Prince and his collaborators knew that all was not right. The play was much too long in its three-act form, and there was still some uncertainty about the political and sexual elements. Prince also knew that for all the daring innovations that married Brecht to Isherwood, the show was soft in the center, particularly in the underdeveloped roles of Sally and Cliff, the sentimentality of Schultz, and some of the cabaret numbers. At a run-through prior to the Boston opening, Robbins, who was invited by Prince to offer comments, remarked that the show was wonderful but that any dancing that didn't occur as part of the cabaret acts should be cut altogether. Field, who had staged the marvelously inventive "Telephone Song," where one couple met and kissed without breaking their embrace throughout the number, was virtually devastated. If Robbins's suggestions were to be accepted, this would have eliminated the brilliant number as well as the engagement party dance that Lenya did with the sailors. Fortunately, Prince did not act upon Robbins's suggestion.

Just before leaving for Boston, Prince ran separate performances of the show, one for Abbott, and the other for Stephen Sondheim. As he explains in *Contradictions*: "They are the two I most like to hear from at that stage. They never waste your time with the obvious; they figure you see it and you'll get around to it in good time" (Prince 1974: 135).

Sondheim's comments are not on record, though Prince gave the impression that his friend appreciated the firm sense of what the evening was about. As for Abbott, the old master is said to have remarked: "Do it in two acts instead of three; I can't figure out where the curtain falls." Prince couldn't figure it out either, so when Ruth Mitchell suggested that he combine the first two acts, that's what he did. "Abbott was right," Prince admits. "The show played better in two acts." *Cabaret* had enticing mystery. Its metaphor shaped the entire piece, the orchestration did not depend on piano for its melodic or harmonic lead, the lyrics filled their respective scenes, and the director evidently succeeded in preventing an audience from relaxing in an atmosphere of musical comedy.

The first night Boston audience sensed that it was witnessing theatrical innovation, though it was rather stunned by certain things in the show. As Joel Grey remarked years later to Richard Alleman in *Playbill*, "it was like...CRACK! From the opening number you were standing there, and you knew that whatever it was you were doing from your gut or heart that it was not a safe musical—but that it also connected with the audience." Why did the show stun so many in the audience? "I think one of the successes of the show is that it wasn't a formula. It took a lot of chances and, in that atmosphere of taking chances, it came up with a lot of fresh things."

The Boston critics were generally enthusiastic. Samuel Hirsch of the *Boston Herald* was taken with everything from the "large, glittering, prismatic mirror" that was "like a rectangular peeping eye reflecting a preening, prancing, prurient world intent on destroying itself in the jazzy age in Berlin just before Hitler poisoned the world" to the performances, especially of Lenya, whose voice he called "the voice of Germany." The most notable of the critics, Kevin Kelly of the *Boston Globe*, praised the "authentic period ring" of the score, with its "Kurt Weill flavor...polished with its own originality, a sour note reality that is perfect." He also approved of the "flawless settings," the costumes, and the dances— especially the cabaret numbers that he described as being "full of spirit, zing, rosebud leers, stalwart low sex and high-flying lust." He reserved highest acting honors for Lenya, for her "heartbreaking dignity" and "the courage of a woman who has seen too much." But he pinpointed two basic problems with the show. The first he described as "the staggering clutter of the first act which tries to define characters and country all at once" but with nothing much really happening apart from the meeting of the young pair of lovers; the second was Jill Haworth's pallid Sally, who "simply lacks the magnetism to make her the quixotic girl she is supposed to be."

Kelly's second point was to prove prophetic in light of subsequent New York critical reaction, but Haworth did draw some good reviews. Hirsch in the *Boston Herald* liked her "pleasant voice" and "dancer's lithsome [*sic*] grace." Alta Maloney of the *Boston Traveler* wrote: "Jill Haworth is absolutely great. She gets beneath the beautiful exterior of the English girl." There was no denying the hard edge to her voice and its capacity to be brutal when required. The actress used three differently colored wigs, one for each act. Kander comments: "Sally Bowles was supposed to be so bizarre and crazy and baroque that she was going to be a blonde, a redhead and a brunette. And I remember thinking, 'This sounds weird!'" (Guernsey 1985: 145). But the black wig she wore for her title song put her in a more bizarre mode and worked well with her green fingernails. Besides, she remained sexy.

But the key problem was not this single stroke of casting. Alan Bunch of the *Christian Science Monitor* claimed that the musical was "almost void" as drama because it mostly contented itself "with setting up contrasting moods—strident voices and gesticulating shadows on a screen [a reference to the menacing expressionism that Prince eventually eliminated]; cavorting entertainers and patrons; the amoral self-centered lovers." The title of the show apparently had not prepared audiences for what they would see, and Masteroff was discouraged by the same spectacle every night: "The name of the show was *Cabaret*, and they expected it to be a normal kind of Broadway musical. Within ten minutes, they had seen these not-so-great looking chorus girls, and the show seemed to be a little on the grim side, and people began trooping up the aisles. Believe me, we were all very depressed about it!" (Guernsey 1985: 143). In fact, Masteroff snuck up behind Ebb during a preview and said gloomily: "You realize, of course, this is a big flop. The critics will like it because it is brave, but the audience will hate it" (Bryer and Davison 2008: 102).

The three-act problem was relatively easy to solve. Of course, some good songs were lost, including "The End of the Party" at the end of the second act, but the show felt tighter. However, Ebb was frightened that losing good musical moments meant that he would also lose good reviews. The night it went into two acts, he took to his bed in the Bradford Hotel, with Kander holding one hand on one side and Joel Grey doing the same on the other. Both friends assured him, "It's not a disaster." However, the first preview in New York—where tickets were $100 a seat for charity—spelled disaster. At the intermission, the theater nearly emptied. Ebb recalled: "They just left in droves. All you could hear outside was frantic screaming, 'Taxi! Get me out of here!' They just really hated it" (102).

The biggest difficulty related to "If You Could See Her through My Eyes." At the opening performance, the audience first laughed at the spectacle of the Emcee romancing a gorilla in a tutu, but then some people realized what they were laughing at and stopped in embarrassment. When the song concluded, they clapped with nervous politeness. But toward the end of the Boston run, the producers started to receive letters of protest. One was from a rabbi who (according to Ebb) lamented that "the graves of six million Jews were pleading for us not to do this" (Guernsey 1985: 141). For the time being, Prince stuck to his guns, and the show moved to Broadway.

CHAPTER 8

BROADWAY PRESENTATIONAL

PRINCE OFFERED LOWER TICKET PRICES BEFORE THE OFFICIAL BROADWAY opening on November 20, 1966. This was part of a system he had begun with *Superman*. Mail orders were accepted as of October 17, and tickets that were purchased before the opening of the Broadhurst box office qualified for discounts up to 33 percent. As a result, the preliminary sales totaled $351,219. Of this amount, preview theater parties accounted for $107,572, mail orders (at discount) for $51,219, and regular theater parties for $192,428. No other Broadway producer favored this system—not even David Merrick, who commented: "It's too complicated to handle." Prince disagreed: "I'm delighted that people want to see a musical that is serious at its core. I think there are a lot of happy people holding orchestra tickets who paid $7.90 for them instead of the regular price of $12 or $10. That's because they bet on the show before the reviews came in" (Prince Papers).

There was only one uneasy moment in the advance sales system. At an audition for theater party sales (usually dominated by high-society women from some guild or other) a grim man, with his hair sticking out, frowned at Fred Ebb, who was hosting the affair at his apartment and offering a preview of the score. As Ebb recalls in *Broadway Song & Story*: "He kept frowning at me, and I got a fix on him. I did the whole show, and I didn't think I did it very well. And I thought this particular person really hated it." The comic irony was that this frowning man was Boris Aronson, the set designer, who had shown up just to hear the material. Thinking he was an escort for one of the theater party "ladies" threw Ebb into "a real panic" (Guernsey 1985: 144).

Poster for Cabaret *(1966) (Photofest)*

There weren't many new musicals the season of *Cabaret*'s premiere; in fact, 1966–67 began with notable revivals of *Guys and Dolls* and *Show Boat* before *The Apple Tree* (a collage of three one-act pieces inspired, in turn, by Mark Twain, a Frank R. Stockton short story, and fiction by Jules Feiffer) and two foreign-language musicals (*Gilbert Bécaud on Broadway* and *Let's Sing Yiddish*). So, the advent of *Cabaret* was a great occasion for Broadway, signaling that a musical could combine the derivative (Brecht–Weill) with the daring (politics–history–promiscuity). Advance word had heralded *Cabaret* as having a rich dramatic subject that was made meaningful by a concentration on the decadent ambience of the period. In short, audiences could expect skill and temperament, heightened musical technique and accurate realism. Many prospective patrons had heard of the huge tilted mirror and the mixture of Nazis and sentimental lovers, glittering vaudeville turns and seedy scenes, a nonlinear narrative and a subtextual level, but all of this was as—yet-unrealized, though enticing, hype.

What unfolded opening night was brilliant but schizophrenic.

The first scene set the presentational style by its elements of kitsch, parody, lewdness, and disguise. The performance world of the Kit Kat Klub—a blacked-out stage caught in its own suspended, distorted mirror—was obviously a reflection of prewar Germany's wish to escape its own true image. As Walter Kerr noted in his review in the *New York Times* (Nov. 1966), the first thing the audience saw as it entered the theater was itself. Boris Aronson's "strings of frosted lamps converge[d] toward a vanishing point upstage centre," and the mirror, which occupied this vanishing point, showed an audience, some at café tables, awaiting a floor show. Everything to be seen and learned during the evening was going to be done (as Kerr put it) "through the tipsy, tinkling, angular vision of sleek rouged-up clowns"—really brassy women, mincing homosexuals, raucous dancers, and a pink satin–vested Emcee heavily rouged with red cupid-bow lips, shiny pomaded hair, and mascara eyes in a death's head white face. More marionette than human, he twisted, turned, and lightly tapped his way in tails and bowtie to "Willkommen," using his cane as a prop, his exotic accents for parody, and his lewdness as a tantalizing force. His grotesque charm held in the garish lighting, as the hefty, rock-faced all-girls band set up the notes for what Edward Winter's Ernst called the "hottest spot in all Berlin."

The opening, of course, did not change everything in Broadway's stale bipartite pattern of storytelling and song-and-dance, but it lunged

Joel Grey as the Emcee/
Master of Ceremonies in
Cabaret *(1966) (Photofest)*

forward with Joel Grey's Emcee (as Kerr described) "to insist on music as mediator between audience and characters, as lord and master of the revels, as mocking *conférencier* without whose ministrations we should have no show at all." The jangle of cabaret music was "the fundamental beat of the entertainment, just as the garish images of the Kit Kat Klub Kittens and a pushy, lipsticked, sinuous M.C. [became] the distorting mirror through which we peer[ed] at an actual world." Instead of putting the narrative first and the singers and dancers into small corners, the show immediately popped "the painted clowns and gartered girls directly into our faces, making them, in effect, a brightly glazed window—with a musical staff scrawled all over it—*through* which we perceive the people and the emotional patterns of the plot."

As Grey completed his "Willkommen," the train that had brought Cliff to Berlin disappeared upstage, and the club regained the central focus. The principal form of narration was established surreally. This was clearly not naturalism, but an expression of self-absorption. By dissolving the train scene and its brief, almost perfunctory, exposition of Ernst and

Cliff, master smuggler and aspiring novelist, the cabaret became the dominant, immediate world.

The first gesture of the show was one of welcome—a sign repeated in Lotte Lenya's rooming house welcome to Cliff as a sinister tremolo pulsed in the background—but it was a movement from a mask, as it were, for the cabaret created a face whose demonic grin and painted charm kept revelers up until midnight (as Kerr phrased it) "making false faces at the hangman."

The sense of masks and faces, of the silver tinsel and neon trappings, as a form of eavesdropping was carried through in Prince's metatheatrical presentation. As Kerr (1968: 202) later wrote: "The show [is] a mask made of musical numbers, Peeping Tom humming a tune," and the angle of vision is made explicit by means of a spiral iron staircase curving to nowhere alongside the proscenium arch. And always someone was wandering up and down, pausing to stare. There was spectacle enough for voyeurs: Bert Convy's straight-backed Cliff was a writer who hardly ever wrote; Jill Haworth's Sally was a performer who sang in fishnet stockings and scarlet garters, never seeming as if she would be a star; and Lenya's landlady succumbed ruefully to Jack Gilford's Jewish grocer who bore her exotic fruit.

Joel Grey (top center) in Cabaret *(1966) (Photofest)*

Although Haworth excelled at comic phrasing (particularly in her songs) and played with spirit, her Sally did not register strongly enough to make the role the central pivot as it had been in Christopher Isherwood's Berlin stories or John van Druten's *I Am a Camera*. The failing had less to do with the actress, however, than with the role as written by Joe Masteroff, or with her foil, a sexually uncharismatic Cliff despite Convy's musical charm and earnestness.

With his thinning hair and shy hopefulness, Gilford produced first-rate comedy in his wooing scenes, spinning himself and his partner into dizziness and then exploiting the spoken-sung "Meeskite" for all its worth. He and Lenya were the veritable scene stealers of the story-end, though Lenya was the audience favorite with her quivering husky voice, worldly-wise shrug, and defiantly curled lip. Her throatily warbled "So What?" caught the desperation of an era and the resignation of her own life, and her pineapple duet with Gilford managed to transcend the clichés with touching tenderness.

The tacky, rattling music, the garish glamour, the strident, forced gaiety in the club all made wicked fun of darkening lives. The first act was filled with many wonders: Aronson's black, silver, and scarlet scenic design (in which a gray-green fruit store, in contrast, came up, in Kerr's phrase, "like a warm summer dawn"); Patricia Zipprodt's gaudy German expressionist costumes; and Ronald Field's parodies of Jazz Age social dancing and frenzied nightclub routines. But could the expectations raised by the brilliant components ever reach ultimate fulfilment?

This was a musical in which the music and dances were as important as the libretto. The cabaret numbers related the plot and action to themes presented in song. Apart from "Willkommen," the signature piece of the Emcee and his world-as-cabaret, there were five pieces of theatrical lasciviousness, militaristic patriotism, and materialism. They were lowbrow or, at best, middlebrow entertainments whose moods and gestures often slid along the edges of vaudeville or burlesque while registering some agitation. "The Money Song" and "Two Ladies" were characterized by a degenerate showiness. "Tomorrow Belongs to Me" swelled with brazen imperiousness. And the cumulative effect registered only at the end of act 1, for in the very moments of their performance, they seemed ex-centric or outside the story's center. They promised happiness while staving off time.

The dramatic highlight of the first half was the disrupted engagement party. When Peg Murray's defiantly vulgar Fräulein Kost informed

Ernst Ludwig that Gilford's Herr Schultz was a Jew, the merry mood changed abruptly. As Edward Winter (Ernst) attempted to leave after urging Lenya to change her marriage plans, Murray held him back, reprising "Tomorrow," and wearing his Nazi armband. In the background dancers swayed slowly as more armbands were passed around. The moment synthesized significance, for as Richard Gilman was to write in *Newsweek* (1966): "To the middle-aged engaged couple it means an end to loneliness, to the young lovers their passion, to the whores their extended fate, to the Nazis their cruel triumph." This was jolting enough to the audience, but Prince was not finished yet. The cabaret world surreally imposed itself on the human drama by the "Tomorrow" reprise as Grey's cigar-puffing Emcee appeared atop the spiral staircase. The choric figure had once again become both spectator and part of the spectacle itself. First he studied the scene; then he descended as the people onstage froze against a black background. Slowly crossing the stage, looking at everyone, he turned to the audience, shrugged, smiled, and exited as a blackout engulfed the scene. The ensemble froze, suggesting a photograph or *tableau mort*, which he had apparently willed into being by his special power to be voyeur and magician of transformation. In his earlier cabaret acts he had adopted personae of a bizarre host, devilishly gleeful libertine, and parody plutocrat, so it was well within his nature to be a compendium of characters, a spectacle in himself, as he remained demonically detached. The first act finale gathered up all its elements into what Gilman called "a single moment of beauty and anguish."

In the very brief opening scene of act 2, the Emcee was in transvestite disguise as one of the Kit Kat Klub chorus girls. Once again, it was music and staging rather than text itself that formulated the world-as-cabaret metaphor. The opening dance disintegrated into ominous drumming as the audience became aware that the song had become a military version of "Tomorrow Belongs to Me." The Emcee and his girls goose-stepped offstage. The imagery was a reordering of reality: cabaret girls were now Nazis; their leader, an aggressive androgyne blending, by his own demonic energy, into the harsh spectacle. It was a spellbinding moment, designed to send chills up the audience's spine while extending the cruel significance of the image.

"If You Could See Her" was a real coup, beginning precisely after a brick was hurled through Schultz's shop window, as Grey bounced from the portals to grab a gorilla in rose tulle. With prim delicacy, the pair

Joel Grey and gorilla in "If You Could See Her" in Cabaret *(1966) (Photofest)*

waltzed to the suggestion of a world gone mad. But this shock was dissipated, and the show began to repeat its effects as old plot conflicts widened without necessarily making the characters count for more than compromises.

Haworth's Sally continued to have charm, but as Richard P. Cooke wrote in the *Wall Street Journal*, cast in "the nostalgic tradition of lost heroines" she couldn't triumph over the limitations of the script to make the audience care about what she did. Her climactic song, the title number, had edge, though her botched romance with Convy's Cliff had almost none. As for Gilford and Lenya, they found, like the ill-fated young couple, that their story was sandwiched and finally flattened between the cabaret scenes. As Martin Gottfried complained in his review in *Women's Wear Daily*, "the differences between the cabaret and the plot halves of [the show] could not be more striking. On the one hand there are unique ideas, striking uses of lighting and movement, a sense of the bizarre. And on the other the same old romance, secondary romance and sketched-in complications." It was the cabaret that won the evening's honors while defeating Masteroff's libretto.

The play's frame was reasserted in the final scene where, as Cliff's train pulled out of Berlin and he began to write a remembrance of the city and sang the opening bars of "Willkommen," the scene dissolved into the cabaret world. Grey's Emcee emerged and moved his lips soundlessly to Convy's singing, and as Cliff stopped and the train disappeared upstage, the Emcee took over, reprising the show's opening number. The Kit Kat Klub rematerialized, though now the picture and mood were disturbingly different from what they had been at the outset of the play. The all-girl band still looked provocative—but this time not because of flesh above black hose, but because they wore German uniforms and swastika armbands. In another staging coup, Prince developed an almost hallucinatory vocal and musical kaleidoscope as Schultz, Fräulein Schneider, and Sally reappeared within a moving crowd and repeated lines from earlier scenes as in a montage. Haworth had one more passage from the title song before she vanished into the darkness, along with the other characters, leaving Grey's Emcee alone onstage for the wrap-up. Facing the audience for his valedictory to a drumroll, he asked: "Where are your troubles now? Forgotten? I told you so! Here life is beautiful—the girls are beautiful—even the orchestra is beautiful." He took five beats, looked around the empty stage. "Auf wiedersehen!" Three beats. "A bientôt!" And he bowed as cymbals clashed, then vanished into darkness.

In this epiphany, what had once been the site for spectacle now was the site for meditative meaning on the nihilism in the story. The jangled music, perversely posturing dancers, and frenzied gaiety were swept away, and left behind, in the emptiness, was a palpable sense of Germany's degeneracy. Hitler and his hordes could not have come to power without the acquiescence of the populace, and the cabaret, where nobody ever openly questioned the content or ambience and where the Emcee reigned with a Mephistophelean smirk, was a gaudy emblem of cynical entrapment and delusion.

This symbolic enlargement was lost for the most part on the Broadway critics, who generally applauded the show's ambition while decrying its compromises. Martin Gottfried's complaint about the uneasy, irreconcilable halves of the show was echoed by Julius Novick, who, in a *Village Voice* review, denounced the show's lapses into "hackneyed Broadwayism." Clive Barnes also found fault with the structure when reviewing the 1987 production, praising the first half for its brilliance but cautioning "ultra-sensitive people" to leave once this zenith had passed and not bother with the "genteel decline."

Some critics thought that the largest mistake of the show was Jill Haworth as Sally Bowles. The actress had already suffered in Boston where, despite some approving reviews, carping critics had branded her as pallid and unmagnetic. At the end of the Broadway opening, she burst into tears of relief for having survived the early setbacks. More suffering was in store for her, however, when the reviews appeared. Norman Nadel, in the *World Journal Tribune*, charged that she lacked "seasoning in musical theater." Gottfried added that she "had neither the vulnerability nor the spunk necessary for Sally" and that she could "barely manage the beginnings of an English accent." This censure of her accent was ridiculous: she was, after all, authentically English by birth. She should have consoled herself with the fact that John Chapman (in the *Daily News*) and Richard Watts Jr. (in the *New York Post*), as well as Richard P. Cooke had kind words for her, but, as is often the case with performers, she dwelled on the negative notices, the coup de grâce of which was delivered by Walter Kerr, who called her "the one wild wrong note" in "a stunning musical." After praising the decor, music, choreography, and performances of Grey, Lenya, Gilford, and Convy, he zeroed in on what he believed was "the evening's single, and all too obvious, mistake." With his characteristic gift for vivid imagery, he likened Haworth to "a snowball in white fur, and sporting that pancake tam that girls of the 20's used to wear whenever they were going to be photographed having snowball fights." But "her usefulness to this particular project," he decided, "end[ed] there." Although he found that at some angles she looked "astonishingly like Clara Bow," he called her "trim but neutral, a profile rather than a person," and given the difficult things the show was trying to do, he termed her "a damaging presence, worth no more to the show than her weight in mascara."

John Kander suggested in *Broadway Song & Story* that Kerr's assault had been provoked by "rather bad letters" the critic had received "about the fact he had gone overboard for women stars" (Guernsey 1984: 144–45). Kerr had raved about practically every female star that season (including Mary Martin in *I Do! I Do!*, Louise Troy in *Walking Happy*, and Barbara Harris in *The Apple Tree*), and Kander intimated that he tried to compensate by slaughtering Haworth. It didn't seem to matter to Kerr or some others that Haworth played Sally without undue sentimentality, as an attractive gold digger, a hardened, amoral adventuress rather than as a real showbiz celebrity in the making.

Deeply sensitive to Haworth's pain at the critical battering, Lenya went out of her way to be compassionate. She rushed to Haworth, consoling her with the fact that she, too, had received poor notices in her career. "She was very supportive," according to Ebb. "It was almost noble, really, the way she took Jill under her wing during that show." (It was only three weeks later, after Haworth began to complain that she was "so bored" with the show, that Lenya snapped at her: "Then get the hell out of the theatre. You have no right to be here") (Farneth 1998: 187).

Of course, with the profuse praise lavished on her own performance, Lenya could afford to be sympathetic and caring. Once more the darling of critics and audiences, she refrained from ever acting grandly. At Sardi's she was gracious to people who stood to applaud her entrance, and when a number of waiters of mid-European extract paid her homage with courtly bows, she accepted this with great grace and charm. And her humor never deserted her. As her biographer Donald Spoto reports, she cried out "Bombay gin!" when a dinner companion specified the brand in a drink order. "I've never heard of it!" she said. "If only we'd known of it back in Berlin—what a title for a Brecht–Weill song—'Bombay Gin'!" As ever, she loved life, especially the strangest haunts she could visit on the Lower East Side and in Greenwich Village, and she remained the eternal optimist. She dismissed excessive compliments on her artistry, knowing full well that her "rasping voice that could sandpaper sandpaper" (as Harold Schonberg put it in a *New York Times* feature [Spoto 1989: 259–60]) was more the result of nature than nurture. She downplayed her technique. "What is so hard?" she used to ask a friend rhetorically. "You stand perfectly still, you open your mouth, and you feel the song—that is all there is to it!" But she genuinely enjoyed her success in *Cabaret*, telling a visitor from the *New York Times*: "For sixteen years I've been the widow of Kurt Weill. Now I'm me" (Spoto 1989: 262).

At the opening night party at Sardi's, Ebb went over to his mother after the first reviews—all raves—came in. "It's a huge hit!" he exclaimed excitedly. "Good," she responded. Feeling buoyantly generous, he offered to buy her a mink stole. "It's about time," she declared. When he asked her opinion of the show, she did not seem unduly impressed: "The show? Well, it didn't have to be so dirty, big shot" (Leve 2009: 14).

Notwithstanding the less than ecstatic remarks of Ebb's mother, the show quickly recouped its initial investment. Indeed, the day after the official opening, the 134 backers were mailed 10 percent of their outlay. *Cabaret* ran for 1,166 performances, was voted the year's best musical by the New York Drama Critics Circle, and won Tony awards for best musical, best supporting actor (Grey), best supporting actress (Peg Murray), director, composer and lyricist, costume design, set design, and choreography. Gilford lost to Robert Preston (*I Do! I Do!*) as best actor, Lenya to Barbara Harris (*The Apple Tree*) as best actress. Lenya didn't mind because it was more important to her to be in a long-running hit. Besides, she had already won a Tony, as best supporting or featured actress in a musical, for *The Threepenny Opera* in 1956.

The show's creators were all surprised by the enormous success, for as Masteroff recalls in Spoto's book on Lenya, he, Prince, Kander, and Ebb would have been pleased if it had run for one year successfully. After all, it was a show about unpleasant subjects—Nazis, abortion, deceit, and crime—and the chorus girls were unattractive. Moreover, virtually every character met an unhappy end.

Well, not completely. An important compromise was made in the cabaret personality, which, though garishly vulgar, was not fully horrifying as a metaphor for soul sickness. A compromise was made as well (as nearly every critic recognized) with romantic conventions of Broadway musicals, for the quartet of lovers appeared to have been manufactured for broad appeal. And the most dramatic compromise came in the ending for "Meeskite," the song that had brought Jewish protests in Boston over its concluding line. After the second preview in New York, a thin woman in a sweater accosted Ebb at the back of the theater. With clipboard in hand, she asked if he was the lyricist. He said yes, indeed, to which she responded by threatening action from pressure groups if the offending line of the gorilla song was not immediately changed. Upon learning of this, Prince became deeply worried. At a meeting in the theater itself, he relented and changed the line from "She wouldn't look Jewish at all" to "She isn't a *meeskite* at all."

The original line did resurface on special occasions, such as at the Actors' Fund performance or when distinguished guests were present. In these instances, Grey would deliver it straight, as if he had forgotten the injunction against uttering it. Kander could never understand the fuss. As he explains in *Broadway Song & Story*, the song was to trick the audience into first laughing and then realizing how easy it was to "fall into a trap of prejudice." The Jewish members of the audience, his family included, thought the song was insulting to Jews by showing they were as ugly as gorillas. "It's a puzzle that has never been solved" (Guernsey 1985: 142).

What was solved was the matter of box office earnings. The show opened with a top ticket price of $12, but it became an established hit, multiplying its profits in 1968, when Prince moved *Fiddler on the Roof* from the Imperial to the Majestic, making way for *Cabaret* at the Imperial. In this way, both shows were able to earn larger weekly gross receipts. Prince also liked the show better "a distance removed from the audience" (Prince 1974: 85). Audiences certainly did not fret unduly that the story element in *Cabaret* sometimes undercut the musical. They accepted the show's mixture of heightened musical technique and realism, of pungent drama and romantic comedy, of symbolism and nonlinear narrative. Although John Gassner (1968: 575) complained that the story element remained "unstylized and thus unprojected," and Lehman Engel (2006: 330) objected to "a series of floor shows interspersed with two ersatz love stories," audiences preferred to share Walter Kerr's view that the production was "sufficiently original in concept and secure in execution."

Later, in a long essay for the *New York Times* (December 4, 1966), Kerr maintained that *Cabaret* opened the door "part way at least—to a fresh notion of the bizarre, crackling, harsh and yet beguiling uses that can be made of song and dance." Pointing to the "mocking, elongated, circuitous fantastications of Gunter Grass, Thomas Pynchon, Joseph Heller, Ralph Ellison, et al," with their "structural openness," "free-association logic," and "irreverence," Kerr thought the show was fateful enough to pave the way for picaresque themes in musical theater. It certainly was something to think about.

CHAPTER 9

REINCARNATIONS AND REVISIONS

THE 1968 LONDON VERSION

After his show had run eighteen months on Broadway, Hal Prince took steps to launch a production in England. On a visit to London to cast this version, he auditioned several British leading ladies of theater, including Vanessa Redgrave and Dorothy Tutin (who had already played Sally in John van Druten's *I Am a Camera* in the West End), but he surprised everyone by casting five-foot-two Judi Dench in the role of Sally after seeing her shine in *The Promise* by Aleksei Arbuzov. Dench was undeniably versatile, but going from the Russian play to a musical role was a stretch even for her. She had never been considered a singer, so when her agent, Julian Belfrage, rang to say that Hal Prince wanted to see her for his production of *Cabaret*, she said: "You have to be joking." Belfrage took her to lunch, she bought a feather boa, drank two glasses of wine, and when she arrived at the theater, she sang from the wings (Miller 2006: 69).

Prince took one look at her and decided she was Sally Bowles. He would comment later: "It was extraordinary, all that energy. Sally shouldn't be a great singer, or a comfortable performer, she's a show-off and she's edgy, she is a little hysterical, she's irresistible and she's very sexy. Judi had all that stuff, and she's got great looks, that girl. It was fun to have her audition, and it was just about two seconds later that everybody said, 'Well, do you think she'll do this thing? If she'll do it, we'll have to have her'" (93).

Prince advised her to read Christopher Isherwood's *Goodbye to Berlin* to see why she was so right for the part. Sally was a middle-class girl from

England who couldn't sing and could never be a musical star. However, Dench was still lacking in confidence. Her friend and fellow actress Barbara Leigh-Hunt had presented her with a copy of the Broadway cast recording, but Dench was unable to listen to it once she was offered Sally. When the musical director in London was about to go to New York during rehearsals, he asked her if there was anything she wanted him to bring her, and she promptly replied: "Yes, the top note from the end of *Cabaret.*" Prince overheard her and said, "If you can't get the top note, act that you can't get it" (Miller 2006: 69). The remark suddenly released her from insecurity, though she never was reassured about her vocal deficiency for a musical role. Her dressing room at the Palace Theatre was in a half-basement, so she could easily hear the conversations of passersby as well as see their legs from the knee down. Just before the opening night, she saw two pairs of trouser legs and heard a voice declare: "Judi Dench in *Cabaret?* No one will go see that, dear, no one" (94).

She worked hard preparing for the part. Her first preparation was to take stock of the large theater auditorium. She took care about her diet, going off to a health farm and losing a stone in weight. She took singing lessons from Gwen Catley, who after hearing her, said: "Well, yes, you're not a singer. But I can teach you to sing in your way." Dench considered putting up a notice in the foyer of the Palace Theatre, where the show was running: "Miss Judi Dench does not have a cold. This is her normal speaking voice" (9). Her voice, as her biographer John Miller points out, was actually a strong suit when it came to acting, with its slight huskiness, almost as if there was a crack in it. "It adds texture and depth, and sometimes pain and melancholy, to whatever character she's playing. When you hear it you know that, even if she's in a major-key role, the possibility of moving into a minor key exists" (9).

She adored working with Prince because he had such wonderful command and a sharp antenna for false acting and staging. In rehearsal for the Sailors' Dance, there was a moment when she jumped and they caught her. Prince scolded: "Oh no, cut that musical crap. Everybody does that. Don't do that." He had fresh ideas about the number, and she thought he was good fun. For his part, Prince marveled at how she could instantly spot a falsehood in her own performance. "I remember watching her in rehearsal trying something and almost editing it, out of some shame, because it was too easy, calculated, adroit, crafty. What's worth mentioning about Dench is her thing about telling the truth; when you know you're working with somebody who just plain says what's on their mind all the time, you don't go home and worry about them" (95).

Alas, when the show opened on February 28, 1968, London did not follow New York in taking *Cabaret* to heart. Part of the problem was the stage technology. *Cabaret* did not have huge spectacle or special effects. The set was essentially a big black velours stage with a tilted mirror and some lights, but the timing of scene changes was very specific. As Prince explains: "In those days we had winches, eight-inch high plates that bring on scenery. We started with a sound system for cueing, and the poor people in the first few rows could hear the fly-floor, 'Warning on 6…bring in 6.' Then we went on to more sophisticated stuff and light cues." The theater crew found that the new technical demands stretched the old Palace's capacities almost to the breaking point. Assistant stage manager Chris Cooper remarked that many in the company were nervous because they did not know whether or not they were going to be run over by the scenery. "There were huge bits of scenery rolling all over this small stage, and many times it ground to a halt, and we'd have to wait for fifteen minutes or so to get the whole thing back on tracks again" (97). The lead performers had to improvise and ad-lib to cover. On one occasion, Peter Sallis, playing Herr Schultz, told jokes and made up business for twenty minutes before he could do his number while the chorus appeared and sat around like his audience. On another occasion he read out some invented telegrams.

The producers were anxious about audience reaction to a musical set in a Berlin nightclub during the rise of Hitler. Through her dressing room window Dench heard a woman scold her husband: "Arthur, you told me it was all about nuns and children!" She also heard another audience member who was disappointed that comedian Frankie Vaughan was not in the show. She had expected him to show up and sing what he always sang on his television show: "Come to the Cabaret" (95).

Misplaced expectations were not confined to the audience. The English critics expected too much or simply quite different things from what the production offered. Most of their negative comments concerned the casting. Ronald Bryden wrote in *The Observer* that Kevin Colson's Cliff was never more than "a shadowy lay-figure" and that Dench, an expert actress, was "simply too big a performer to cramp herself into Sally's frailty." In his *Times* review, Irving Wardle commented that Dench's Sally was "essentially an affectionate home girl with none of the glittering inconstancy of the unattainable original" and concluded that because her performance sometimes suggested "the thwarted fantasies of a Pinner secretary," you wondered how she ever got to Berlin. Indeed, the English critics spoke almost as a single chorus about the actress, finding that she lacked the right physique for a flapper and the "frenetic gaiety" for the "glittering inconstancy" of the second-rate overreacher. Lila Kedrova as the voluble, vivacious landlady was praised for her ability to be more than simply "an unshakable veteran of the twentieth century" (Wardle). But Peter Sallis's Schultz seemed to have sunk into massive sentimentality. Of the London cast, only American Barry Dennen as the Emcee won high praise, obtaining approval from Charles Marowitz of the *Village Voice* for managing "to bridge the gap between the world of Pabst, Brecht, the degenerate Berlin'20s, and the normal-as-blueberry pie American musical of today," though Frank Marcus, in *Plays & Players*, was a dissenting voice: "For the record: he doesn't (and couldn't) equal Joel Grey in New York, who is not only one of the greatest artists I have

Judi Dench (right) as Sally Bowles in the 1968 London production directed by Harold Prince (Photofest)

ever seen but also made the first ten minutes of the show into the kind of experience that leaves one with tears in one's eyes, electric shudders running down one's spine, hair standing on end, and generally limp from shock and incredulity."

The English critics found much to praise in Prince's direction, Aronson's decor, and Rosenthal's lighting, but almost all found the libretto weak and compromising. Herbert Kretzmer (*Daily Express*) called the show an "astonishingly inventive production" in which "one can almost smell a country going slowly to rot in the lurid and garish pictures [the director and designers] create." Eric Shorter (*Daily Telegraph*) called it "brash," "colourful," "staged with brilliance and performed with uncommon verve and feeling" but thought it needed "a more precise musical evocation." Peter Lewis (*Daily Mail*) held that the cabaret set and dances were "ingenious," though he faulted the music for entirely failing to get "the injured howl into it that Kurt Weill did in, for instance, 'Mac The Knife.'" The most considered judgments came from Marcus and Bryden, both of whom felt uneasy finding fault with a show that had several strokes of genius. Bryden pointed out that "What *Cabaret* does best is create the atmosphere of a civilization dancing on the brink of catastrophe.... But in its eagerness to evoke the approaching fall of the Weimar Republic, the musical neglects the moment-to-moment vitality of its main characters." He added: "The show's Sally, Fraulein Schneider and other butterflies are scarcely given a chance to flap their wings before the wheel of Juggernaut crushes them. In the shadow of their oncoming doom, they're too pallid to command attention." Calling *Cabaret* "so nearly the best American musical since *Guys and Dolls*," Bryden complained that it was "maddening to have to qualify one's praise by a warning that to enjoy it you had best put out of your mind any memories of Christopher Isherwood's Berlin stories, on which it is based." If Bryden felt maddened, Marcus became pathological: "The good things in *Cabaret* are great. The bad ones bring one near to despair. To say that I was in two minds about some of it is the understatement of the year: I left the theatre a manic-depressive." Nevertheless, the show ran for nine months.

The original cast albums of the Broadway and London productions also left patrons split in their reactions. The New York recording, under Goddard Lieberson's direction, was not wholly satisfying. Certainly, Joel Grey's performance was persuasively perverse; Lotte Lenya's, lusty and plangent; Jill Haworth's, far more accomplished than one was first led to believe. But the brilliance of the music was complemented onstage by

Ron Field's choreography that, of course, could not be experienced on disc. Lieberson, however, devised a clever strategy to minimize the loss, urging the orchestra to double the tempo of Field's numbers in order to provide some hint of the excitement of live theatrical performance.

The London album featured Barry Dennen's obscenely ingratiating Emcee, who sounded richer than Grey's epicene version. London had no one to match Lotte Lenya or Jack Gilford, but Judi Dench managed to make her acting technique prevail over a mediocre singing voice. Her Sally was intermittently more vulnerable than Jill Haworth's had been.

THE 1972 FOSSE FILM

Music connoisseurs had to await the film soundtrack, in which Grey redefined the Emcee with sharp, spiky, salacious detail while Liza Minnelli re-created Sally Bowles almost entirely in her own idiosyncratic mode. As Kurt Gänzl (1990: 411) wrote: "Forget Isherwood, forget the silly, self-deceiving lass from Chelsea, London: Liza Minnelli's American Sally Bowles performs her on-stage numbers with a sophisticated vigour that would have got her out of the Kit-Kat Club into a job at the Folies-Bergère in a flash." Wiping away all vocal competition with her knock-down belting, she dominated the recording, prompting Gänzl to remark: "I don't suppose Sally Bowles has been played as she was written since, and I don't suppose she ever will be. This is what you call taking a role and making it your own."

While Minnelli's reinterpretation was radical, acute, and glittering, it was a deliberate star turn that perversely altered Isherwood's texture and Sally's importance. It grew out of a rethinking of the Berlin stories, and it was something that was guided and enlarged by the filmmakers, who did not want their movie to follow the Broadway show's focus, look, or structure. Moreover, the film was directed by Bob Fosse, not Harold Prince, and was accordingly informed by a different sensibility. Prince could not get the director's job for the Allied Artists/ABC Pictures film because he was about to go into rehearsal with a new Stephen Sondheim show. Besides, while he was a rocketing success on Broadway, Prince had not amassed any reputation as a film director after his debut with *Something for Everyone* (also known as *The Cook*) in 1970, a black comedy shot on location in Bavaria about an amoral, bisexual young man (Michael York) who manipulates the family and staff of an impoverished Countess

(Angela Lansbury) to his advantage. Prince's busy schedule proved to be Fosse's glorious opportunity, though Fosse had to wait nervously while the chief executives of Allied/ABC (who had optioned the work in 1969 for $1.5 million) first considered Billy Wilder, Joseph Mankiewicz, and Gene Kelly for the job. "I've got to do it," Fosse insisted to Cy Feuer, the film's producer and an old friend who had backed him for *How to Succeed in Business without Really Trying* and *Little Me*. "It's my last shot. I can't get arrested in Hollywood."

Fosse was referring, of course, to the fact that his film of *Sweet Charity* (1969), starring Shirley MacLaine, Chita Rivera, and Sammy Davis Jr., had been a resounding failure where, as Martin Gottfried (1990: 197) complained, "the dark story and street musical numbers faded into the background, upstaged by the fledgling director's movie pyrotechnics." Fosse hadn't yet understood the difference between stage and screen and by making the film too realistic had lost the intriguing style of the Broadway version. As Feuer (2003: 242) explains: "You can get away with suggestions and fake sets onstage; you can't do that in a movie. In the theatre an audience can see a stagehand in the wings and it doesn't bother them. On the screen if they see a shadow of a camera, they lose interest in the entire film. It's a completely different set of rules."

Fosse had gone $3 million over *Sweet Charity*'s $7 million budget, something Feuer knew. The entire budget for *Cabaret* was supposed to be $3 million, and the film was being made at Bavaria Studio in Munich, not simply for atmosphere but also for economy. However, Feuer had a hunch that Fosse had learned his lesson. The two of them met for lunch (Feuer had pasta; Fosse, a pack of cigarettes!), and Feuer explained that because Manny Wolf, the head of Allied Artists, and Marty Baum at ABC wanted a big-name director, Feuer would have to see the other directors. "If I don't see them, I'll seem unreasonable. But after I see them, I'll tell Marty that I've talked to everyone and I want Fosse" (243). Feuer first went to Billy Wilder, an old friend, who declined because he had already seen too much of Germany. He had, in fact, fled the Nazis. He was simply not the least bit interested in the subject. Next, Feuer saw Gene Kelly, another old friend, but felt, after their discussion, that Kelly would not have made the kind of film Feuer wanted. "He could have made the movie, but it wouldn't have been the same picture. It would have been more...frivolous. It wouldn't have Fosse's dark side" (243). The simple truth is that Feuer was set on Fosse before he met with Wilder and Kelly.

Feuer made a convincing case to Baum by explaining that the eight musical numbers for the Kit Kat Klub and its small fifteen-by-twenty-foot playing area all had to work or the film would flop. They had to protect the musical numbers, and there was nobody better in that area than Fosse. Baum responded: "You have to do it. It's your call. But you have to watch the budget." As far as the cast was concerned, Feuer knew he could hold the line on salaries, and he assured the executives that he would keep Fosse in check.

Before the actual production, however, and before Fosse was signed on, Feuer had serious doubts about the project. He had seen the stage musical's road company in Seattle, but that visit simply reinforced his initial reaction. "The entire secondary story—that soupy, sentimental, idiotic business with the little old Jewish man courting Sally's landlady by bringing her a pineapple every day—had to be thrown out. I couldn't stand it. Besides, it was dull and uninteresting" (240). However, Feuer loved the parts dealing with the Kit Kat Klub and the diabolical Emcee. Picking up a magnificent limited edition copy of George Grösz's book *Ecce Homo*, its sixteen watercolors and eighty-four drawings depicting, in Grösz's unique style, the "cruel decadence of Berlin between world wars," Feuer realized at once that "this depravity had a deep-seated heritage" and that he could create something important on film. He told Baum (a former Broadway casting agent as well as head of ABC Pictures): "If you throw out the pineapples and put in a decent secondary love story— something that could appeal to young people—I'll do it" (240).

Besides the problem of the landlady and her Jewish grocer, Feuer was troubled by the lack of sexual definition for the English teacher, Sally's admirer. Feuer felt that in earlier versions of the play and musical "the exact sexual inclination" of the man was "either fudged or eliminated." His opinion was that if the character was not a homosexual, he would not have avoided sleeping with Sally or preferred merely observing her many trysts. Feuer wanted the issue of the man's sexuality dealt with "in a forth-right way. Berlin and the Nazis were all tied up in knots with sexual perversion and repression. The business of sex and violence was at the heart of their craziness" (240–41). In his own less than sophisticated way, Feuer was articulating what some intellectuals (such as Camille Paglia and Susan Sontag) would see as one of the fascinations of fascisman: an aggressive and compulsive sexual adventurism that includes sadomas-ochism. As Sontag (1980: 102) outlines in her famous essay "Fascinating Fascism": "Much of the imagery of far-out sex has been placed under the sign of Nazism. Boots, leather, chains, Iron Crosses on gleaming torsos, swastikas, along with meat hooks and heavy motorcycles, have become the secret and most lucrative paraphernalia of eroticism." According to Sontag, fascist leaders in prewar Germany had a predilection for sexual metaphors, and though Feuer's notion of these metaphors was sketchy, it was sensitive to theatrical forms of sex and violence—and to connections between sex and politics.

Turning to stylistic matters, Feuer was bothered also by the appearance of songs outside the Kit Kat Klub. The problem was really a generic one, having its roots in the nature of movie musicals in which "people keep bursting into song in the middle of the street for no apparent reason." This could not happen in *Cabaret*, he told Baum. "There's a reality about the movies that will not accept it. This is a show-business story and the singing takes place on the stage of the Kit Kat Klub. Period" (Feuer 2003: 241). Baum agreed, trusting Feuer's movie instincts and intelligence. Feuer was to be the sole producer, with Ernie Martin remaining in the background because he was not terribly interested in film and was more about securing money for shows. In this instance, the money was coming from ABC Pictures and Allied Artists. Besides, an entirely new script had to be developed, and that area was not Martin's interest.

The first person Feuer put to work was Jay Presson Allen, the screenwriter, whom Martin had suggested for the job. Feuer told her his ideas about necessary changes in the story. He wanted to use Sally Bowles from Isherwood's Berlin stories and the homosexual from van Druten's *I Am a Camera*, and he wanted to keep the sexual tension high. Feuer also thought that the script should have a new secondary love story—between a young Jewish heiress and a gentile. As he explained: "The drama comes from the fact that she doesn't know that he really is not a gentile, but a poor Jewish schnook trying to pass" (242). Allen agreed with Feuer about the English teacher's sexuality. He was to be bisexual ("a switch-hitter"), who accordingly could have an affair with both Sally and the German baron romancing Sally (242). Allen went to work with relish, but she did not at first please Fosse, who was also unhappy that he couldn't get Robert Surtees (his cameraman from *Sweet Charity*) as cinematographer. None of the executives wanted Surtees. For one thing, he would be too expensive (a minimum of $50,000 more than any of the European cameramen). For another, his work on *Sweet Charity* had not impressed Feuer or his business partners. When Fosse kept pestering Feuer about Surtees, Baum suggested that they cut their losses, pay Fosse off, and get another director.

Bob Fosse as shown in Bob Fosse: Steam Heat *(1990)* *(Dance in America,* *PBS TV) (PBS/Photofest)*

Feuer refused because he was convinced that Fosse was the right person to direct. He suggested to Fosse that they have a close look at all the leading cinematographers—from Geoffrey Unsworth in England to Sven Nykvist in Stockholm. "Okay," Fosse agreed, "as long as you keep an open mind about Surtees." "It's open," Feuer retorted, "as long as you know I don't want the guy" (Gottfried 1990: 207).

However, he did have to break his promise about keeping an open mind over Surtees. This betrayal transpired in the Hotel Vier Jahreszeiten, Munich's finest, a reconstructed prewar building with walls thick enough to resist radiation. Feuer had no reason to suspect that his private telephone conversation with Baum (who was in Los Angeles) would be over-heard by Fosse, but Fosse's room was next door, and he could easily eavesdrop. What Fosse heard was enough to detonate his friendship with Feuer. As Fosse related to Bob Aurthur (a film writer and producer), it was a terrifying experience because Feuer had promised him he would fight for the cameraman Fosse wanted, but then Fosse heard him say, "No, no, I won't let Fosse have him." It was a nightmare for Fosse, who sat an hour listening to the conversation and feeling utterly deceived (208). This led to an explosive confrontation in which Fosse accused Feuer of being "a two-faced shit." "Listen, prick," Feuer responded. "You don't know what was going on at the other end of that conversation. The guy wants to fire you, and I can just pick up the phone right now and do it. But I'm not going to do that, because I want to make this picture, you stupid son of a bitch" (209). Feuer knew Fosse was very insecure after the disaster of *Sweet Charity* and that, therefore, he would not dare quit this new project. After a volatile exchange laced with profanity, Feuer finally asked: "Okay, Bob, what do you want to do?" The ball was in Fosse's court, but Fosse had been expecting something like this. "If you want me out," he declared, "you're going to have to fire me." There was a charged silence as the two men stared at each other, until Fosse turned and walked to his room.

Fosse would not quit, and Feuer did not fire him, but Fosse never forgave his former friend. "After that phone call, I couldn't look at Cy or talk to him. I couldn't help it." In fact, Fosse would remain angry at Feuer for the rest of his life. Forced into accepting Geoffrey Unsworth, an excellent craftsman in his own right, Fosse plunged into the film with all the professional spirit he could muster—leaving time, of course, for his sexual dalliances, a proclivity not unknown to his wife Gwen Verdon.

Whereas there was no longer any close friendship between the two men, being with Fosse was intensely stimulating for Feuer as the two traveled to Munich and Hamburg to check out locations. Fosse's sharp eye for detail was impressively ingenious—as was duly noted by Feuer. Fosse seemed to look at everything as through a camera lens. He found a very nice castle in the little town of Eutin, just outside Hamburg, that had an enormous ballroom, "sixty feet across, high ceilings, and great big fireplaces at both ends." He used it for a scene in which the three principals—Sally, Brian, and the baron—stage a drunken seduction (Feuer 2003: 244).

In order to avoid further blowups with Fosse, Feuer had to take precautions in his dealings with other collaborators. For instance, though he was friendly with Wolfgang Glattes, a German first assistant director, Feuer had to insist that the two of them pretend they had a purely business relationship. There was to be no social exchanges at all. Fosse was so difficult to deal with that Feuer had to restrict his dealings with him to film matters: "He'd discuss the setups with me. We'd talk about lighting. We'd watch the dailies together. But beyond that, nothing. He wasn't just hard on me, he was hard on himself, working twelve, fifteen hours a day. Rehearsing endlessly" (249).

Hugh Wheeler was commissioned to improve the screenplay, but he came under enormous pressure from ABC Pictures to bowdlerize the script. *Love Story* (1970) had convinced the executives that all movies should be sentimental and have a noble, suffering heroine. Wheeler resisted their promptings, but he agreed to make Sally Bowles American and transplanted her, like Louise Brooks, to Germany. Herr Issyvoo, Cliff on the Broadway stage, was now turned into Brian Roberts, a rather pallid introvert, though bisexual rather than heterosexual as he had been in the stage musical. As Marjorie Garber points out in *Vice Versa*, it took a long time for the Christopher Isherwood projection to "come out." In van Druten's stage play, he was "disarmingly reticent" about his sexuality, even though the playwright was himself gay and "cognizant of the possibilities." Instead, the play "displaced the question of dangerous sexuality onto Sally Bowles, permitting her (especially when played by the 'boyish' Julie Harris) to traverse the territory from androgyny to promiscuity." Sally used double entendres. Garber cites her allusion to the landlady's bosom ("I say, Fräulein Schneider's got a big one, hasn't she?") as a code of "her extravagant and unaccountable behaviour as a gay male, while the 'real' gay male in the story, played in the film version for added spice for those in the know by bisexual actor Laurence Harvey, became Chris, a 'confirmed bachelor,' wedded to his writing" (Garber 1995: 489). The phrase "confirmed bachelor" has usually been a euphemism for a gay man who lives alone discreetly. In his only overt heterosexual move in the film, after lamenting his inability to work, Harvey's Chris, fueled one evening by too much wine, makes a pass at Sally, suggesting that, "despite his writer's block, he is not entirely impotent." Punning on the word "pass," Garber interprets this act of making a pass as his attempt to pass as a heterosexual before actually passing up his opportunity (490).

Fosse's *Cabaret* constitutes the third transformation of the male lead, though Isherwood himself decried the bisexual identity of the protagonist as "fundamentally anti-gay in attitude" (Stoop 1975: 62). By the early seventies, the gay liberation movement had begun to affect the social and cultural image of homosexuals, and Isherwood found Michael York's Brian Roberts to be offensively "off-again, on-again." But Fosse was not concerned with gay liberation. He used Brian's bisexuality to make the erotic triangle (Brian, Sally, Max) "the primary unit of desire" (Garber 1995: 491). The narrative shows a ménage à trois as Max, Sally, and Brian dance together. After a drunken Brian passes out, Sally and Max go off together. Sally never misses a sexual opportunity but is not seen in bed with anyone but Brian. Instead, the camera seems to favor the progress of Max and Brian's affair. In the Bavarian beer garden scene, for instance, they are shown exchanging glances of sexual interest. In the backseat of Max's car, they are shown to be preoccupied with each other. Max's divinely sexy masculinity is used as a goad by Sally to taunt Brian: "Screw Maximilian." Brian retorts, "I do." Sally tries to trump him: "So do I." Then Brian, after a little pause, says, "You two bastards." Sally hisses, "Two? Two?" Brian comes back, "Shouldn't it be three?" The exchange is followed by a transition to the grinning, cross-dressing Emcee in a chorus line at the Kit Kat Klub. In revealing the drive to be both sexes, the film confirms the decadent thirties as well as the ambivalent seventies. In other words, again quoting Garber, "Brian's bisexuality marks both the difference and the similarity between the time period the film is *describing* and the time period in which it was *made*" (495).

A decision had already been made by Fosse to excise the Broadway show's subplot romance between Herr Schultz and Fräulein Schneider. Fosse wanted to substitute Isherwood's material about Natalia Landauer, a wealthy Jewish girl, and her suitor, who had been passing for gentile. Feuer was in favor of omitting all musical numbers that would not pass for songs sung in real life. Adjustments to the plot necessitated adjustments to the music, or at least to the treatment of music. As Fosse asserted in a *New York* magazine interview, he got "very antsy watching musicals in which people are singing as they walk down the street or hang out the laundry." He thought it looked "silly": "You can do it on stage. The theatre has its own personality—it conveys a removed reality. The movies bring that reality closer" (Gardner 1974: 59). Having learned a costly lesson from the failure of *Sweet Charity*, Fosse realized that *Cabaret* was going to need a musical logic that would relate every number to the dramatic action and not simply indulge a composer's urge to have entertainments. This meant, of course, that the stage production's "Telephone Song" and the Schultz–Schneider duets would have to be dropped. As Martin Gottfried explains in *All His Jazz*, a biography of Fosse, the screenplay would immediately cut from a laundry where Sally flirts with the German baron, Max, who owns an expensive automobile, to the cabaret where she and the Emcee perform the satiric "The Money Song." In this same fashion, a scene would be followed by a musical number related to it or a scene would follow a number. The only song outside the cabaret was

"Tomorrow Belongs to Me," a Nazi anthem spontaneously sung by the public in a beer garden, and it was the only musical number Fosse regretted (Gottfried 1990: 206).

The film uses only five numbers from the original stage show plus parts of a couple of others. Kander and Ebb composed new numbers: "Mein Herr" (which replaced "Don't Tell Mama"), "Maybe This Time" (Sally's one brief moment of honesty), and "Money, Money" (that took the place of "The Money Song"). "Mein Herr," in the words of Archer Winsten (1973: 13), was "a perceptively developed replica of a bouncy, tacky, mindless bit of cabaret come-on," while "Maybe This Time" was a torch song for which Fred Ebb devised lyrics that were "more sophisticated than those that were common in the twenties." This way the musical burden was placed more squarely on Minnelli and Grey—a good thing in terms of musical quality, though not necessarily in terms of fidelity to Isherwood's Sally Bowles or of getting to know the chief characters through their songs, as Ethan Mordden complains in *The Hollywood Musical* (1981: 221). Sally never sounds like a vulnerable, self-deceiving girl from Chelsea; she is far too musically sophisticated. However, Grey's vocal performance is in the right salacious style for the Emcee, enhanced greatly by Ralph Burns's arrangements, which have "an agitated brightness that always seems just on the verge of turning sour" (Winsten 1973: 13).

Fosse and his assistant, Wolfgang Glattes, poured over drawings by George Grösz and Otto Dix and then scouted bars, clubs, and neighborhoods in the towns of Charlottenburg, Lubeck, Eutin, and Dohlem, visited the narrow alleyways near Savigny Platz, and ventured into the Tiergarten. Glattes served as interpreter as Fosse scouted these locations and studied faces of the population. The faces were to play an important part in the film, being used as a mirror of German attitudes to the unfolding decadence and horror. In the finished film version (as Gottfried points out), the recurring image in the eerie, grotesque cabaret is one of "immobile German faces, the faces of burghers vacantly observing contortionists, transvestites, even whippings, as if they were entertainment." While the stage show of the cabaret was not evil in itself, the audience's unresponsive, insensitive, soulless, impassive faces suggested evil. The only gleeful responses that Fosse allowed the audience were in response to female mud wrestlers (Gottfried 1990: 215).

Liza Minnelli (who had been rejected by Prince for the Broadway show) was cast as Sally on the basis of her kooky persona in several movies and for her strong singing talent. She had already been offered several Walt Disney musicals but had turned them down, hoping (as she confessed in her father's autobiography, *I Remember It Well*) that she would one day land a movie musical that would allow the public to make a final comparison between her and her legendary mother, Judy Garland, and so conclude: "There she is in a musical movie. And that's what her mom did. *And* she's holding her own." When she first announced to her father that she was going to play Sally Bowles, he asked: "What are you going to look like?" She went blank and said, "I don't know. What should I look like?" Vincente Minnelli was himself at a nonplus: "I don't know." The conversation ended abruptly, but three days later when she walked into his room, she found books and pictures on his bed that were meant to help her. Marlene Dietrich's high cheekbones and sophisticated look came to mind, as did Louise Brooks's Lulu makeup and helmet-like coiffure. But Liza's father cautioned: "It has to be a version of you, if you were in the Thirties" (Minnelli 1974: 16).

Fosse drove her hard by badgering her once to work late. She just turned around and walked off the set. Feuer (2003: 249) comments:

Liza Minnelli in the 1972 film version of Cabaret *directed by Bob Fosse. (Allied Artists/ Photofest)*

"No one could ever accuse Liza of being lazy, and she had gone as far as she was willing to go on that particular day. She knew that if she stayed, they'd end up saying things that couldn't be fixed." As it turned out, Liza found a great assistant in Gwen Verdon, Fosse's wife, who helped find most of the costumes for the role after Fosse's dissatisfaction with the film costume designer. Fosse wanted a special sleaziness and hated the heavy brocade on many of the designer's dresses. He could not find the costumes he wanted anywhere in Munich. The population was still in a state of denial about the Third Reich, and all vestiges of that era had been destroyed or removed. As Minnelli told Rex Reed in a 1971 *Daily News* interview: "I asked for some real '30s clothes, slinky, no bra. I said 'It should look like before the war' and the Germans all said, 'What war?' I mean, they don't want to know! So they came up with costumes that made me look like Joe Namath—wide Joan Crawford sleeves, padded shoulders and pleats."

Consequently, Fosse enlisted Verdon to hunt all the antique shops and flea markets in Paris, where she found a purple embroidered chemise with a black, fringed sash belt, and a beaded centerpiece for Sally's title song. After she and Minnelli settled on these and a few other costumes and props, including a gorilla mask found in New York for the "If You Could See Her" number, they discovered that Bavaria Studio had all the old costumes from prewar German film locked away for fear that *Cabaret* would re-create the Nazi era too unpleasantly. Fosse himself completed Liza Minnelli's look and transformed her into a spectacular dancer. "Right before our eyes," said Kathryn Doby (one of his favorite dancers and film assistants), "she was becoming a star" (Gottfried 1990: 213).

But the process was not easy. Fosse strove to make realism the key to the film. "As with the songs," notes Gottfried, "there were no dances where there would not have been dances in real life." Consequently, there was little choreography other than an occasional and brief entrance of chorus girls to start a floorshow, and the cabaret stage was only ten by fourteen feet, a size it would actually have been in a Berlin nightclub. Fosse never allowed it to "grow" through movie magic and accommodate more than six girls. He remarked: "I tried to make the dances look not as if they were done by me, Bob Fosse, but by some guy who is down and out." In other words, the vulgar choreography was meant to look like the creation of someone who worked in cheap cabarets and clubs. And to execute these dances perfectly, he drilled his dancers ruthlessly. Minnelli had to sing "Mein Herr," composed especially for the movie, in a very awkward and physically taxing position, "perched on a chair with one leg in a squat and the other extended flat out" (Gottfried 1990: 216). The choreography was obviously influenced by Marlene Dietrich's famous "Falling in Love Again" from *The Blue Angel*, but where Dietrich merely toys with her chair, Minnelli uses hers like a toy or sex object, and her energy is frenzied rather than slyly sexual—as was Dietrich's in the much earlier film.

Fosse hired only two American dancers for the film (Doby and Louise Quick) because he wanted an authentic look of buxom, well-fed German women as they might have appeared in the early thirties. He hired thickset Germans and asked them to eat a hearty breakfast every morning. "It was the only time I remember he tried to make his dancers *gain* weight," Quick remarked (Grubb 1989: 149). In a further drive for the vulgar look he wanted, he forbade them to shave under their arms, causing considerable protest. It was only after the musical numbers had finished filming that he rewarded them with razors and soap at a party.

He kept books on Grösz's art in the makeup room so that the dancers could derive ideas for bizarre effects. Quick found the books helpful but thought Verdon was even more inspirational when she showed her how to melt crayons in a spoon over a candle, dip a little mascara brush in it and apply the melted wax to their eyelashes. "They got awfully thick that way," Quick noted in *Razzle Dazzle*, "but the thicker they were, the more Bob liked them. So, on top of the two or three pairs of eyelashes I was already wearing, Gwen and I melted green crayon and dripped the beads on the tips of the lashes. The effect was rather startling" (Grubb 1989: 150).

As Mitchell Morris (2004: 148) explains, Fosse took charge of the choreography, "slanting his distinctive synthesis of jazz and vaudeville dance styles toward the camera's love of detail." Individual dance numbers evoked "freneticism," "expressionism," and other qualities "that would mark the cinematic representation of Weimar bodily stage decorum, and yet small features of finger motion or eyebrow position were made to carry the momentous poetic weight that would be invisible on a Broadway stage." Ironically, this was a kind of realism, though "focussed on representational efficacy rather than one or another kind of verisimilitude."

The composite design of pudgy, gartered thighs, unshaved armpits, bored or obscene smiles, garishly painted faces, and oddly cut costumes captured a macabre spirit of sensual decadence. Sexuality was turned grotesque on the cabaret stage. It had leer, strut, mockery, and disgusting self-consciousness. Its foil was in the figure of Brian Roberts, Isherwood's alter ego, played by English actor Michael York, whom Minnelli at first thought was wrong for the role. But York was a fine actor, trained in the classics, who had done everything from small walk-on parts and pallid secondary characters to Hamlet, Romeo, and Prometheus. He also had valuable film experience, having appeared in movies directed by Joseph Losey, George Cukor, and Franco Zeffirelli. York had heard through the grapevine that the film was to be made, so he urged his agent in New York to get him the role. "I've now read the screenplay," the agent reported, "and couldn't be more disappointed." The role was "straight, dull, square, and boring as a character." It had no songs, and was really just support for Minnelli, so the agent was proceeding cautiously (York 1991: 220). However, he did secure an audition for York, at which Fosse and Feuer read all the other roles, including a gruff Sally! Bob Fosse had tested many for the part of Brian Roberts, but found none who quite so matched his conception as York did. Fosse didn't want an effete or book-worm personality for the role, and he liked York's prize-fighter look. "It's too easy to fall into that limp-wristed fag stereotype," he told *After Dark*, adding that he liked to "startle the audience" and make them "rethink their perceptions of what a gay man looks like." He wanted to disabuse people of the notion that sexual experimentation was exclusive to the sixties, for in *Cabaret*, another sexual revolution was ending with Hitler. "Men and women were trying *everything*. So you could have someone who looked like Michael York sleeping with a man. It was perfectly logical" (Stoop 1975: 62).

However, as he reveals in his autobiography, *Accidentally on Purpose*, York was unimpressed by the script, finding no role to play in the "pallid screen *doppelgänger*, even though contemporary permissiveness now allowed his bisexuality to be overt." He felt the part was "another introspective literate Englishman in the Darley mode, another dull foil to all the brilliant extrovert characters enlivening the story" (York 1991: 231). To his delight, he discovered that Fosse agreed with him and promised to make changes in the screenplay. Fosse reassured him that he intended to review and rehearse the dialogue during the two weeks scheduled for the song and dance rehearsals and that Hugh Wheeler would be present to supervise revisions. Wheeler, who had been engaged to revise the script, complained about "ghastly pressures from ABC to bowdlerise" the screenplay. "*Love Story* has made

Joel Grey (far left) in a scene from the 1972 film version of Cabaret *directed by Bob Fosse. (Allied Artists Pictures/Photofest) (photographer: Lars Looschen)*

them all convinced that all movies must now be *Rebecca of Sunnybrook Farm*" (229).

York and Minnelli improvised dialogue, embellishing the script and creating real characters, though their contribution did not impress Isherwood, who objected to the fact that Brian's homosexuality was treated "as an indecent but comic weakness to be snickered at, like bed-wetting" (Grubb 1989: 154). York's part was recognizably English, but the actor had to leave unchallenged "such distinct Americanisms as 'horse's ass' for idiot, as this could be justified as coming from Sally's growing influence" (York 1991: 232). Minnelli renounced her earlier misgivings about her co-star, crying out to Fosse, "Oh, Bobby! Was I wrong! He's sensational, that mysterious personality, and that terrific face, that broken nose" (Gottfried 1990: 217).

York shared his director's dissatisfaction with the costuming and asked permission to scavenge for more appropriate apparel in the junk shops of London, where he was briefly returning while the musical numbers for the Kit Kat cabaret were being recorded in Munich. King's Road provided

Michael York and Liza Minnelli in the film 1972 film version of Cabaret *directed by Bob Fosse (Allied Artists/Photofest)*

a "rich trove—authentic old jackets and an ancient period raincoat" (York 1991: 232). He also unearthed an old, worn camel hair dressing gown that had belonged to his father when he was a student in the 1930s, the same era as in the film.

Grey was repeating his role as Emcee, though Fosse insisted that the character had to be more literal than symbolic because now he was in close-up. At the first rehearsal for "Two Ladies" Fosse took him aside and asked him to do an acrobatic trick. "What trick?" Grey asked, incredulous at the demand. When he tried to demonstrate a black flip the way he had done in his prime in such films as *Kiss Me, Kate* and *Give a Girl a Break*, Fosse forgot he wasn't young anymore and landed painfully on his face. What made it even more horrifying, Grey remembered, was the bizarre sight of a swollen-face Fosse on the set for days after, a cigarette hanging out of the corner of his puffy mouth.

Fosse believed he was making "the first adult musical" and was half in love with Grey's character as the Emcee. He nicknamed him "Mister Porno." But his fascination did not mean that he would abandon his dictatorial work habits. His first time before the camera in white chalk face makeup, Grey was stopped by Fosse, who told him he wasn't to play it as he had on stage. When Grey contended that that was the way he had conceived the part, Fosse retorted: "Joel, you're before the camera. Theater and film are two entirely different animals. In films, use restraint." It took the actor about a week to adjust, but he dug deeper into the role than he had on Broadway, discussing with Fosse where the Emcee slept and lived, what his food, politics, and sexual preferences were, and what the Kit Kat girls had had to do for him to get their jobs. Fosse and Grey even developed a subtextual relationship between the Emcee and Sally, expressed (the actor claims) "in shorthand, an exchange of glances between Liza and me, or just pursed lips. It was enough. It didn't matter whether he had actually slept with her" (Gottfried 1990: 212).

The sleaze, that had been part of the actor's vaudeville and nightclub experience and which Prince had encouraged for the Broadway show, was extended. As Gottfried remarks in *All His Jazz*, sleaze was "part of Fosse's strip-joint childhood," and the director "was starting to perceive in lowlife show business a metaphor for all existence as being tainted and vulgar. He seemed to be concluding that life was innocence corrupted, the strip joint extruded to its slimy essence, that in life as on

Liza Minnelli and Joel Grey in the 1972 film version of Cabaret *directed by Bob Fosse. (Allied Artists/ Photofest)*

stage, flash succeeded rather than quality" (212). "The Money Song" would be performed as if it were "a vaudeville turn done in a moral abyss, a jolly evil."

Fosse wanted the all-girl band in the club to sound as seedily bad as those he remembered from working in cheap clubs before achieving success on stage and film. So orchestrator Ralph Burns hired musicians from the lowest German union (ten played behind the cameras for the eight on screen), but they didn't have the bad sound that Fosse wanted, so Burns moved all the way up to Class "A" musicians, requesting that they play like bad musicians. "That was *too* terrible," he told Gottfried. "Finally we said, 'Play it good,' and then it sounded bad the right way" (213).

Fosse was "a coiled dynamo of charged energy," according to Michael York. He was lean and squinted as he concentrated, but "the haze of smoke from the permanent cigarette, dropped down to the butt that tinged his mustache with a yellow aureole," so that he looked like "the antithesis of the *danseur noble.*" Yet his angular, sexy choreography matched the mood of the cabaret, and only once did he offer direction that York rejected. That came at the climactic moment when Sally and Brian were making love for the first time. The script required each of them to look down at his tumescent member while York was to burst into a Shakespearean quotation. York would neither look down at his member nor utter any such quotation, and Fosse had to accept this refusal (York 1991: 234–36).

Grey remarked that Fosse worked "as if his career was on the line. He was intent on proving himself a director of drama as opposed to musicals." This drive was fueled by a sense of perfectionism that manifested itself in such details as the Berlin accent for Grey, the smoky congestion of the club, the female mud wrestlers, the special look for Minnelli, and the strategic use of color filters. "As soon as we started seeing [the] dailies, we all knew that we were involved in something special," said Grey. "And we were lucky to have Geoff Unsworth as the cameraman because he had exactly the same vision as Bob." Fosse, for his part, backed away from the filtered look of *Sweet Charity*, ensuring that the look of *Cabaret* was not overdone, but he still could not forget Feuer's betrayal, conceding that Unsworth "turned out great," while adding, "He was still my third choice" (Gottfried 1990: 215).

Minnelli made periodic long-distance calls to her father in California. "I don't know if I'm doing it right," she would moan. "In the rushes," he asked, "do you see yourself or do you see somebody else?" "I think I see somebody else." "Then you're on the right track" (Minnelli 1974: 372).

The atmosphere on the set was electric as everyone in the company felt that the movie was turning into something very special and that Minnelli was becoming a major film star. Fosse's attention to everything from makeup to the transitions between the musical numbers and the dramatic story outside the Kit Kat Klub was creating flawless tone and texture. Grey was rehearsed until his Berlin accent was perfect. The outdoor scene for the German youths' rendition of "Tomorrow Belongs to Me" necessitated the construction of a beer garden. Moreover, the extras playing Germans of varying ages who were to join in the swelling Nazi anthem had to learn how to move their lips in synchronization to the English lyrics, though none of them knew English. Another problem was getting all the youth in the scene to get haircuts so that they would look authentically in period and not like longhaired kids of 1971. The studio had to offer "hair payments" as a bribe. The twelve-year-old kid who started to lip-synch the song needed to look like an innocent Boy Scout, but he had hair trailing down his back which necessitated a surprise rape of his locks with the consoling bribe of a joyride in a jeep for the day to survive a crisis. Next, the filmmakers had to find a voice to dub him. Feuer tried the Vienna Boys Choir but couldn't match the right voice to the boy. The right match turned out to be someone in a Hollywood rock band (Feuer 2003: 250–51).

The filming began to wind down in the spring, but as yet without the anti-Semitic duet that Grey was supposed to sing to a female gorilla ("If You Could See Her through My Eyes / She Wouldn't Look Jewish at All"). This was essentially a vaudeville number in soft-shoe rhythm where the gorilla, dressed in a pink-veiled hat and a flower-covered ballet tutu, would be partnered by Grey wearing a straw boater. Fosse was dissatisfied with the look of the gorilla and with how dance assistant John Sharpe performed the part. He wanted the gorilla to seem feminine in her movements, so he asked Louise Quick to don the gorilla costume, but there was still no satisfactory head for it. Fosse had already rejected all the gorilla heads brought in from costume shops, secondhand dealers, and toy stores. In desperation he phoned Verdon in New York and asked for her help. She turned up on the set within a week with an enormous and unusual gorilla head in her arms. Although it had a ring through its nose, the head looked very much like a persona of Verdon! (Gottfried 1990: 218).

After the film wrapped, it was edited and given a private screening in New York before a specially invited audience. Fosse sat in the last row of the darkened room, nervously studying the audience for hints of boredom or disapproval. When there was no applause at the end, he was paralyzed with fear that he had produced another "bomb." But then Vincente Minnelli, famed for his own musicals, such as *Meet Me in St. Louis* and the Oscar-winning *An American in Paris*, arose. Overcoat in hand, he walked slowly to the exit. When he reached the last row, he saw Fosse, stopped, took his hand, and said: "I have just seen the perfect movie." In his autobiography, Minnelli praised the film's style, calling it more vivid than the stage musical's, and the "evocative cinematography," which captured "the hard and cynical mood of the era." Minnelli also noted: "*Cabaret*'s sophistication was singular. This wasn't the empty-headed joy which characterizes the musical genre. *Cabaret* was about something" (Minnelli 1974: 372–3).

One thing the movie was about was revolt. As Pauline Kael noted in her review, the revolt was against old-style musicals of the sort where "performers once again climb hills singing" or where "a chorus breaks into song on a hayride." But *Cabaret* revolted against not only "the wholesome approach of big musicals" but also "the pseudo-naturalistic tradition— the tradition of *Oklahoma!–South Pacific–West Side Story*…which requires that the songs appear to grow organically out of the story." As Kael pointed out, the "organic" big show had become the "white elephant of Broadway," and on-screen this animal clumped in the worst sense to go into numbers "naturally." "It was as if there were something the matter with song and dance," Kael complained, "as if they had to be excused by being worked into 'a life situation'—or one of those damn dream ballets" (Kael 1973: 515).

As many who saw it were to realize, *Cabaret* turned the conventions of recent big-musical movies inside out. Its subject was often raw or sleazy, its tone detached and objective, its style garish or obscene, its energy animalistic and violent or determinedly camp. Virtually every character in the story was corruptible, and the film reveled in decadence—but always without losing its control.

Fosse made realism the rule of his film. No song or dance was ever an affront to realism. So, while the film has palpable musical staging, "there is little choreography other than an occasional (and abortive) entrance of chorus girls to start a floor show" (Gottfried 1990: 215). Fosse and his film editor, David Bretherton, never let an audience forget the sinister

Cabaret (1972) film poster. (Allied Artists/Photofest)

history-in-the-making both inside and outside the club, achieving by their deft crosscutting and montages a succinct expression of prodigal decadence. From the opening image of distorted, unrecognizable figures reflected in a giant, polished mirror to Joel Grey's demonic doll of an Emcee, the movie adhered to a careful design of Nazi encroachment, corruption, and control. The chorus girls, with their slow bottom shimmying and obliquely angular choreography, moved slyly from high kicks to a goose-step as the camera peeked from under their crotches and legs opened like scissors at the performers and the grinning audience as well. The editing often established parallel narratives, crosscutting, for instance, between the cabaret's zany slap-dance (with the Emcee and his girls in shorts and suspenders) and the brutal Nazi battery of the club owner on the dark street outside. The sportive stage violence interlocked with the real street violence, as if both were part of the same design. Similarly, the crosscutting between Sally's torch song rendition of "Maybe This Time" in a virtually empty nightclub and her boudoir scene with Brian set up an ironic juxtaposition of false hope and doomed romance. Sometimes the point was satirical and pointed, pithy and pictorial, as the camera moved, for instance, from Sally's awe at Max's chauffer-driven car to her bawdy, gaudy duet with Grey in "The Money Song," an anthem to vulgar capitalism. Sometimes the point was too simple and sentimental, as in the cut from Fritz's dramatic announcement "I am a Jew" at the Landauer mansion door to the Orthodox Jewish marriage ceremony for him and Natalia in a stained-glass synagogue, but sometimes, too, the parallel narrative made telling political and moral points, as when the movie cut from Grey's cavorting in drag with goose-stepping chorus girls in helmets to Nazi vandals baiting Jews.

The (often grotesque) choreography, garish transvestites, and female mud wrestlers in the club; Brian's translation of Herr Ludwig's pornography; the silent recording of Nazi street crimes; and the rousing alfresco rendition of "Tomorrow Belongs to Me" provided abundant evidence of a country on the skids. And the several suggestions of androgyny—the transvestite in the men's urinal, the Emcee's paganism, and Brian's bisexuality—made for sexual permutations, sometimes in an almost unnatural stillness. The spectator's eye was invited to linger but in an unmistakably coercive manner. Beauty for its own sake was relatively rare in this decadence. Apart from Natalia's innate beauty and stylish glamour and the young blond Nazi tenor in the garden scene, the Apollonian ideal was absent or demonized.

Minnelli's Sally was more a parody of the femme fatale (being, as York's Brian acidly noted, "about as *fatale* as an after-dinner mint"), as she embellished her appearance with extravagantly patterned chemises, a glinting black helmet of hair, dark eyelashes, full red lips, green finger-nails (her "divine decadence"), and a frequent manic energy. Although she certainly caught the character's bubbly capriciousness and play-acting, untidiness, perverse selfishness, and amorality, she lacked inti-macy in her scenes with York, and her powerhouse singing—particularly in her opening and closing numbers—canceled Isherwood's point of Sally being a dreamer lost in a false dream of artistic success. This Sally could have belted her way vocally to top billing in any premier nightclub in the world. Minnelli's raw singing power, rattling pace, and brash American manner left little room for delicate shadings, though she stamped Sally with indisputable *folie de grandeur* in going after fame and stardom with exuberant tackiness.

Minnelli effectively turned the story into a diva musical—as defined by John M. Clum in his book *Something for The Boys*—a category that includes, for example, *Gypsy, Hello, Dolly, Mame, Sunset Boulevard, Applause, Coco, La Cage Aux Folles,* and, in its gender-reversal way, *Hedwig and the Angry Inch.* As Clum (1999: 168) puts it, "the diva musical is about a woman's escape from the humdrum. Whether it's Dorothy being whirled from Kansas to Oz, from black-and-white to color, a metamorphosis sym-bolized by glittering red shoes, or Rose (*Gypsy*) getting out of a dismal trap in Seattle through show business, or Eva Peron sleeping her way from the hinterlands to the Big Apple, the diva fights for liberation from stasis in a grim, everyday world." Minnelli's Sally has a dream as big as Madam Rose's but one that the actual actress's own talent could accom-modate. Looked at from outside the context of the film itself, Minnelli's performance is in a crucial sense an attempt to escape her own mother's diva legend by forging her own fierce, showy, brash, vulgar self-apotheo-sis. In effect, the "Cabaret" number becomes her version of "Rose's Turn" but in the opposite way. It doesn't show her to be a victim of fatal self-delusion but, rather, a showbiz headliner with an ego much larger than decorous good taste would allow.

Minnelli's performance drew divided reactions. Its detractors were led by John Simon, who threw darts at the film in general before thrash-ing the actress. Allowing for the fact that the film was "handsomely pho-tographed" and "much the best reincarnation" of Isherwood's stories, Simon faulted the movie for pretending to say more than it actually did.

He found Grey to be "wonderfully sinister" but the other actors merely adequate or deficient. The subsidiary love story fell flat, he complained, owing to "the dull performances or personalities of Marisa Berenson and Fritz Wepper," but "even the main threesome" suffered. His biggest target was Minnelli, whom he branded "the film's irredeemable disaster." He savaged her for heavy-handed acting, disjointed speech, and "unfeminine and unattractive" appearance and movement. She could not even sing Kander and Ebb's "admittedly inferior songs," and she was sung off the screen by Greta Keller's intermittent background rendition of "Heiraten" (Simon 1982: 69).

Clum and Kael took a radically different position. In his book *Something for the Boys*, Clum calls Minnelli's Sally her defining role and notes how terrific her musical numbers are. He points out that "Minnelli's Sally is doomed by her looks, not her talent, never to be the star she dreams of being. Minnelli also captures Sally's neediness and confusion. Sally is always over-the-top, always 'on'" (Clum 1999: 155). Kael was more extravagant in her praise, calling the film "a big musical that doesn't feel like one, and the first really innovative movie musical in many years," and she waxed lyrical about Minnelli. "Sally is no longer just an innocently and adorably mad gamine, older sister to Holly Golightly," Kael asserted. "This Sally has grown claws." The singular achievement of the interpretation was that Minnelli made you believe "in the cabaret as 'life'" because she came "fully to life" only when she sang. And the way she sang—leading with "her truculent shoulders, her small flapper-head like a predatory bird's"—suggested the prurience displayed in Toulouse Lautrec's Moulin Rouge posters and so was quite in keeping with the general "grinning vividness" of a rotting period (Kael 1973: 517).

Minnelli's film performance brings this book full circle in a sense, for it achieves a centrality for Sally Bowles that Harold Prince never wanted. Despite its flagrant distortions of Isherwood's conception, Minnelli's radical reinterpretation of Sally Bowles is part of cinema history and legend. It does jar any viewer who cannot forget the Sally of the Berlin stories, but it cannot be erased as screen iconography. More vivid and effective than Audrey Hepburn's Eliza Doolittle, Rosalind Russell's Madam Rose, Natalie Wood's Maria, Betty Hutton's Annie Oakley, or Mitzi Gaynor's Nellie Forbush, it reincarnates Sally Bowles and reveals her anew. This Academy award–winning performance (the film won a total of eight Oscars) epitomizes quixotic capriciousness and certainly gives a distinctive pitch, timbre, and style to the songs. This Sally, it is true, shares similarities with Minnelli's other madcap screen heroines, and sometimes she is too much a junior Auntie Mame on the lam in Berlin, but her deft comic timing, tumble of dialogue, gangling body and features, and wry persona are undeniably impressive. The revision of Sally into a brash, provocative American at, once base and fascinating, does allow the actress to color the role vulgarly. With show business in her very genes, as it were, Minnelli appears to have an instinctive understanding of a girl who wants to be shockingly original. The show business side is overstated but real, vulgar but forceful. The actress's intensity and the character's desperation are fused such that this Sally Bowles is charged to be decadent with a vengeance, reveling in her modes of power. Her theme is always self-assertion, pure presence, and she relishes her opportunities to shock Natalia with sexual conversation and to taunt Brian about his homosexuality. Even her cabaret performances are variations on the theme: she is spectacularly on display even as she seduces her audiences. Her choreographic style is erotically spasmodic and contorted while her vocal style is authoritatively robust. Her mobility is an excessive sequence of immediate impressions in which passion and ambition are interlocked.

But the undeniable fact is that Minnelli's Sally, a real singer, a sexy dancer, and an inveterate star, changes the tone and scope of Isherwood's original creation. As Roger Copeland (1999: 25–26) maintains, Minnelli's Sally is "a chirpy, fast-talking, irrepressible American" who is "dementedly zany" and "benignly bonkers" but "hardly a tragic figure." Her "acquaintance with the darker side of bohemia [is] pretty much confined to green nail polish, soigné cigarette holders and casual sex." Perhaps, as Copeland suggests, she is the result of an American wish that is essentially a contradiction: a tragedy with a happy ending. To purists, she is only an American cousin to Jean Ross, the real-life Sally Bowles—so much so that when Judi Dench, who had played Sally in the London musical version, tried watching the film on television, she rapidly decided that "this wasn't the story of a failure but of a huge success" and switched off her set.

The Minnelli issue aside, the Fosse film, as musicologist Raymond Knapp (2006: 102–3) argues, provides an important link between two eminent movie musicals—Baz Luhrman's *Moulin Rouge!* (2001) and Rob Marshall's *Chicago* (2002)—that position themselves as metamusicals "about the relationship between MERM [Musically Enhanced Reality Mode] and real life, but from nearly opposite perspectives." MERM involves moving across space and time, as well as real and imaginary

states, in a fluent way. Its use can be traced back to such early movie classics as *The Wizard of Oz* (1939), *Meet Me in St. Louis* (1944), *Singin' in The
Rain* (1952), and any number of Esther Williams aqua-musicals. In
MERM, as Knapp shows, there are polarized impulses toward "the spon-
taneity and enhanced realism of live performance and toward an overt
artificiality" (67). To take just a single vivid example, *The Wizard of Oz* uses
black-and-white (actually, sepia tone) for the Kansas scenes and then
switches to brilliant color for the land of Oz. MERM uses technology to
impart an extra charge to sung performance: in many films, lip-synching
to prerecorded song tracks is common. In the cases of *Moulin Rouge!* and
Chicago, there is an intermixture of reality and playacting on various
levels: the Luhrman film has an eclectic mix of familiar stories and songs
in order to suggest "that we learn how to live our lives through musicals,"
whereas *Chicago* "sees reality itself—and quite a cynical and grim reality
that is—in terms of elaborate musical numbers" (103). However, both
these musicals owe a debt to Fosse's film version of *Cabaret*.

Right from the "central situational details" in Luhrman's film—
Christian's pilgrimage from England to turn-of-the-century Paris (caught
in a fraught historical moment), his descent into the underworld of the
club, his romance with Satine (the nightclub's star), and the all-seeing
gaze of the cynical proprietor—the main plot facts find direct parallels in
Fosse's *Cabaret*. After all, Brian is English; he travels to Berlin (a city
caught in a particularly fraught historical moment of its own), descends
for a while into the perverse, tainted world of the Kit Kat Klub, has a
romance with its star, and his and Sally's story is played out under the all-
seeing-eye of the Master of Ceremonies. Moreover, there is the camp
element that links the two movies. Indeed, camp is "the most distinctive
feature of [*Moulin Rouge!*], the key to every exaggerated gesture and
indulgence in cinematic and/or MERM-based excess" (109). The camp
is in the mode of storytelling rather than the story itself. It "ratchets up
the emotional charge of each particular within the story, investing every
object, every sentiment, and every person with sufficient exaggeration
that they might be taken either 'straight,' with deepened significance, or
as complete jokes, a travesty of what they seem to be. Or both."

As for *Chicago*, Knapp also sees a strong camp element in the presentational mode. Many of the numbers have an exaggerated cynicism, but
the film undercuts its own cynicism at times by substituting "a grim,
all-too-believable reality, which confronts us whenever MERM falls
away" (114). *Chicago* offers yet another doubleness, "similar in kind to

the disturbing ways that *Cabaret* has its cake and eats it too." In *Chicago*, "the idea that jazz and its associated lifestyles have warped Roxie, so that these societal ills and not she herself should be held accountable, is put forth cynically, as a way to evoke public sympathy but not as a real explanation." In other words, Roxie's fixation on an imaginary world of MERM "has led her to disconnect from the real world, discounting its meanness and the harsh consequences of her own immoral actions" (115). The MERM effectively reduces the cynicism to jazz and its dance forms "so that content and its campy mode of delivery merge: medium thus becomes message, and message medium."

In effect, then, Fosse's *Cabaret* set a trend for such metamovie musicals as *Moulin Rouge* and *Chicago*. In this sense, Fosse was extending his aesthetic influence just as he had on Broadway with *Sweet Charity* (1966), its cynicism and laconic, world-wise, world-weary tone establishing his quirkiness of attitude and style. Formulaic in its "prostitute with a heart of gold" theme and fatalistic failure of its heroine, *Sweet Charity* bore similarities to the stage version of *Cabaret* as well as to Fosse's *Chicago* in 1975 in that all three stage musicals had no reliable moral compass and thus marked a distinctive break between moral idealism and "corruptive" performance. This trope in the musical (both onstage and in film) is a feature that now defines the genre, so it will be interesting to see what mode or form it will generate in the twenty-first century.

THE 1987 PRINCE REVIVAL

Barry and Fran Weissler planned to go into rehearsal in early 1987 for a revival. Their idea was to have a national tour (to Delaware, Miami, Chicago, Los Angeles, and San Francisco) before opening on Broadway. They invited Joel Grey to star in the revival, and he agreed, offering to direct it as well. The Weisslers said delicately that they had been thinking of Hal Prince to take on that task. "That would be great," Grey retorted, "but Hal *never* redirects a show." True enough in the sense that Prince would never make a carbon copy of an original. "I wouldn't have been tempted to come back to it unless we made a lot of changes," Prince told William B. Collins. "Under the circumstances, it was probably a wise idea to keep the love story extremely romantic and may be a bit unreal." However, he asked Joe Masteroff to rewrite the book so that they could be braver with the leading characters. Herr Schultz was to be played by Werner Klemperer, so "Meeskite" would be dropped. "Jack Gilford was wonderful, but he was more Jewish than German, and that's not true of German Jews. They're more German than Jewish. The Jews in Germany were assimilated: that's why they were tempted to feel over-secure. And that's what was so horrifying about what happened to them" (Ebb Papers). Regina Resnick, who was enticed to play Fräulein Schneider, had concerns about her role. In a December 23, 1986, letter sent to Masteroff, Kander, and Ebb, Prince outlined them:

Fellas,

I had a good meeting with Regina Resnick. She thinks straight and cre-atively and she has one problem which could turn to an advantage. She thinks the stretch of the show from "Pineapple" through "Married" doesn't illustrate the stuff in Schneider which culminates in "What Would You Do?" And I believe she's right.

Since I do want to move away from the sentimentality we had with Lenya and Guilford [sic], it might be worth while seeing whether we could, around the "Married" number (since they are monologues), provide Schneider with some facts—that she's a man's woman, that this is her last chance, that she sees Schultz's foibles but she's pragmatic and that pragmatism, of course, would be echoed later on in some fury.

For Resnick this is a role in which she can lose herself. For Lenya it was an extension of her personality. And Lenya could play against how she looked and sounded and be more sentimental than most people. This lady could use some text: possibly words going to the song; possibly words and a verse going into the song; possibly words going into the song and a musical bridge. I don't know the shape of it, but it interests me. Please give it some thought.

Have a happy Christmas.

Love—

Hal

(Ebb Papers, box 9, series 1: Scrapbooks)

Gregg Edelman's Cliff would have more character, with a sexual past of his own as well as a present with Alyson Reed's Sally. He would be slow with women because he was attracted to men. He would no longer sing "Why Should I Wake Up?" a song that implied he was sleepwalking through life. Now he would sing "Don't Go," a plea of mounting desper-ation, as he looks on Sally as his last possible heterosexual attraction. Masteroff put less stress on her craziness, making her a little more knowing and a little less naive (Kuchwara 1987). There would also be a difference in the way Grey's Emcee would interact with the dramatic scenes. He would be far more aggressive than he had been in 1966, becoming from the outset a vividly poisonous character, lethally in control of the cabaret. In other words, he would have less naughty charm than before and become less apologetically evil. As Prince commented in an article by Diane Solway (1987: 32) in the *New York Times*: "The first time, Joel was predominantly feeding on all those years he had as a kid in vaudeville and in the Borscht Belt—in other words, show biz. The interim years have been about humanity and life biz. That's a big qualitative change of emphasis."

The essence of change, however, was connected with the temper of the times in America. Post-Stonewall (1969) America made it possible to acknowledge homosexuality openly in musical theater—certainly more so than in the sixties. As Knapp (2006: 238) contends, "Berlin—like Morocco for an earlier generation—was widely known as a place one could indulge in homosexuality without fear of official censure, particularly in the years immediately preceding June 1934, at which point the Nazis cracked down on homosexuality." Broadway could enjoy greater freedom in indulging sexual license, especially when it came to "bad girls" of the ilk of Sally Bowles. After all, there had been Gypsy Rose Lee in *Gypsy*, Mrs. Lovett in *Sweeney Todd*, Velma Kelly and Roxy Hart in *Chicago*, and neither Margo Channing nor Eve Harrington was exactly saintly in *Applause*. The movies had already presented *Lady Sings the Blues, Victor/Victoria*, and *The Rose*, so audiences had already been exposed to a wide range of perverse sexuality or addiction by women.

The original Broadway production had been a cautionary tale for the United States in the 1960s because of the often brutal and violent opposition to civil rights activists, both black and white. In the late 1980s, however, Prince noted that his country was emerging from a period of self-hypnosis during which Americans had believed that everything was wonderful. They were deluding themselves, in Prince's view, because if they had really looked around them, they would have seen more homeless people and more desperation. People had kept looking away from the reality but finally were changing their perspective. Said Prince: "Nobody is taking at face value what other people are saying to us on television. We are beginning to engage again and make our own decisions." The new clarity brought a loss of confidence in the government as well as a cold recognition of a world where it was still possible to deny genocide

(Jewish, Armenian, et cetera) and to fall victim to terrorism. In this context, *Cabaret* could become a different cautionary tale: a parable about what happens when people look away from what is happening. On the first day of rehearsals for the 1987 version, Prince offered his cast the observation of how, while walking up Central Park West in the snow, he had seen a man huddled among his bundles on a bench. Prince looked the other way. "In Germany, in the thirties and forties, some people say they knew what was happening and looked the other way; others insist they didn't know what was going on." The question the play was asking, he added, was what would you do? "This is a show about survival and about how most people unheroically look the other way in order to survive" (Hirsch 2005: 40, 42).

Prince was a little concerned about the design of the opening set for this new production. As Carol Ilson reports, he requested that the first set as well as all the others in the show be based on Boris Aronson's 1966 designs, understanding that the audience must be given the initial, original image that Aronson created because that had been innovative. Everyone who remembered the first version recalled the mirror and the neon sign, but as Prince explained, there were also "trolley-car cables and globe street lamps which went upstage diminishing in size to give a sense of distance. It was strong and abstract and definitely Berlin pre-war" (Ilson 1989: 340). However, that scenery was too difficult to tour. Lisa Aronson, Boris's widow, was consulted for all the rest, but sacrificing the original image provoked the disapproval of Frank Rich, coauthor with Lisa, of the superb book on Aronson's career. Rich (1987: C3) attacked the "cheesiness" that softened Prince's "hard-edged conception" and exposed "just how old-fashioned and plodding 'Cabaret' was when dealing with musical-comedy specifics rather than in directorial metaphor."

In fact, the new version got mixed reviews. Howard Kissel of the *New York Daily News* (1987) loved it, claiming that Prince had "recreated a brilliant show brilliantly" (Kissel 1987). Reviewing the show in Washington, David Richards thought that the production took into account the original without betraying it. "The results," he concluded, "fall curiously between betwixt and between. 'Cabaret' is not what it was, but the creators have stopped short of the full-fledged overhaul that might establish the show on a new footing altogether." For instance, Edelman's Cliff was no longer a robust heterosexual and no longer gave in blissfully to Sally's charm. By cutting down on the Schultz–Schneider subplot and eliminating "Meeskite," the production imparted "a matter-of-factness to the twilight courtship" and displayed "an underlying reluctance on the part of both participants to abandon the protective anesthesia of despair." There was also a loss and a gain in Grey's performance. Where the Emcee had been wickedly charming in luring the audience into his embrace before tightening his grip on it, thereby resulting in "a tantalizing ambiguity," he was now unapologetically evil. So, instead of heating up the temperature on the Kit Kat stage, he now produced only a chill. The review also suggested that some of the flaws in the production derived from Prince's decision to "attune 'Cabaret' to our more cynical times" (Richards 1987: B4). Clive Barnes disagreed. His review in the *New York Post Weekend* praised Prince's decision to "enhance" the show in time and coloration "to offset the always dulling comparison with memory's impossible brilliance." He liked the fact that Prince took the slightly harsher tone that the film adopted. Things were more pointed: Cliff's bisexuality, Nazi anti-Semitism, and Grey's duet with the gorilla. Reed's Sally was "a much tougher little English cookie" than that suggested by Jill Haworth. As for Grey, he was always better than the show, and still was, though he was never going to stop his role from being "peripheral to the story." More than ever, he remained central to the theme, giving it "the backbone" the show needed. Barnes was the first critic to recognize that Grey's interpretation owed nothing to Isherwood and his world (Barnes 1987).

After listing the new version's evident virtues—Grey ("scarlet grin cracking his clown-white skull in two"), Resnik ("in perfect voice for the brilliant pastiches"), the musical as a whole ("two simultaneous demi-romances struggling against the wild tide of quick pleasure and growing fear that leers from a mirror overhead")—Walter Kerr (1987) zeroed in on Reed's Sally, finding it "something of a puzzler"... "efficient enough in its practiced, matter-of-fact way to keep the essential machinery going." Reed was "a clockwork professional, cool glossy, and experienced beyond feeling," but this "only gives us a glimpse of the kind of performing Sally does, it doesn't tell us much about the kind of person she is." In Kerr's view, Reed was unable to present an image that would define Sally.

This revival ran on Broadway until June 1988 and then resumed its national tour. Prince was pleased with the reception, despite the critical cavils. Perhaps there was a more radical reason for the objections than any particular shortcoming in casting or design. As Kander told Greg Lawrence: "When *Cabaret*, the show, first came out, it was

*Joel Grey in the 1987
Harold Prince revival.
(Photofest)*

considered highly innovative and it later influenced other shows. But by the time the first revival was mounted in 1987, it no longer seemed new to people. Even with some changes in the score and staging, it was more or less a re-creation of the original production" (Kander and Ebb 2003: 72). Nevertheless, at the very least, this version confirmed Prince's expertise in craft. Prince confirmed that he was "the best director of musicals around by far"—as Stephen Sondheim had maintained in 1984—because of his sense of the function of music in a show and his daring risks. As Sondheim elaborated: "He has a sense of dignity of the musical theatre and thinks it's the highest form of theatre....He's not condescending about musical theatre" (Ilson 1989: 373).

What any revival needed to be was (in Kander's terms) "a renewed experience" whereby "the show suddenly seems innovative and daring in the way the original production seemed" (Kander and Ebb 2003: 72). *Cabaret* had to wait for a new collaborative team in order to achieve this utterly daring creative renewal.

*Joel Grey in the 1972 film
version of* Cabaret *directed
by Bob Fosse. (Allied Artists/
Photofest) (photographer:
Lars Looschen)*

THE 1998 SAM MENDES BROADWAY PRODUCTION

The daring came, unexpectedly, out of England. Sam Mendes's 1998
production, starring Natasha Richardson and Alan Cumming, offered
the most incisively accurate tone and interpretation of the story. From
theater setting to casting to choreography and stylization, this production was everything a revival was meant to be, except that it wasn't so
much a revival as a daring, hypnotic, rethinking of the material. The
production originated in 1993 at the Donmar Warehouse in London's
West End, where in 1992 Mendes and Caro Newling had become artistic
directors of the newly formed theater organization. *Cabaret* was "up
there with *The Crucible* or *The Homecoming* or any other play of the twentieth century that deserves to be reinvented and rediscovered generation to generation. It's a great piece of theatre," asserted Mendes (Wolf
2002: 38), who was attracted to "the embryo of a dangerous show that
was wrapped in a conventional Broadway wrapping" (Sunshine
1999: 12). But how could it be communicated anew? Mendes believes
that in order to make a play work, you need to ultimately feel as if you

REINCARNATIONS AND REVISIONS • 165

have a *secret* about the work. "A secret that only you have and that, in the end, you make available to the audience" (Wolf 2002: 38). Mendes's unique secret was to be the environmental mode of presentation: he would turn the stalls of the Donmar into the Kit Kat Klub, where performer and spectator could share complicity in what Matt Wolf calls "the poisonous seductions of an age poised for collapse" (38). When audiences walked into the reconfigured Donmar, they were seated at tables and served food and alcohol by waitresses as tattooed, bruised, and pierced chorus boys and girls dragged musical instruments onto the small stage and doubled as the orchestra. The stage itself was stripped to a bare minimum, with no more than six wooden chairs at any time and an overhead fan to replace the automated train scenery used by Prince. Mendes also refused to distribute playbills until after the performance in order not to disturb the mood or distract from the story (Sunshine 1999: 12–13). Mendes explained in *Playbill:* "It's really about the central mystery of the twentieth century—how Hitler could have happened. And it's important that we go on asking the question whether or not we can find some sort of answer." His central metaphor was the club—a second- or third-rate one where an audience could see runs in the chorus girls' stockings, broken light bulbs, and overall tackiness. However, the club's atmosphere and entertainment would pull the audience in and show them what they had become part of by being there. "It turns out to be the club that puts on the story rather than a story that contains within it a club" (99).

Like others, Kander realized that this idea was not new as a directorial conceit, but what was novel was Mendes's kind of talent and imagination. "When *Cabaret* was first done, it was fresh and imaginative and no one had ever seen anything like it. And in a funny way, that's what Sam did for a whole other generation: we got back the feeling that *Cabaret* had had the first time out" (Wolf 2002: 40). Mendes pinned pictures by Grösz and his contemporary Otto Dix to the rehearsal room walls. The cast had to read Ebb's lyrics for a long while without singing them. Chorus members were made to invent their own characters' histories. Stephen Spender, Isherwood's writer friend and colleague, paid a visit and fascinated the cast with his gentle recollection of life in coffee bars and cafés and the gay cruising scene in Berlin of the period. Musical director Paddy Cunneen taught nine members of the ensemble to double as musicians who could join the four principals of the Kit Kat Band. The stage size was reduced on all sides by almost a meter. The house was transformed into a club but one with a working environment. Jane Horrocks, who had mimicked Liza Minnelli (among others) in her Olivier-nominated role in *The Rise and Fall of Little Voice*, was concerned about being judged as Sally against Minnelli's film performance (Wolf 2002: 40–41).

Another anxious performer was Alan Cumming, who was rehearsing the Emcee while playing Hamlet at night. He was worried that he would be the target of every musical theater actor in London for landing this plum role. Moreover, he had a radical problem with musicals: "I had a problem, and still sort of do, about ending a sentence and bursting into song." After articulating his objections to Mendes, Cumming was able, however, to find a way by which the Emcee could bring a dark theater to life, becoming virtually the eyes of the audience, luring them yet challenging them once they were his captives (41). In his opening number, only the fingers of one hand showed in a small spotlight as he beckoned the audience to leave their troubles outside. Then, as the beam widened, he was shown to be wearing a black leather jacket that he shed only after he introduced the Kit Kat band framed behind and above him in a lit picture frame—the production's replacement for Aronson's tilted mirror. Under his black jacket, he wore a white tuxedo, black bowtie, black trousers, and spats. However, he was bare-chested and had two gleaming kiss curls as sideburns. With nicely outlined eyebrows and red lips, he became increasingly suggestive in a sexual way, his fingers miming a Japanese fan unfurling and spreading, as the Kit Kat dancers cavorted in red light. Of course, his white tuxedo jacket had to come off, and when it did, he was shown with livid bruises on his arms—a result of his drug addiction. He also was shown to be in a harness that went down to his crotch. This gear helped to accentuate every pelvic thrust and groin movement, and the actor was certainly explicitly sexual, rubbing his crotch on some lines while leering at the audience. Vocally, Cumming was sometimes harshly emphatic ("Happy to see YOU"), almost yelling his exhortation "Leave your troubles outside."

His sexual exhibitionism continued in succeeding scenes. He caressed Cliff suggestively on the train bringing the American writer to Berlin, insinuating the sexual lure of the city and its cabaret. In the raunchy "Two Ladies" number, during which he wore boxer shorts, suspenders, and a bow tie, his pelvic thrusts and crotch rubs left nothing to the imagination, and he cavorted as a transvestite in a female kick line number after the "Married" duet between Fräulein Schneider and Herr Schultz. Even in his soft-shoe with the gorilla ("If You Could See Her") he

Alan Cumming in the 1998 Sam Mendes Broadway production of Cabaret *(Photofest)*

modulated from flirting coyly to grabbing her crotch. However, he played a multiplicity of roles and functions, sometimes introducing a new scene, facilitating a new number, performing a torch song ("I Don't Care Much"), and inserting himself as a comic (the Pineapple Song) or dramatic chorus (the Kristallnacht moment). In scene 8, for instance, he squatted on his haunches while playing a gramophone record of "Tomorrow Belongs to Me," suddenly stopping the song in the middle of a line to utter the final words with a ferocity that presaged the dark and chilling tone of other things to come.

The show became the first of a Donmar series of Christmas musicals, but it was a super hit and not just a show that came and went quickly. With Adam Godley as Cliff and Sara Kestelman as Fräulein Schneider, it played like "a study in isolation and loss" in the midst of a "sometimes horrific march of history" (44). Kestelman's Jewish landlady was without any razzmatazz, cutting to the emotional quick of the role, and winning the actress an Olivier award for best supporting performance in a musical. Olivier nominations also went to Mendes, Cumming, and the production itself (for best musical revival). It played to 106 percent (standing room included) over sixteen weeks (December 2, 1993–March 26, 1994), became the turning point for everybody, and was the first Donmar production to be taped for television (by Carlton Television in December 1994). It also facilitated Mendes's move four years later to Broadway, where it fully realized Mendes's artistic vision in a glittering new production headlined by Cumming once more as the Emcee and Natasha Richardson delivering a *cri de coeur* as Sally (in place of Horrocks).

Mendes spent more than two years looking for a site in Manhattan that could duplicate the cabaret setting for his London production. Under the auspices of the Roundabout Theatre Company, the Broadway run opened in the long unused Henry Miller's Theatre, which had been renamed the Kit Kat Klub and turned into a late-night dance club where rows of orchestra seats had been removed in favor of small round black café tables adorned with small red Tiffany lamps and straight-backed black chairs for four. At the rear of the auditorium were banquettes, and audiences were reminded by this transformation that they were part of the evening's entertainment, even as the patrons at the tables could order drinks (from waiters or waitresses dressed in black like the chorus and band onstage) or be invited by the Emcee to dance onstage with him at the beginning of act 2. Despite these gestures of socialization, glamour of any sort was distinctly out of the question. The Kit Kat dancers, far thinner and paler than the garish, lumpy ones in the film, had ripped stockings, dingy underwear, and bruises on their bodies as if from some invisible but palpably felt wounding by life outside the café. They wandered onstage before the opening to do their stretches, splits, backbends, and somersaults, and they ogled and flirted with patrons. Their fanny-waggling and grotesque squats suggested, as Vincent Canby noted in his *New York Times* (March 29, 1998) review, that dancing was merely a sideline. Their world was too aggressive, too subject to Nazi perils to permit any indulgence in something purely diversionary or professionally glamorous. If anything, the "girls" suggested ugly distortions of George Grösz and Otto Dix because the lines and angles of their dancing were skewed or exaggerated. "It's like choreographing everything twice," commented Rob Marshall in *Dance Magazine* (March 1998): "I'd say to myself, 'No, fray it purposefully with people on the wrong foot or out of step.'" (Sunshine 1999: 20).

The stage was bare except for two black doors, black metal staircases and ramps, and a tilted gilt picture frame with lights that took the place of Aronson's famous suspended mirror. This frame overhanging the main space was a literal frame for the Kit Kat band made up of male and female musicians dressed in black caps, sleeveless undershirts or filmy underwear, and black boots. The only glitter, apart from the gilt frame, was a large silver-fringed curtain that sometimes concealed the band. The lack of high gloss and razzle-dazzle extended to the characterization of the Emcee and Sally Bowles, which were far more incisive in incipient hysteria and ferocity than the portrayals by Grey or Minnelli. Alan Cumming's Master of Ceremonies was no sleek demonic doll. He entered in a long black leather coat and boots, his lips a blood red, his eyes highlighted in blue eye shadow and tinges of red. When his coat was off, audiences saw his nipples, rouged and glittery, and his bruised torso, with needle marks on one forearm and a tattoo on his upper left arm. In the center of his half-nude upper body was a bowtie attached to a harness made up of multiple straps that wrapped around his body—including his crotch. As Nancy Franklin noted in her *New Yorker* (April 6, 1998) review, he was "a spectacle of mixed messages" that forced the audience to ask itself what it thought it was seeing and what it all meant. Thin and sinewy, he used his long hands and fingers as semaphores of Eastern dance, beckoning the audience to leave their troubles outside and join the cabaret world. Continuing his portrayal of the most candidly carnal Emcee in living memory, Cumming engaged in explicit sexual byplay with "boys" and "girls," allowing his hands to grope and explore their breasts, buttocks, and genitals in uninhibited exhibitionism. Throughout the show he acted as a persistent voyeur, watching the audience watching him as he roamed the entire rim of the stage. At times, he crouched like a monkey on a platform above the stage, and his posture linked with his gorilla number when he sang the satirical song resonant in mockery of anti-Semitism.

The Emcee played an entire range of roles, from host to commentator to kick line dancer to supernumerary. He was the all-knowing, allseeing one, whether posing as a uniformed guard on the train bringing Clifford Bradshaw to Berlin or dancing in cross-dress in the club or serving as a prop man during the "Pineapple" song or baring his swastikaemblazoned buttocks to the audience at the finale of act 1. He shared the production's highest individual honors with Natasha Richardson's Sally, the one and only Sally of stage or screen to actually reflect the extravagant but foolish romantic that Isherwood portrayed in his Berlin diaries. The interpretation was not only credible and accurate; it was, in a paradoxical way, a radical transformation of what had already existed on the printed page by simply being presented without fussy elaboration. It revealed Richardson as one of those rare performers who are said to possess "a remarkable transparency," a phrase recalled by Canby in his *New York Times* review, defining it as "the quality that allows us to see the heart of the character being played, while the woman we watch on the stage never appears to get in the way" (Sunshine 1999: 47). With short, dirty blonde hair and untended, short green nails, Richardson's Sally was, as Franklin put it in the *New Yorker*, "not interested in finishing touches." She drank alcohol, smoked, snorted cocaine, enjoyed her own jokes about sex, and had a silly exuberance. Jill Haworth had looked winning in her fur; Liza Minnelli had had perfectly lacquered hair and long, spectacular nails. Although attractive in her beloved, ratty, rain-stained fur coat that she sometimes fondled as if it were the dearest thing in the world, Richardson was the most feline in movement of the three actresses who played Sally in the versions discussed in this chapter. She captured the self-delusion and pathos of a northern English mill owner's daughter who aspires to reinvention. Fintan O'Toole (1998) adjudged her Sally to be "obviously a child of privilege" who could "easily have been the wife of a landed gentleman. Her jolly, gangly manner is almost that of a frightfully nice fox-hunting girl. And this makes her descent into gin-sodden promiscuity all the more moving."

Natasha Richardson as Sally Bowles in the 1998 Sam Mendes Broadway production of Cabaret. *(Joan Marcus/Photofest)*

Her husky voice was well suited to the raucous "Don't Tell Mama," but it was modulated for the more lilting "Perfectly Marvelous" number with John Benjamin Hickey's Cliff. Its biggest test came, of course, with the title song, where Richardson was both boisterous and melancholy, showing a tangle of emotions, with desperation behind the cosmetics, fear insinuated into the bravado. As Roger Copeland (1999: 26) eloquently described in a brilliant essay entitled "Cabaret at the End of the World," Richardson suggested "a ritual of self-hypnosis" as she worked hard to convince herself that her story was going to end happily. As she prepared to sing the line "But when I saw her laid out like a queen," she closed her eyes and paused, suggesting something ominous. Her halting delivery helped her place the emotional emphasis squarely on the word "corpse." Her eyes opened wide, and she seemed to be staring into a coffin—not so much Elsie's as her own. Then, her hands quivering, she knocked over the microphone stand at the end and stumbled off. It brought a kind of hysteria and hypnotic enchantment to the moment, and the number became a sort of "suicide note" (as Mendes puts it) "about staying in a city that Sally knows is going to end in rubble" (Wolf 2002: 45). Possessed of the character's desperately mad heroism, Richardson's performance was like that of Angela Lansbury's Rose in *Gypsy*—an incisive, powerful reinvention of a role, and it was hailed by the *New York Times* as "a radiant performance that lights up the year."

Mendes's production (co-directed and choreographed by Rob Marshall, who later won an Oscar for his work on *Chicago*) showed the motive and scope of reincarnations by generating the excitement of something new, something disturbing, yet something spellbinding. Dangerously inventive, it made real revisions of the original, enlarging the libretto by quotations from Isherwood's Berlin diaries. It cut three songs from the original score, replacing them with three from the Fosse film, including "Mein Herr," the hot, sultry number sung by Sally in the company of cigar-chewing girls with wild hair. It removed the glitz of the show numbers, making them raw and immediate. Mendes did not want "a produced sound" from his singers; he wanted "the singing voices" to come out of "their speaking voices" (Sunshine 1999: 65) As previously noted, runs could be seen in the chorus girls' stockings, many of the club's fixtures had broken bulbs, and a general tackiness was evident beneath the glitzy veneer. William Ivey Long's costumes were purposefully rough looking. In addition to the Emcee's crotch-accentuating harness, Sally wore a signature corset made of

Natasha Richardson as Sally Bowles in the 1998 Sam Mendes Broadway production of Cabaret. *(Photofest)*

whalebone and three different kinds of lace. It was skintight and covered all of her intimate parts yet was flexible enough to withstand strenuous choreography. She wore a leather jacket for "Mein Herr" as if she were prepared for a bit of kinky fetish. Under their corsets, bras, panties, and garter belts, the women wore two pairs of underwear, including bras with microphones sewn into the seams. Long's costumes were deliberately "deconstructed." They would begin as full costumes, but pieces were eliminated one at a time until Long achieved the desired effect.

The Kit Kat Klub band (that had to double as characters in the story) was selected after nineteen casting sessions and the rejection of many fabulous dancers who could not put aside their slick technique. Rob Marshall devised more dancing than had been done in the London version, but he wanted the dancing to be "uncomfortable to watch" rather than slick and smart. He deliberately choreographed everything to look frayed and on the wrong foot or out-of-step.

One of the production's most striking innovations was its presentation of the spectrum of sexuality. An obvious—and superficial—example was in the Emcee's risqué introduction of the girls: Rosie and her rosy buttocks; lesbian Lulu ("You like Lulu? Too bad. So does Rosie"); Texas, "a very cunning linguist"; Frenchie ("I like to order Frenchie on the side"); Helga ("I'm like a father to her, so when she's bad, I spank her"); and Fritzy of the voracious vagina. Another lewd example was in the lyric for "Two Ladies" with lines such as "We switch partners daily to play as we please" and "There's room on the bottom if you drop in some night." Where the first production of *Cabaret* in 1966 presented a heterosexual romance, thereby betraying the ambiguous sexual politics of its literary source, Mendes's version had a far more complex treatment of sex, love, and desire, building, it seemed, on the advancements in Fosse's film. In Prince's initial production, the protagonist–narrator was Cliff Bradshaw, an American novelist, and his romance with Sally Bowles was, as John M. Clum (1999: 277) contends, quite a conventional Broadway romance "set within an unconventional musical framework." In it, boy met girl and boy lost girl without the happy ending. Fosse made the Isherwood character, Cliff, bisexual, renaming him Brian Roberts and turning the stage musical romance into a bisexual love triangle. In Prince's 1987 revival, Cliff became an unhappy gay man who saw in Sally (says Clum) "a way back into the closet." The only unrepentant homosexuals in this revival were Bobby and Victor, but they were stereotypical mincing queens. Masteroff set to work to make Cliff bisexual, though the character was most reluctant to show any interest in men who wanted to bed him.

Mendes changed all this. Despite a sexless but warm Fräulein Schneider by Mary Louise Wilson (light rather than sourly wry) and a paint-by-numbers Cliff from John Benjamin Hickey (a performance that was explicitly bisexual in tone yet without any cutting edge), Mendes's cabaret site was not simply a place of escape from the reality of the outside world; it was "a site of sexual liberation" (Clum 1999: 278). Same-sex desire was presented as "a necessary part of the musical world *Cabaret* celebrates." Cumming's Emcee was more androgynous than Grey's demonic doll. With red sequined pasties on his nipples, Cumming's Emcee seemed to relish changing gender, passing from the "naughty, oversexed boy" of burlesque comedy in the first act to a drag performer in "Two Ladies" and continuing the drag act in a sequined dress for the torch song "I Don't

Leenya Rideout (left), Alan Cumming, and Michele Pawk in the 1998 Sam Mendes Broadway production of Cabaret. *(Joan Marcus/Photofest)*

Care Much." Between these two numbers he slow-danced with Bobby during a reprise of the Schneider–Schultz ballad celebrating marriage.

Mendes further charged his production with a grim apocalyptic vision. As Clum shows, Isherwood's original stories had focused on the advent of Nazism and the Holocaust; Mendes's production was concerned with the doom about to befall homosexuals in Berlin. On the last line of "If You Could See Her" the mood changed from burlesque to grotesque. According to Mendes, this is where the musical turned into "a black-as-pitch play" (Sunshine 1999: 14). The Emcee's revels were a fascinating exhibition that, nevertheless, presaged the doom to come: examples of the polymorphously perverse but, ironically, also a tocsin of impending Nazism, and Mendes showed us the world Nazism would destroy. At the end of the first act—when the audience was a willing participant—the Emcee dropped his trousers to reveal a swastika painted on his buttocks, mocking the encroaching Nazi movement. The final sequence of the second act went even further. The doors of the club were suddenly shut from outside, making the audience feel trapped. The music changed tempo, and a new setting was shockingly revealed. Clum (1999: 279) explains: "The final image is of the emcee in a concentration camp uniform ornamented with both the yellow star and the pink triangle. The cabaret setting flies out revealing whitewashed brick walls and a gunshot rings out as the lights black out."

Mendes could be charged with the exploitation of heavy-handed imagery and symbolism for "messages," something that Prince had eliminated for being superfluous and of the wrong tone. For some people, the finale felt like a sledgehammer, as the stage seemed to be stripped down to the bare grey pipes and smoke slowly filled the scene. The characters began to resemble figures from a concentration camp. The Emcee sensationally reinforced the image by uncovering his coat to reveal the costume of a Nazi camp victim. This moment pushed the production into sentimental propaganda, without, however, negating the central paradox. More aggressively insolent and madly idiosyncratic overall than either the Fosse movie version or Prince's original Broadway production, Mendes's version had "the scary, hypnotic fascination of one of those nightmares from which you feel you can wake yourself at any time, but somehow you never do" (Franklin 1998).

For Michiko Kakutani of the *New York Times* (April 26, 1998), the production was the perfect *Cabaret* for the 1990s because it was "darker, raunchier and more disturbing than its predecessors, and by turning the entire theatre into the Kit Kat Klub . . . it implicate[d] the audience in the frenetic escapism, and coming horror, of 1930's Berlin." Isherwood's understatement was replaced by Mendes's "fierce in-your-face stage magic to break down the fourth wall." Cumming's Emcee, "part 'Clockwork Orange' droog, part George Grösz demimondaine," was "more complicated and ultimately more threatening" than Grey's Emcee in the Fosse film. "Isherwood's narrator was a passive observer who believed you could watch history from a safe remove; Mendes's tour guide is Cumming's leering EMCEE, the sexy boy toy turned cosmic demiurge, who reminds us that history makes no concessions to voyeurs." Quoting Grösz on his own art—"I felt the ground shaking beneath my feet, and the shaking was visible in my work"—Kakutani (1998: 624) concluded that "the same might be said of the work of Cumming and Mendes in their dazzling reinvention of 'Cabaret'— the difference is that they make it impossible for the audience not to feel that shaking, too."

THE 1987 AND 2008 STRATFORD SHAKESPEARE FESTIVAL OF CANADA PRODUCTIONS

Founded principally to mount Shakespearean plays, the Stratford Shakespeare Festival of Canada has often entertained audiences by producing high-caliber musicals. In 1987, Brian Macdonald staged a colorful production of *Cabaret*, starring Sheila McCarthy as Sally, Scott Wentworth as Cliff, and charismatic Brent Carver as the Master of Ceremonies. Very much influenced by Prince's two versions of the musical, this one was (in the words of one critic) "an artefact of dazzling precision," from the leg-snapping Kit Kat girls ("sober and calculating as judges") to the carefully arranged tableaux. Ray Conlogue of the *Globe and Mail* (June 2, 1987) felt that the director had given "equal weight to all aspects of the show" and that some of the business he created was "almost plodding." He had mixed feelings about McCarthy's Sally, finding her to be very different from other interpretations, "much frailer and more vulnerable," but finally feeling let down by her voice, which he thought was "too slight for barroom belting" and given to softening the ends of lines.

Other Toronto critics found the production more delightful, praising especially Brent Carver's Emcee, whom all agreed was a spectacular dancer with dangerous sexiness. Carver could execute rapid pirouettes with a lunatic grin on his face, and his struts were done with mocking *and* erotic arrogance. "This is an Emcee who loves the little cupidon dots of red on his cheeks and the twirl of his cane," remarked Conlogue. Another critic saw a sophisticated line of development in Carver's performance, starting with his pouting and campy first appearance, when, white-faced, he glided across the stage with the Kit Kat girls, pinched a few rear ends, and did not give away the creepy elements he would introduce later— such as the boiling rage with which he screamed the punch line in "If You Could See Her": "She wouldn't look Jewish at all!" Trouble was, he did not have a leading lady with the power for the final anthem. Though girlish, giggly, and wacky, McCarthy was not a vocal dynamo, and she lacked sexiness—as did Scott Wentworth, who otherwise was a dignified Cliff, managing to combine naïveté with intelligence. The Schultz and Schneider pair (Denise Fergusson and Richard Curnock) divided the critics, who found them either engaging or monotonous. For much of the time it was left to Carver to supply the sexual force and personality, and he was magnificently androgynous, roguish, and sinister for the production in which Eric McCormack (before he became an American television star with *Will and Grace*) played a transvestite waiter in the Kit Kat Klub. Just like his later Tony award—winning performance as Molina in *Kiss of the Spider Woman* (1993), Carver's performance as the Emcee should have been one for the ages, but the production has receded in memory, perhaps because it did not reimagine the libretto in a vivid and altogether convincing fashion.

For any director who wishes to engage this musical, the leading question is just how many more major interpretations *Cabaret* could possibly engender. Illinois-born Amanda Dehnert directed a significant reimagining of this musical in 2008. She took as her starting point the socioeconomic conditions in Berlin prior to 1929–30. Her research uncovered the fact that after World War I, where many millions of people were killed, severely injured, or simply lost, German society "was

Brent Carver as the Master of Ceremonies in the 1987 Stratford Shakespeare Festival of Canada production (Michael Cooper/ Stratford Shakespeare Festival Archives)

really upended." Following the armistice of November 1918, a series
of violent uprisings, strikes, and mutinies shook the country, and rival
political groups (Social Democrats, Sparticists, Munich "Reds,"
Dadaists, et cetera) led to savage street fighting in Berlin, where Left
battled Right, wounding the Weimar Government that turned to
sources of power from pre-republican days (Appignanesi 1984: 84).
People were trying to live in a difficult socioeconomic time, and
everyone seemed to be engaged in defining what the country should
become. In the Roaring Twenties, Eastern European refugees, English
visitors, and indigenous artists, black marketers, drug addicts, pimps,
prostitutes, speculators, and assorted bohemians thronged to Berlin.
This was when Berlin cabaret had manifold expression, spawning satirical revues with a primacy on music and dance. However, the welter of
activity contained seeds of anxiety and desperation. Was Germany
defining itself out of a celebration of its own cultural strength, or was
it attempting to stave off some vaguely sensed apocalypse?

One of the most influential books Dehnert consulted was Mel
Gordon's *Voluptuous Panic* (2000), a collection of documentary material
about debauchery and erotica in 1930s Berlin, the city once referred to
as "Sodom on the Spree." Gordon's title is derived from radical sociolo-
gist Roger Caillois's contention in *Les Jeux et les hommes* (1958) that one
can be temporarily liberated from the burden of memory and social
responsibilities when experiencing the "voluptuous panic" of vertigo—
induced by sex or drugs or even a carnival ride. Through the book's
compilation of photographs, snippets of memoir, interviews, playbills,
postcards, erotic art, *verboten* travelogues, illustrated "Moral Histories"
(*Sittengeshichten*), underground tabloids, sexy hotel brochures, and
naughty guides about what to do after dark, Dehnert was able to get a
strong sense of the decadence of the place and era. In the interwar
period, Berlin had more than six hundred sex establishments—massage
parlors, sex clubs, cabarets, brothels, and private torture dungeons—
and a range of female prostitutes that was astounding and grotesque, as
was the repertoire of homosexual types. A partial typology of the latter
included Androgynes, Aunties (older, larger framed gays), Bad Boys
(mostly youth in packs), Bubes (handsome working-class men),
Breslauers (men with huge penises), Cellar-Masters (Tops), Kitty
Receivers (Bottoms), Line-Boys (teen prostitutes), and Wild Boys (homeless young teenagers). The famous writer of that period, Stefan Zweig,
wrote of powdered and rouged young men sauntering along the

Kurfürstendamm and of the "perverse balls of Berlin," where hundreds of men costumed as women and hundreds of women costumed as men danced under the indifferent eyes of the police. "Even the Rome of Suetonius had never known such orgies." The city's cabarets, too, were remarkable for their perversities—the most notorious being The Cabaret of the Nameless, where promoter Erwin Lowinsky lined up horribly untalented and mentally ill performers, stopping performances of anyone remotely competent in the process. If it is accurate to represent this period as Berlin's golden age of cabaret, it is only because every night could feel like New Year's Eve and every sort of licentious pleasure could be bought for a price.

Gordon's book proved to be an advantage to Dehnert because it provided the sort of erotic documentation that was not available to the researchers on Fosse's film who had complained that only literary routines and political satires remained of the old cabaret routines. But *Voluptuous Panic* was profusely stocked with provocative visuals that brilliantly captured the cabaret and social life and moral degeneracy of Weimar Berlin, leading Dehnert to experience a revelation about the country. "I had thought of all these people who gathered in the nightclubs as being really abhorrent," but the book changed that perception. She realized that the clientele was a cross section of German society at a time of multiple social and political movements, though the literary cabarets drew a more select audience than did the political ones. She came to the conclusion that the rise of the National Socialist Party came out of this period of Berlin decadence, though this party was really one of several movements also arising out of a period of profound social and economic chaos. Before Hitler and the Nazis, people of the dominant culture could live their lives any way they wished and had tried to live their lives in a full, beautiful way. There was a peculiar optimism in that various groups were engaged in trying to decide what sort of Germany the country would become. "I suddenly began looking at *Cabaret* as much more of a historical piece than I had as yet imagined. It was a part of history; it was in history; and it was a moment of history. I wanted to make a production that was somehow coming from that place, not from any sort of *judgment* about that place. I really wanted to capture a free sense of Berlin in this time—to capture something that was not Harold Prince's world, not Bob Fosse's world, and not Sam Mendes's world. Honestly, it's quite difficult because everything that could have been done had seemed to be done" (interview with the author, July 17, 2009).

The first issue was which of the existing scripts to use. There was the first published version of 1967—the one used in the original Broadway production. There was the film script of 1972. Prince then used a revised libretto for his 1987 production and Mendes yet another in 1998. Some of the changes involved rearrangements and eliminations of scenes and deletions of songs that were replaced by new ones. (Some of these changes have been mentioned above.) There was also a question about orchestration. Dehnert and her musical director, Rick Fox, wanted their show to have the feel of a dream-like revisiting of an actual Weimar cabaret, so Fox redid most of the orchestrations, pointing out that while a few of the songs have a Weimar texture and sound, most of the original orchestrations (especially for the book scenes) were more representative of a sixties Broadway sound, which is to say a brasher orchestration because of advances in sound technology.

However, the main question was how to treat the role of Cliff, a character she felt was very much at the center of the story because Sally felt like a cipher. Dehnert wanted to focus on him as the American outsider because she was aware that "Americans tend to go voyeuristically into other people's cultures, take things, and get out again." They remain outsiders to other cultures. (Interestingly enough, Isherwood also thought of himself as an outsider, even in 1956, when he wrote in his diary: "I not only take it for granted that I'm an Outsider but I really am only interested in modern books if they are written from an Outsider's point of view.") (Isherwood 1996: 652). Dehnert understood Cliff to be an interloper because his purpose, while not quite that of "a recording angel," was to document the time. He was "someone who could write it down, someone who could bring it back." Perhaps she saw him the way Isherwood viewed himself: "The Outsider stands outside the modern conformist world, looking in—but with passion, with sincere involvement, with heartfelt hostility" (652–53). She also wanted to underline his sexual journey—something that was "not transparent in the sixties script at all," though it was "far more transparent in the eighties script," the film, and the Mendes version.

The principal thing was to find a way "to span the here and now," to link Weimar Berlin to 2008. "The story itself takes place around 1929–30, and it's a history. So I wanted to acknowledge that, and I wanted somehow to make the action be about uncovering that time." She viewed Walter Ruttmann's 1927 silent black and white documentary *Berlin: Symphony of a Great City* (*Berlin: Die Sinfonie der Grosstadt*) that shows a full day of mundane life in Berlin, beginning at dawn and ending in deepest night. This gave her a sense of the imagery of the city. She elected to use Brechtian techniques, multimedia, moveable platforms, symbolism, and expressionistic lighting—everything that was commonly used in the theater and cabaret of that period. She wanted, as it were, to recall the dead-like ghosts from that era, so she and Stratford's design coordinator, Douglas Paraschuk, went for a setting that looked like an abandoned, derelict railway station dominated by a huge gate and overhanging clock. A spiral staircase, steep ship's ladder, and a fire pole completed the decor. The site could have once been a meeting place or served any number of different functions before the war when it, possibly, suffered a bombing. The war is present, of course, in this musical as an event both past (World War I) and approaching (World War II), and the set, looking like remnants of a world, was eerie at first under Kevin Fraser's lighting—a site of ghosts of the past—but Dehnert had a marvelous trick up her directorial sleeve. Wanting the story's opening to be a festive occasion or celebration, she set it in the morning after a really big economic collapse after nearly a decade of solid success, and she used the idea of a play-within-a-play as her main framing device. To put it another, more trenchant, way, this was not *just the world of a cabaret*; it was *the whole world as cabaret!*

Each character was a voyeur of everything that transpired within and outside the Kit Kat Klub. The club itself was part of a proscenium arch stage (the Avon Theatre, once an opera house in days long gone). Some of the characters functioned as stagehands who operated the spotlights, the stage revolve, the heavy doors, and the fuse box or who moved the set pieces. The show began as a flickering black-and-white movie reel, replete with scratched and blurred celluloid, with the Emcee (numbers drawn all over his body) doing a countdown in a traditional German expressionist way. When the movie strip ended, the Emcee (Bruce Dow) entered through a beaded curtain accompanied by four musicians. Where the Prince versions had used a full pit orchestra and a five-piece Kit Kat Klub band, and where Mendes's production had used actors to play musical instruments in place of an orchestra, Dehnert and Fox were content with a four-piece klezmer band (violin, accordion, euphonium, ukulele) and an orchestra. In chalky white makeup, white shirt, black trousers and wearing a parted Mohawk, the Emcee snapped his fingers, and low-wattage candelabras lit up in the auditorium as he introduced himself and then gave the cue for the ensemble to make an explosive entry—like characters from a past era being recalled to life. The twenty-six-member ensemble obviously represented a cross section of Berlin society. Gone was the fleshy all-girl band of the original Prince staging. Instead there was a topless aerial acrobat (with pasties) who recalled a circus routine as well as Marlene Dietrich on a swing in *The Blue Angel.* The space became a sort of colorful circus in the bold shades of a Grösz or Dix (albeit within a railway station that was disintegrating with age), rife with a sense of vibrancy and urgency, turning the opening of the musical into a thrilling, luridly colorful, startlingly sensational piece of metatheater led by the portly, dough-faced Emcee, who now wore a long red overcoat (resembling a circus ringmaster's) and a red top hat modeled to resemble a woman's corset. Beneath the coat he wore black-and-white pin-stripe trousers and spats. Costume designer David Boechler had apparently taken inspiration from the flamboyant costumes of punk rocker Marilyn Manson but also had taken care to add period details to his designs, especially in the boxer shorts for the Emcee and the union suit for Bobby and Victor that was really a combination of shorts, singlet, jacket, and trousers to be shared as twin halves by the two actors. Boechler's costumes were all of "found" materials. Many had been costume pieces from other productions or street clothes used in a different way. But everything was of the Berlin period.

Because the Emcee's part is not defined in stone by the libretto, Dow could find his own interpretation for a character who had no book scenes all his own. Though very talented, he was not anybody's immediate idea of a Berlin *conférencier,* so his approach (in concert with his director) was to strip the audience of its preconceptions and present a new image that spoke about the material and the history in an entirely fresh way. He elected to treat the role as that of an artist who had observed the entire story and provoked reactions to it. As Master of Ceremonies, he was to lead the audience through the experiences of those he had loved but were now lost forever. He was to direct an audience's attention so that it would not miss anything or, perhaps, to sinisterly misdirect its attention. His role was a very clear use of *Verfremdungsteffekt:* it drew attention to the differences between his feelings and those of other characters. Sometimes a song would put a twist on what an audience might think it had just experienced. The Emcee was the only participant who was conscious that everything we were seeing was in the past. Therefore, he knew what would happen to all of the beautiful people onstage. He could neither stop fate, nor make it happen. He did have the power to make some

Monique Lund as Max, Paul Nolan as Bobby, Ashley Burton as Gabriella Marcialla, Stephenos Christou as Sven, Bruce Dow as Emcee, Robert Yeretch as Herr Zweig, Tessa Alves as Edna A., Deirdre Halley as Alicia Graff, Lindsay Croxall as Elsa Bundchen, Sam Strasfeld as Kalman Ratz and Jewelle Blackman as Angelique Rivera in the 2008 Stratford Shakespeare Festival of Canada production (David Hou/Stratford Shakespeare Festival Archives)

things happen but only in so much as they could reveal to the audience something from the past.

He needed an audience because he had a story to relate and be understood, though not necessarily agreed with. In an interview for the Festival's *The New News* (June–July 2008, no. 1), Dow stated: "The Emcee needs Cliff to write this story. He needs the audience to hear it, because his viewpoint is this: 'I don't think you know how wonderful these people were. And if you don't hear our story, it will be as if we never lived at all.' " In the second act, with the frolic and frivolity of the first act considerably diminished, the Emcee showed a sentimental side in "If You Could See Her," evidently uncomfortable at having to play to the audience in this number. He uttered the final line not as a joke, but with contempt for those who might find it funny, and he adopted a benign, protective attitude toward the gorilla lady. A formerly grotesquely mischievous figure, the Emcee was now a warm-hearted, empathetic Everyman who nevertheless had no illusions about the invidious corruptions and flaws in the society that had bred him. Perhaps this sentimentality was linked

Bruce Dow as the Emcee in the 2008 Stratford Shakespeare Festival of Canada production (David Hou/Stratford Shakespeare Festival Archives)

to Dow's overall interpretation. His Emcee was not the highly sexualized host in the Cumming manner. He was almost paternal. Dow played him a bit like a Prospero driving the action and a bit like a Shakespearean Fool who saw the truth and was able to crystallize it for the audience.

Sex and bawdiness were strongly imprinted on the production. Victor and Bobby were explicitly gay, with Bobby planting a lingering hot kiss on Cliff's mouth and lifting him up like a sex object. In "Two Ladies," sex was friendly fun, and the point made was that sex could be done in manifold ways and with lots of different partners. The Emcee (in period underwear and socks) began it almost childishly, toying with two little rag dolls before the release, when the number expanded into raw lewdness where everything was magnified. Dow emerged from under a bed, lifted a sheet and leered at Sally (Trish Lindstrom) and Cliff (Sean Arbuckle) having sex. He then smacked a kiss on Cliff's bottom and mimed anal intercourse.

Sally Bowles was not a sweet innocent struggling to make it in Berlin cabaret. She was often in black lingerie and had a rough-hewn quality. Harsh and mercurial, she was not always likable as a character. Lindstrom looked a lot like Patti LuPone and conferred some of that diva's attack and force in the songs. Like Richardson in the Mendes version, Lindstrom was not interested in finishing touches; her Sally was seedy and unrefined to an aggressive extreme. Her first number ("Don't Tell Mama") had a naughty lesbian element, as she delivered it in the company of girls all backing her up in a song about having dirty sexual fun. "Mein Herr," with its loud staccato stamping of chairs on the floor (emblematic of the Nazi goosestep?), began with a party that you might never want to leave, with everyone at play and wet. Boisterous, sexy, casually amoral, and a little melancholy, she lacked a satiric touch, and her comedy fell a little flat. She did make the neurotic desperation compellingly dramatic, except in her anthem song—where it counted most, though the director did not regard this number as a breakdown. Lindstrom sang it like a final goodbye wave at what was about to disappear with the tides of history. According to Dehnert, Sally is standing up for the world she is in, whether it is in good shape or bad. "It's a complicated song because on one hand, the world that she is singing about is long gone. On the other hand, it is giving a political message. 'I will live my life the way I choose to live my life. The way I live my life is the way I want it to be. And I will be doing that regardless of all the forces against me.'"

A crucial dialectic in the musical is the contrast between the internal world of the cabaret and the external world, but the production eliminated this dichotomy by having the Kit Kat Klub assimilate the external world as part of total theatrical illusion. As the program credits showed, every performer had a stage identity, down to the musicians, prostitutes, boyfriends, sailors, et cetera. The Euphonium Player was called Gottfried; the Violinist, Angelique; the Ukelele Player, Kalman Ratz. The Working Man was Herr Zweig; the Circus Girl, Gabriella Marcialla; the Runaway, Alicia Graff; and so on. There was an important point to be scored by suggesting that all Berlin was caught up in a collective illusion or delusion, yet no character had genuine autonomy. Although Dehnert sought to make Clifford Bradshaw the chief outsider, Arbuckle in the role did not evince a lasting vividness because his role as narrator was swallowed by the director's concept. Instead of being Isherwood's camera, he became merely part of the play-within-a-play, a functionary rather than a protagonist who marked the boundary between the cabaret fantasy and

Trish Lindstrom as Sally
Bowles and Omar Forrest as
Victor in the 2008 Stratford
Festival of Canada
production (David Hou/
Stratford Shakespeare
Festival Archives)

the real external world. True, Dehnert choreographed his movements well, making him the careful voyeur of Sally's performance in "Mein Herr" as he sat at a table to observe who she was and what she did. Accordingly, the first part of the song was done as a live-action film, with a very large close-up of Sally's face on a screen. After the first verse, Sally and her chorus broke out into their full-scale presentational mode, revealing to Cliff the real scope of the seductiveness of this world.

Elsewhere, the metatheatrical mode turned characters into presentational types more than authentic flesh-and-blood figures. Fräulein Kost (Diana Coatsworth) and her sailors were always vaudevillian in a sense, but the vaudeville extended to other things as well. Nora McLellan's Fräulein Schneider sang "So What?" with exultant defiance, acknowledging the audience's applause, incarnating their director's sense of starting within the body of a scene and letting it grow in a Brechtian way to be a performance directly played to an audience. She and Frank Moore's Herr Schultz became a charming duo, especially in the Pineapple Song ("It Couldn't Please Me More"), during which the Emcee fanned white paper confetti into the scene as if they were in an early ballroom–dance hall. Extending the use of symbolism, "The Money Song" used the prop of a metallic cash register and showed the Emcee in a silver jacket, hat, and tiara, while the chorus wore pig snouts to denote greedy capitalists. Stratford's use of "The Money Song" contrasted with "Sitting Pretty" used initially in the first Prince production, "Money" in the film, and a mix of the two in the second Prince version. Dehnert used "The Money Song" as a riff on Cliff's experience with the underworld of smuggling and as a parable that spanned the Weimer period into our own time. The director wanted to mark this song as the point after which everything starts to go wrong for Cliff and Sally, especially as the number followed "Don't Go," a song that Kander insisted be kept in the show because of its importance to Cliff's wish to make his relationship with Sally work. "Tomorrow Belongs to Me" was begun as a solo before building into a choir-like chorus, except that the singers were not choir members. They were misfits and social outsiders, drawn one by one into the number. The reprise of this number was performed with the houselights on and the performers moving down the aisles while invoking (with the obvious complicity of the audience) the true significance of the song. It ended with a sudden blackout.

Instead of hitting her audience over the head with Nazi evil, Dehnert subtly indicated how fascist energy infiltrated the cabaret world. She used four Nazis (their faces covered) to stand in for an entire invading force. The second act showed more of a distinct difference between the book scenes and the cabaret ones, as the performance pieces either imparted a greater sense of social awareness or clung nostalgically to the past. With the Nazi presence onstage, the question became what the characters would do about it. What would Cliff do? In answer to her own question, Dehnert added a little cabaret table and chair downstage that Cliff sat at through all the cabaret numbers. This was to suggest that he was trying to work out what to do about Sally.

As the drama deepened and the lighting grew darker to mark evil closing in, the number of characters onstage dwindled gradually but evidently. There was a touch of symbolism in this, for the production was suggesting something that was happening to a specific segment of the German population as Hitler's plan for genocide took root. Dehnert elected intimation rather than explicit comment, just as she insisted on not judging the main characters for their particular choices in life: "I don't really judge the characters before a show. I think they do what they do, and I think it's important to get it all in context. But I always have a hard time deciding if they are right or wrong. I wouldn't have done what Sally did, but knowing who she is as a person, I understand why she did it. She was probably wrong. We know the ending of that period, but thousands of Berliners did not know what was happening." Dehnert reminds us that even Isherwood did not ultimately understand Sally or why she kept returning to the cabaret.

The production's "Finale Ultimo" was the only moment outside the play proper for the audience and for Cliff. The Emcee appeared in a newsreel and later asked Cliff if he had enjoyed his stay in Germany and if he had found the country beautiful. Cliff replied: "Yes, I found it—beautiful," adding to this what he had begun to write in his journal: "There was a cabaret and there was a master of ceremonies and there was a city called Berlin in a country called Germany...." Cliff's reading of the words was a way of repeating what had just been brought back onstage, and it completed the frame for the action. The actual show ended with a gunshot and a photographic montage of the entire ensemble, the photograph performing as a kind of ghost of frozen time.

By foregrounding history and its own form, Dehnert's production helped open up areas of inquiry into *Cabaret* the musical. One question it helped provoke was: what other forms of staging could work for this musical? Two sensational productions were in 2006: Rufus Norris's production at the Lyric Theatre, Shaftesbury Avenue, London; and Molly Smith's Arena Stage, Washington, D.C., production. Both elicited radically contradictory critical responses. Norris's version took the politics of the show to an extreme, asserting that late Weimar decadence became the fertile soil in which Nazism flourished. Its key point was the rancid atmosphere of the cabaret: owing a debt to thirties expressionism and to Grösz and Dix, the Kit Kat Klub was not only *louche*, it became a site of "furtive fantasy in which bums [were] bared, the crotch [was] the focal point of the choreography and a mediocrity like Sally Bowles blithely flourishe[d]" (Billington 2006). Norris's Berlin was a "wantonly, self-absorbed, liberal society carelessly dancing its way to destruction and letting xenophobia creep in en route" (Basset 2006). Even before the show actually started, patrons were given an inkling of things to come: a large stage screen with the word "Willkommen" spelled out in metallic letters stared down at them, almost an instruction rather than a greeting, as the word was split into three lines: "Will Kom Men." The central "O" was designed as a camera shutter, out of which the Emcee (a robust James Dreyfus) appeared in black lipstick, his fat, waxen jowls and glittering eyes creating an image of depravity. Its Sally Bowles (a blonde Anna Maxwell Martin) performed her first number in a vertical cage where she appeared as a nun in satin knickers. This cage would turn into a bed at Fräulein Schneider's "sex-saturated" lodging house (Billington 2006). Norris seemed to have been influenced by Leni Riefenstahl's propaganda films featuring blond Aryans and naturist lifestyles because he filled his ensemble with gorgeous nude or nearly nude men with superb physiques and added half-naked girls and boys in black tights who flung themselves up ladders and landed in the odd bed.

In many ways, this was a vigorously inventive production. Katrina Lindsay's abstract design, characterized by sharp angles, skewed perspectives, and lack of comforting corners, was threatening. Sliding panels in asymmetrical shapes suggested a culture of twisted values while also demolishing the distinction between the Kit Kat Club and the external world. Colored in fin de siècle mauve and violet, and lit by Jean Kalman, it bred ever-looming shadows that collected and thickened. Choreographed by Javier de Frutos, noted for his use of nudity, this *Cabaret* turned sex into energetic self-indulgence. A music hall threesome had gag penises swinging around like pale sausages. There were lots of pats on lots of perky bottoms. Nudists leapt around with joyful athleticism. But politics were never forgotten. Dressed in an inflated costume, the Emcee spat out paper money during "The Money Song" as two dancers used pins to pop the balloons in his trousers and deflate his sense of worth. This added irony to the economic theme: money was a flimsy basis for identity. During "If You Could See Her," the Emcee wore a suit on his front but a pig costume on his back, a reminder of the anti-Semitic imagery used by Nazis. There was another spectacular use of symmetry. At the end of act 1, naked men and women danced in the background of Sally Bowles's bed before looking upward at the sky as they climbed a ladder, cold, white light shining on their naked bodies. But at the end of act 2, this intimation of heavenly optimism was completely negated as one by one the metallic letters spelling "KABARET" were knocked down by a Nazi officer. The naked ones, their backs to the audience, huddled together upstage, but this time their faces were not turned upward, but outward—toward death, the sound of hissing gas, snow whirling around what was now a death camp.

Though mainly approving, the London critics expressed a radical division of opinion about the show. While none questioned the enduring brilliance of the musical itself, some of the lead performers drew negative reactions. As is customarily the case with actors playing Cliff, American actor Michael Hayden was faulted for being bland or won sympathy for his largely thankless role. Though she was described as graceful, appealing, and touching, Anna Maxwell Martin was also adjudged not strong enough a singer or even a hedonist, and her Sally was panned for being "as raddled as a nursery-rhyme milkmaid" (Clapp 2006). James Dreyfus's Emcee was called "magnetically reptilian" and "emphatically tawdry," but there was also sneering disapproval of his "leering drag artist of the Grand Guignol-going-on-Ann Summers school" (Basset 2006). Sheila Hancock's Fräulein Schneider ran off with the most praise, winning an Olivier for her performance. The overall production was called either a work of genius or heavy-handed. Critics generally praised its explicit social and sexual politics, as well as its liberation of the anarchic side of the Weimar, but there were jeers from some quarters for this "circus of the damned." Writing in *The Observer* (October 15, 2006), Susannah Clapp found the show to be "too emphatic" and "too purple" and complained: "No one ever has missed the politics in *Cabaret*, but this time the audience more or less gets a guide book....The smut is vivacious—but much too energetic." Michael Coveney (2006) was in general agreement, finding the production "misguidedly cast" and "disappointing....Right from the start you know Norris is making things too complicated." While acknowledging that this production had its moments, Benedict Nightingale of *The Times* (Oct. 11, 2006) felt it lacked the excitement of the Sam Mendes version, "still less the class of the [Bob Fosse] movie."

Far more classless and extreme was Molly Smith's production at Washington's Arena Stage, where men in rouge and fishnet stockings belted out "Tomorrow Belongs to Me." *The Washington Post's* Peter Marks targeted this production for looking beyond the rise of the Nazis all the way forward to Dame Edna! The director's "re-engineering" produced, he complained, "a shrill sandwich sign for all manner of editorializing." At one point, Nazi hoodlums pummeled one of the main characters and then posed with their victim in mimicry of the photographs from Abu Ghraib. The director's "sledgehammer approach" made earlier versions' (including Mendes's) tinkering "seem pantywaist." For instance, the gorilla number was performed with a cage rising in the middle of the stage, and the gorilla was shoved into it at the end of the number, its mask yanked off, and the creature sent down a trapdoor to its doom. The cast, apparently enraptured by booze, broke into the anthem "Tomorrow Belongs to Me" during the engagement party of Fräulein Schneider and Herr Schultz. These inventions made the show seem like "I Am a Billboard," commented Marks, adding that Brad Oscar's Emcee snarled menacingly from the start and became increasingly monotonous. Such an extreme makeover of the show underlines the danger of reinvention when it is exercised desperately and without respecting the tone and texture of the libretto.

Another crucial question raised by this great musical is whether *Cabaret* (in any of its major incarnations) creates a myth of Weimar Berlin that does not accord with historical fact. Peter Jelavich (a professor of German history at Johns Hopkins University and author of *Berlin Cabaret*) has argued that the Fosse film had little to do with the political and social cabarets of interwar Berlin. The Kit Kat Klub of the film is more leftist and liberal than the actual Kabaretts were, which rarely featured political songs, and if they did, these tended to be right-wing because of the politics of the era. For instance, the famous Kabarett der Komiker, Berlin's largest and longest-lasting cabaret that had hosted such stars as Yvette Guilbert, Rosa Valetti, Paul Grätz, and Ilse Bois, depoliticized itself. While recognizing that there was a flourishing gay and lesbian subculture in Berlin, Jelavich points out that it tended to be segregated and limited to a relatively small area of the city. Jelavich's view is not necessarily invalidated by Gordon's discovery of Weimar erotica and pornography, and Jelavich's dislike of the word "decadent" as applied to that society also raises a problem for any interpretation such as Fosse's, Mendes's, or Dehnert's. His objection is based on his reading of the period's history, and it focuses on the Nazis' deployment of the word "decadent" to attack gay and lesbian subculture by defaming it, though the Nazis were wary of being too aggressive in Berlin because they were not popular there.

Some cabarets did have skits and songs about Hitler, portraying him as a buffoon, but as the Nazis engaged in more and more street violence, they ceased to be a laughing matter. In 1933 many cabaret performers, writers, and musicians had to flee Germany. Some went to Holland, where they were captured and sent to holding camps in the east before their deaths were sanctioned. The ironic lesson to be learned from this history is that the Nazis permitted cabaret because it was a sly way of exposing the dangers of the art form to German society, which was becoming increasingly in thrall to "Aryan" ideology. Their strategy was to permit satirical assaults on the rise of Nazism in the confident knowledge that the satirists could not engage in direct political action. Of course, the counterargument is obvious: any action, overt or covert, can have a political consequence. Speaking or singing one's criticisms of a society may not in itself constitute a revolution, but it is nonetheless a political act—just as silence can be construed as political when it is forced on the artist by decree or elected by the artist as a symbol of passive resistance.

The real point in Dehnert's version would be the historical effects of Nazism as mirrored in the cabaret world. The decadence of her vision, with its open bisexuality, drug use, and pornographic sex, gives a segment of Berlin's population a level of freedom they have never experienced before. Many become so enraptured by this freedom within the cabaret world that they are distracted from or unaware of what is happening outside. When the kick line at the beginning of act 2 segues into a Nazi goose-step, this is an omen, not simply a laughing matter. Sally Bowles, however, would be one who refuses to think of political and social implications. She merely wants a good time, so she uses sex and alcohol to hide from the real world. In contrast, Cliff sees what is happening and warns her against it. But the crux of the issue is the Emcee, who is a principal character as well as a controlling metaphor. Friendly and charming, he is nevertheless dangerous right to the end. Under his perky exterior and musical comedy veneer is a sinister power. While he entices us to leave our troubles outside, he glosses over the fact that our troubles are actually inside the Kit Kat Klub, "pervading every moment of the show" (Miller 1996: 31). He turns reality inside out, telling us that the orchestra and the girls are beautiful when we can plainly see otherwise. He encourages us and watches with special glee as characters are destroyed. When he reprises "Willkommen" at the end, he does not finish the song, and when he bids us farewell, is he, as Scott Miller (1966: 32) trenchantly asks, "saying goodbye to us or Cliff or both? Or is he saying goodbye to the good times in Germany?" Rhetorical questions, perhaps, because he is a bizarre figure in a cautionary morality story with much larger implications for the world outside the cabaret.

CHAPTER 10

THE FUTURE: A CONCLUSION

WHEN I ASKED HAROLD PRINCE IN A LETTER WHETHER *CABARET* COULD generate future radically innovative interpretations, he replied: "You bet there will be. It invites that kind of invention, but I take great pride in knowing that our version was the first" (Prince, letter to author, February 26, 2010). His response also acknowledged that "*Cabaret* has a life of its own. It's [*sic*] genesis was in my office, with Kander and Ebb and Joe Masteroff. And our version clearly led the way to all the subsequent interpretations." When the show first appeared on Broadway, it represented a new musical form because it began with concept and libretto rather than score and because of its provocative subjects (Nazism, promiscuity, abortion). Emma Brockes (2007: 100) maintains that *Cabaret* "turns the traditional morality of the musical on its head" because "the people who pine about the future are the Hitler Youth," whose song ("Tomorrow Belongs to Me") is a Nazi anthem that shows how "we are all, to some extent, self-deceiving; it is merely a question of which deceptions we choose to sign up to." *Cabaret*'s strong literary credentials could be offered in argument against those who think they are too smart for musicals. What adds even further scale to this musical's greatness is that it has given rise to a succession of radical reimaginings that testify to its artistic strength.

Prince's original Broadway production brought Nazism into the foreground and literally turned a mirror over audiences to show them their own features and to ask them what they would have done in place of the characters onstage. In other words, it dramatized the metaphor that was central to the production and invoked German icons (Brecht, Weill,

Dietrich, Grösz, Dix) as a way of justifying the musical's distance from the standard model of the American musical (Morris 2004: 146). The original stage version had limitations that Prince recognizes: "There's no question in my mind but that we fudged a little on the love story, but remember, it was 1966, and throwing the Joel Grey character (really, the lead) at an audience, complete with the unparalleled depression in Germany, which directly led to Adolph Hitler and the National Socialists, was an awful lot to expect of an audience, so we deliberately eschewed Cliff's homosexuality and allowed a more conventional view of Sally and Cliff's love story" (Prince, letter to author, February 26, 2010). The Fosse film (that many British critics used as their standard for measuring subsequent stage versions of the musical) was able to take advantage of social change and went farther into political and sexual darkness, making even its choreography frenetically expressionistic of the decadence into which Berlin was plunged. Then came Sam Mendes's version, which seemed to locate its "master scenario" in Susan Sontag's essay "Fascinating Fascism," with the Kit Kat Klub's swallowing up the reality outside and beyond it. This production was about "life as an entertainment state, where anything and everything—including the symbols and accoutrements of the Third Reich—[could] be reduced to a form of amusement" and where the Emcee was the spirit of the Zeitgeist, though not simply Weimar decadence but "the spectacle of a society (ours!)" in which politics, journalism, and news had all become subdivisions of show business (Copeland 1999: 88–89). Amanda Dehnert turned the show business metaphor into a central conceit in her Stratford Festival production but used German politics, sociology, economics, and sexual practice as points of departure for her metaphor and the libretto.

Each of these groundbreaking productions had "new" interpretations of Sally, Cliff, and the Emcee. Sally went from being a naive English girl who simply was too frivolous to understand the serious demonic changes overtaking Germany to a seedy cocaine-sniffing party girl. Fosse even changed the nationality of Sally by making her flamboyantly American, while almost every director tinkered with the sexual identity of Cliff, making him morph from a conflicted bisexual to a gay man who was either finding a way back into the closet or reveling in the polymorphously perverse character of Berlin. Like Sally, Cliff also suffered a nationality change, going from English to American for the Hal Prince productions, then back to English for the Fosse film, and back to American again after. As for the Emcee, Joel Grey's interpretation for Prince (according to

Roger Copeland) was "pre-sexual" (think Michael Jackson), whereas Alan Cumming's was "pan-sexual" (think "Jim Morrison welded to the androgynous glitter of David Bowie") (Copeland 1999: 26). Grey's Emcee for Fosse did have more of a sinister and sexual edge than for Prince—as did Cumming's for Mendes, but in both these versions the Emcee started as evil and ended as evil, without changing in between, while Bruce Dow's Emcee was a sort of Everyman with the power to select and distort aspects of reality in order to manipulate an audience. James Dreyfus's Emcee was the least charming, most rancid one, though his bloated physiognomy (far past its prime) had a lot to do with the interpretation's sinister elements.

What will the future bring to *Cabaret*, or, perhaps to phrase it in a more intriguing way, what will *Cabaret* bring to the future? As with classic plays, every era can influence the way in which a story is told and the way in which its main characters are delineated. There is, for example, a different Hamlet for every generation, perhaps for every nation. It isn't simply a matter of difference in acting technique or style. Of course, a Gielgud or Olivier or Scofield would look, sound, and act differently in the part, as would a David Warner, Ken Branagh, Ralph Fiennes, or Jude Law. An English Hamlet or an Italian one would be temperamentally different from a German or Russian one, just as a Victorian Hamlet would differ radically from a twentieth or twenty-first-century one. But the options are rather less for characters in a musical, perhaps because the libretto and score permit less experimentation. It seems that we have already had the full gamut of possibilities for Sally or Cliff or the Emcee, so the question becomes what other ways are there to stage this musical? Should the musical modify its libretto by using more of the Isherwood material? Should John Kander tamper with his own score and make it more Germanic? Would *Cabaret* gain from a larger use of German expressionism? Of course, such radical revisions would prompt a serious consideration: would it still be *Cabaret* or a new, quite different musical with a different soul?

Cabaret has already changed a little (or more) with each new revision. In fact, it already bears an international passport, and this means that it is no longer chained to the Ur-text, that is, the first libretto and form of presentation. Apart from the critically acclaimed 1993 Sam Mendes production at the Donmar Warehouse, there have been two other major London revivals: in 1986, at the Strand Theatre, choreographed and directed by Gillian Lynne; and the Rufus Norris version in 2006 at the

Lyric Theatre, which won enough critical favor and audience approval to merit a UK tour with a regional company in 2008–09. Mendes also did an Australian production in 2002 in Sydney and Melbourne. Several international productions have also added to the chronicle of this musical, including a 2003 Spanish production at the Teatro Nuevo Alcala in Madrid, directed by B. T. McNicholl with Spanish performers acting in their native language, and a 2005–06 Mexican production, directed by Felipe Fernández del Paso. France has also seen *Cabaret* in a French-language version at the Folies Bergère in 2006. More exotically, there has been most recently (2008) a Cuban version that performed major surgery on the Masteroff libretto by grafting a new libretto from Nicolas Dorr, with contributions from well-known Cuban dramaturges and directors (Héctor Quintero and Jose Milian) and a Peruvian production (2009) at the Teatro Segura in Lima, directed by Mateo Chiarella. The Cuban version was the most radical: under the general direction of Tony Diaz, it renamed the show *Musical Cabaret,* added musical variations, new choreography, and a distinctly socialist torque that amounted to a fervent denunciation of fascism. It is very conceivable that there will eventually be versions of *Cabaret* in other languages to extend the reputation of this musical's greatness.

PRODUCTION NOTES

ORIGINAL BROADWAY PRODUCTION

Cabaret was first presented by Harold Prince, in association with Ruth Mitchell, at the Broadhurst Theatre, New York, on November 20, 1966. It ran for 1,166 performances. The cast was as follows:

Master of Ceremonies (Emcee), *Joel Grey*
German Sailors, *Bruce Becker, Steven Boockvor, Roger Briant, Edward Nolfi*
Clifford Bradshaw, *Bert Convy*
Frau Wendel, *Mara Landi*
Ernst Ludwig, *Edward Winter*
Herr Wendel, *Eugene Morgan*
Customs Officer, *Howard Kahl*
Frau Kruger, *Miriam Lehmann-Haupt*
Fräulein Schneider, *Lotte Lenya*
Herr Erdmann, *Sol Frieder*
Fräulein Kost, *Peg Murray*
Herr Schultz, *Jack Gilford*
Girl, *Tresha Kelly*
Sally Bowles, *Jill Haworth*

Kit Kat Girls
Maria, *Pat Gosling*
Lulu, *Lynn Winn*
Rosie, *Bonnie Walker*
Fritzie, *Marianne Selbert*
Texas, *Kathie Dalton*
Frenchie, *Barbara Alston*

Bobby, *Jere Admire*
Victor, *Bert Michaels*
Felix, *Robert Sharp*
Greta, *Jayme Mylroie*

Girl Orchestra, *Maryann Burns, Janice Mink, Nancy Powers, Viola Smith*
Two Ladies, *Mary Ebara, Rita O'Connor*
Maître D', *Frank Bouley*
Max, *John Herbert*
Bartender, *Ray Baron*
Directed by *Harold Prince*
Dances and Cabaret Numbers by *Ronald Field*
Scenery by *Boris Aronson*
Costumes by *Patricia Zipprodt*
Lighting by *Jean Rosenthal*
Musical Direction by *Harold Hastings*
Orchestrations by *Don Walker*
Dance Arrangements by *David Baker*

MUSICAL NUMBERS

1. Willkommen
2. So What?
3. Don't Tell Mama
4. Telephone Song
5. Perfectly Marvelous
6. Two Ladies
7. It Couldn't Please Me More (A Pineapple)
8. Tomorrow Belongs to Me
9. Why Should I Wake Up?
10. The Money Song (Sitting Pretty)
11. Married
12. Meeskite
13. Entr'acte
14. If You Could See Her (Gorilla Song)
15. What Would You Do?
16. Cabaret
17. Finale

1987 BROADWAY PRODUCTION

Cabaret opened October 27, 1987, at the Imperial Theatre before transferring to the Minskoff Theatre (June 4, 1988). It ran a total of 261 performances. The cast was as follows:

Master of Ceremonies (Emcee), *Joel Grey*
Clifford Bradshaw, *Greg Edelman*
Ernst Ludwig, *David Staller*
Customs Officer, *David Vosburgh*
Fräulein Schneider, *Regina Resnik*
Fräulein Kost, *Nora Mae Lyng*
Herr Schultz, *Werner Klemperer*
German Sailor, *Jim Wolfe*
Sally Bowles, *Alyson Reed*
Frau Wendel, *Mara Landi*
Victor, *Lars Rosager*
Bobby, *Michelan Sisti*
Max, *Jon Vandertholen*
German Sailors, *Mark Dovey, Greg Shanuel, Jim Wolfe*
Kit Kat Girls, *Laurie Crochet, Noreen Evans, Caitlin Larsen, Sharon Lawrence, Mary Rotella*
Girl Orchestra, *Sheila Cooper, Barbara Merjan, Panchali Null, Eve Potfora, Viola Smith*
Ensemble, *Steve Chandler, Bill Derifield, Karen Fraction, Laurie Franks, Ruth Gottschall, Mary Munger, Aurelio Padron, Steve Potfora*

Directed by *Harold Prince*
Dances and Cabaret Numbers by *Ronald Field*
Scenery by *David Chapman* (after *Boris Aronson*)
Costumes by *Patricia Zipprodt*
Lighting by *Marc B. Weiss, Susan A. White*
Musical Direction by *Donald Chan*
Orchestrations by *Michael Gibson*
Dance Arrangements by *Donald Melrose*

THE 1998 SAM MENDES VERSION

Cabaret opened March 19, 1998, at the Kit Kat Klub (formerly Henry Miller's Theatre) before transferring to Studio 54. It ran for 2,377 performances. The cast was as follows:
(in order of appearance)

Emcee, *Alan Cumming*
The Kit Kat Girls:
Rosie, *Christina Pawl*
Lulu, *Erin Hill*
Frenchie, *Joyce Chittick*
Texas, *Leenya Rideout*
Fritzie, *Michele Pawk*
Helga, *Kristin Olness*
The Kit Kat Boys:
Bobby, *Michael O'Donnell*
Victor, *Brian Duguay*
Hans, *Bill Szobody*
Herman, *Fred Rose*
Sally Bowles, *Natasha Richardson*
Clifford Bradshaw, *John Benjamin Hickey*
Ernst Ludwig, *Denis O'Hare*
Customs Official, *Fred Rose*
Fräulein Schneider, *Mary Louise Wilson*
Fräulein Kost, *Michele Pawk*
Rudy, *Bill Szobody*
Herr Schultz, *Ron Rifkin*
Max, *Fred Rose*
Gorilla, *Joyce Chittick*
Boy Soprano (recording), *Alex Bowen*
The Kit Kat Band:
Patrick Vaccariello, Fred Lassen, Gary Tillman, Bill Sloat, Rich Raffio, Christina Pawl, Bill Szobody, Denis O'Hare, Michael O'Donnell, Kristin Olness, Brian Duguay, Joyce Chittick, Erin Hill, Leenya Rideout, Fred Rose, Michele Pawk, Linda Romoff, Vance Avery
All other parts played by members of the Company

Directed by *Sam Mendes*
Co-Directed and Choreographed by *Rob Marshall*
Dances and Incidental Music by *David Krane*
Original Dance Music by *David Baker*
Set and Club Design by *Robert Brill*
Costumes by *William Ivey Long*
Lighting by *Peggy Eisenhauer, Mike Baldassari*
Musical Direction by *Patrick Vaccariello*
Orchestrations by *Michael Gibson*
Sound Design by *Brian Ronan*

MUSICAL NUMBERS

1. Willkommen
2. So What?
3. Don't Tell Mama
4. Mein Herr
5. Perfectly Marvelous
6. Two Ladies
7. It Couldn't Please Me More
8. Tomorrow Belongs to Me
9. Maybe This Time
10. Money
11. Married
12. Tomorrow Belongs to Me (Reprise)
13. Entr'Acte
14. Kick Line
15. Married (Reprise)
16. If You Could See Her
17. What Would You Do?
18. I Don't Care Much
19. Cabaret
20. Finale

THE 2008 STRATFORD FESTIVAL
OF CANADA VERSION

This version played in the Stratford repertory at the Avon Theatre from May 29 to October 25, 2008, for 109 performances, excluding 9 previews. The cast was as follows:

Emcee, *Bruce Dow*
Angelique Rivera as the Violinist, *Jewelle Blackman*
Gottfried von Schwartzenbaum as the Euphonium Player, *Phillip Hughes*
Kalman Ratz as the Third Sailor and Ukelele Player, *Sam Strasfeld*
Edna A. as the Taxi Man, *Tessa Alves*
Max as the Owner, *Monique Lund*
Alicia Graff as the Runaway, *Deidrea Halley*
Sven as the First Sailor, *Stephenos Christou*
Victor as the Boyfriend, *Omar Forrest*
Bobby as the Boyfriend, *Paul Nolan*

Fräulein Kost as the Prostitute, *Diana Coatsworth*
Tobi as the Second Sailor, *Julius Sermona*
Elsa Bundchen as the Sausage Girl, *Lindsay Croxall*
Louis/Louise as the Boy/Girl, *Jordan Bell*
Rosi Müller as the New Tart, *Naomi Costain*
Erika Mann as the Sister, *Kelly-Ann Evans*
Klaus Mann as the Brother, *Andrew Moyes*
Herr Zweig as the Working Man, *Robert Yeretch*
Gabriella Marcialla as the Circus Girl, *Ashley Burton*
Clifford Bradshaw, *Sean Arbuckle*
Ernst Ludwig, *Cory O'Brien*
Fräulein Schneider, *Nora McLellan*
Herr Schultz, *Frank Moore*
Sally Bowles, *Trish Lindstrom*
Swing, *Marc Kimelman*
Swing, *Carla Giuliani*
Musicians, *Eugene Laskiewicz, Joseph Macerollo*

Directed by *Amanda Dehnert*
Musical Direction by *Rick Fox*
Choreography by *Kelly Devine*
Set Design by *Douglas Paraschuk*
Costume Design by *David Boechler*
Lighting Design by *Kevin Fraser*
Sound Design by *Jim Neil*
Fight Direction by *John Stead*
Video by *Sean Nieuwenhuis*
Assistant Direction by *Phillip Hughes*
Assistant Choreography by *Mike Jackson*
Associate Musical Director *Laura Burton*
Assistant Design by *Katherine Lubienski*
Assistant Lighting Design by *Christina Cicko, Gareth Crew*
Assistant Sound Design by *Brad Stephenson*
Dance Captain *Julius Sermona*
Fight Captain *Phillip Hughes*

MUSICAL NUMBERS

1. Willkommen
2. So What?

3. Don't Tell Mama
4. Mein Herr
5. Perfectly Marvelous
6. Two Ladies
7. It Couldn't Please Me More
8. Tomorrow Belongs to Me
9. Don't Go
10. The Money Song
11. Married
12. Tomorrow Belongs to Me (reprise)
13. Entr'Acte
14. Kickline
15. Married (reprise)
16. If You Could See Her
17. What Would You Do?
18. I Don't Care Much
19. Cabaret
20. Finale Ultimo

BROADWAY AWARDS AND NOMINATIONS

1966 PRODUCTION

· Tony Award for Best Musical (**winner**)
· Tony Award for Best Composer and Lyricist (**winner**)
· Tony Award for Best Actor in a Musical (Jack Gilford, nominee)
· Tony Award for Best Actress in a Musical (Lotte Lenya, nominee)
· Tony Award for Best Featured Actor in a Musical (**Joel Grey, winner**; Edward Winter, nominee)
· Tony Award for Best Featured Actress in a Musical (**Peg Murray, winner**)
· Tony Award for Best Scenic Design (**Boris Aronson, winner**)
· Tony Award for Best Costume Design (**Patricia Zipprodt, winner**)
· Tony Award for Best Choreography (**Ron Field, winner**)
· Tony Award for Best Direction of a Musical (**Hal Prince, winner**)

1987 REVIVAL

· Tony Award for Best Featured Actor in a Musical (Werner Klemperer, nominee)
· Tony Award for Best Featured Actress in a Musical (Alyson Reed and Regina Resnik, nominees)

· Tony Award for Best Revival (nominee)
· Drama Desk Award for Outstanding Actor in a Musical (Joel Grey, nominee)
· Drama Desk Award for Outstanding Director of a Musical (Hal Prince, nominee)
· Drama Desk Award for Outstanding Revival (nominee)

1998 REVIVAL

· Tony Award for Best Revival of a Musical (**winner**)
· Tony Award for Best Actor in a Musical (**Alan Cumming, winner**)
· Tony Award for Best Actress in a Musical (**Natasha Richardson, winner**)
· Tony Award for Best Featured Actor in a Musical (**Ron Rifkin, winner**)
· Tony Award for Best Featured Actress in a Musical (Mary Louise Wilson, nominee)
· Tony Award for Best Costume Design (nominee)
· Tony Award for Best Lighting Design (nominee)
· Tony Award for Best Choreography (nominee)
· Tony Award for Best Direction of a Musical (nominee)
· Tony Award for Best Orchestrations (nominee)
· Drama Desk Award for Outstanding Revival of a Musical (**winner**)
· Drama Desk Award for Outstanding Actor in a Musical (**Alan Cumming, winner**)
· Drama Desk Award for Outstanding Actress in a Musical (**Natasha Richardson, winner**)
· Drama Desk Award for Outstanding Featured Actress in a Musical (Michele Pawk, nominee)
· Drama Desk Award for Outstanding Choreography (nominee)
· Drama Desk Award for Outstanding Direction of a Musical (nominee)
· Drama Desk Award for Outstanding Orchestrations (nominee)
· Drama Desk Award for Outstanding Set Design of a Musical (nominee)
· Drama Desk Award for Outstanding Costume Design (nominee)
· Drama Desk Award for Outstanding Lighting Design (nominee)
· Theatre World Award (**Alan Cumming, winner**)
· Astaire Award for Best Dancer (The Kit Kat Girls & Boys: *Joyce Chittick, Erin Hill, Kristin Olness, Michele Pawk, Christina Pawl, Leenya Rideout, Brian Duguay, Michael O'Donnell, Fred Rose, Bill Szobody*)

THE 1972 MOVIE VERSION

Liza Minnelli, *Sally Bowles*
Joel Grey, *Master of Ceremonies*
Michael York, *Brian Roberts*

Helmut Grieme, *Maximilian von Heune*
Fritz Wepper, *Fritz Wendel*
Marisa Berenson, *Natalia Landauer*
Elisabeth Neumann-Viertel, *Fräulein Schneider*
Helen Vita, *Fräulein Kost*
Sigrid von Richthofen, *Fräulein Mayr*
Gerd Vespermann, *Bobby*
Ralf Wolter, *Herr Ludwig*
Georg Hartmann, *Willi*
Ricky Renee, *Elke (as Ricky Renee)*
Estrongo Nachama, *Cantor*
Kathryn Doby, *Kit Kat Dancer*
Inge Jaeger, *Kit Kat Dancer*
Angelika Koch, *Kit Kat Dancer*
Helen Velkovorska, *Kit Kat Dancer*
Gitta Schmidt, *Kit Kat Dancer*
Louise Quick, *Kit Kat Dancer*
Oliver Collignon, *Hitler Youth Singer* (uncredited)
Director, *Bob Fosse*
Producer, *Cy Feuer* for ABC Pictures
Associate Producer, *Harold Nebenzal*
Original Music, *John Kander*
Cinematography, *Geoffrey Unsworth*
Film Editing, *David Bretherton*
Casting, *Renate Neuchi*
Production Design, *Rolf Zehetbauer*
Art Direction, *Hans Jürgen Kiebach* (as Jürgen Kiebach)
Set Direction, *Herbert Strabel*
Costumes, *Charlotte Flemming*
Makeup, *Susi Krause, Gus Le Pre, Raimund Stangl*
Sound, *David Hildyard*
Dubbing, *Robert Knudson, Arthur Piantadosi*
Editing, *David Ramirez*
Music Conductor, *Ralph Burns*
Music Arranger, *Ralph Burns*
Composer, Additional Songs, *John Kander, Fred Ebb*
Music Editor, *Illo Endrulat, Karola Storr, Robert Tracy*
Stager, Musical Numbers, *Bob Fosse*
Choreograph Assistant, *John Sharpe*
Dialogue Coach, *Osman Ragheb*
Script Supervisor, *Trudy von Trother*

1972 ACADEMY AWARD NOMINATIONS AND WINS

Best Picture (nomination)
Best Actress (**winner**) *Liza Minnelli*
Best Supporting Actor (**winner**) *Joel Grey*
Best Director (**winner**) *Bob Fosse*
Best Adapted Screenplay (nomination) *Jay Presson Allen*
Best Cinematography (**winner**) *Geoffrey Unsworth*
Best Art Direction–Set Direction (**winner**) *Rolf Zehetbauer and Jürgen Kiebach; Herbert Strabel*
Best Sound (**winner**) *Robert Knudson and David Hildyard*
Best Adapted Score (**winner**) *Ralph Burns*
Best Film Editing (**winner**) *David Bretherton*

NATIONAL BOARD OF REVIEW AWARDS

Best English Language Film, Best Supporting Actor (*Joel Grey* tied with *Al Pacino (The Godfather)*), Best Director (*Bob Fosse*), Best Supporting Actress (*Marisa Berenson*)

NATIONAL SOCIETY OF FILM CRITICS AWARDS

Best Supporting Actor (*Joel Grey* tied with *Eddie Albert (The Heartbreak Kid)*)

HOLLYWOOD FOREIGN PRESS ASSOCIATION GOLDEN GLOBE AWARDS

Best Picture (Comedy or Musical), Best Actress (Comedy or Musical) (*Liza Minnelli*), Best Supporting Actor (*Joel Grey*)

BRITISH ACADEMY OF FILM AND TELEVISION ARTS (BAFTA)

AWARDS AND NOMINATIONS

Best Film (**winner**)
Best Actress (**winner**) *Liza Minnelli*
Best Director (**winner**) *Bob Fosse*

Best Promising Newcomer to Leading Roles in Film (**winner**) *Joel Grey*
Best Soundtrack (**winner**) *David Hildyard, Robert Knudson, Arthur Piantadosi*
Best Costume Design (nomination) *Charlotte Flemming*
Best Screenplay (nomination) *Jay Presson Allen*
Best Supporting Actress (nomination) *Marisa Berenson*
Best Art Direction (**winner**) *Rolf Zehetbauer*
Best Cinematography (**winner**) *Geoffrey Unsworth*
Best Editing (nomination) *David Bretherton*

ORIGINAL BROADWAY CAST RECORDING CDs

1966 Original Cast Recording (with Joel Grey, Jill Haworth, Lotte Lenya, Jack Gilford, Bert Convy)
Sony Classical/Columbia/Legacy (**SK 60533**). Original Release Date: June 2, 1998 (the soundtrack originally appeared on disk in 1966)
1998 Original Cast Recording (with Alan Cumming, Natasha Richardson, Mary Louise Wilson)
RCA Victor (**09026 63173**). Original Release Date: June 30, 1998

THE 1972 FILM VERSION SOUNDTRACK

Film Soundtrack (with Liza Minnelli, Joel Grey)
MCA **250 428–2**
Winner of the Grammy Hall of Fame Award (inducted 2008)

Ackerman, Marianne. "Cabaret vs. Shakespeare." *The Gazette*, 2 June 1987.

Atkey, Mel. *Broadway North (The Dream of a Canadian Musical Theatre)*. Toronto: Natural Heritage Books, 2006.

Alleman, Richard. "Back to the Cabaret." *Playbill*, vol. 87, no.11 (Nov.1987): 8–12.

Alpert, Hollis. *Broadway! 125 Years of Musical Theatre*. New York: Little, Brown and Co., 1991.

Appignanesi, Lisa. *Cabaret: The First Hundred Years*. London: Methuen, 1984.

Aronson, Arnold. *American Set Design*. New York: Theatre Communications Group, 1993.

Bacon, James. "New Bid by Convy." *Newark Evening News*, 6 April 1961.

Banfield, Stephen. *Sondheim's Broadway Musicals*. Ann Arbor: University of Michigan Press, 1993.

Barclay, Charlotte. "Lighting a Show Is a Man-Sized Job—for a Woman." *New York Herald Tribune*, 16 April 1950.

Barnes, Clive. "Grey Eclipses." *New York Post Weekend*, 23 Oct. 1987.

Basset, Kate. Review of *Cabaret*. *The Independent* (London), 15 Oct. 2006.

Beckerman, Bernard, and Howard Siegman, eds. *On Stage: Selected Theater Reviews from the New York Times, 1920–1970*. New York: Arno, 1973.

Bergman, David, ed. *Camp Grounds: Style And Homosexuality*. Amherst: University of Massachusetts Press, 1993.

Billington, Michael. "Cabaret." *The Guardian*, 11 Oct. 2006.

Blakeley, Godfrey. "Jill Haworth: Starlet into Star." *New York World Journal Tribune*, 20 Nov. 1966.

Block, Geoffrey. *Enchanted Evenings: The Broadway Musical from Show Boat to Sondheim*. New York: Oxford University Press, 1997.

Blumenfeld, Ralph. "They Applauded." Profile profile of Ron Field. *New York Post*, 23 April 1970.

Bolton, Whitney. "Cabaret." *New York Morning Telegraph*, 22 Nov. 1966. NYPL clipping folder.

Bordman, Gerald. *American Musical Theatre: A Chronicle.* New York: Oxford University Press, 1978.

"Bowles Players." *Radio Times* (London), 20–26 April 1974.

Brockes, Emma. *What Would Barbra Do? (How Musicals Changed My Life).* New York: Harper Collins, 2007.

Brown, John Mason. *As They Appear.* New York: McGraw-Hill, 1952.

———. "Star Bright." *Saturday Review,* 22 Dec. 1951.

Brown, Mark. "For Cabaret, Life Is a West End Battle." *The Guardian,* 12 Sept. 2008.

Brown, Peter. "Cabaret." *The London Theatre Guide Online,* 11 Oct. 2006.

Bryden, Ronald. "Cabaret." *The Observer,* 3 March 1968.

Bryer, Jackson R., and Richard A. Davison, eds. *The Art of the American Musical: Conversations with the Creators.* New Brunswick, N.J.: Rutgers University Press, 2008.

Bunce, Alan N. "Cabaret." *Christian Science Monitor,* 28 Nov. 1966.

Canby, Vincent. "At the Heart of a Spellbinding 'Cabaret,' a Star." *New York Times,* 29 March 1998.

Carroll, Kathleen. "Minnelli and Grey Star in *Cabaret.*" *Sunday News,* 13 June 1971.

Chapman, John. "*Cabaret* Has Fine Production, Good Cast, Downhill Story Line." *Daily News,* 21 Nov. 1966.

Citron, Stephen. *Sondheim and Lloyd-Webber: The New Musical.* London: Chatto & Windus, 2001.

Clapp, Susannah. "Fascism by Numbers." *The Observer,* 15 Oct. 2006.

Clum, John M. *Something for The Boys: Musical Theater and Gay Culture.* New York: St. Martin's, 1999.

Clurman, Harold. *The Collected Works of Harold Clurman: Six Decades of Commentary on Theatre, Dance, Music, Film, Arts and Letters.* Edited by Marjorie Loggia and Glenn Young. New York: Applause Books, 1994.

———. *The Divine Pastime: Theatre Essays.* New York: Macmillan, 1974.

Cole, Gloria. "Life is a Cabaret: Joel Grey Talks about His Years on the Stage." *Fairpress,* 6 April 1989.

Conlogue, Ray. "Something of an Emptiness Inside Cabaret." *Globe and Mail,* 2 June 1987.

Cooke, Richard P. "Princely Entertainment." *The Wall Street Journal,* 22 Nov. 1966. NYPL clipping folder.

Copeland, Roger. "Cabaret at the End of the World." *American Theatre,* Jan. 1999.

Coveney, Michael. "Review Round-up: Critics Willkommen Back Cabaret." www.whatsonstage.com, 11 Oct. 2006.

Crew, Robert. "Come to the Cabaret and Taste Its Delights." *Toronto Star*, 2 June 1987.

de Jongh, Nicholas. "Bowled over by Cabaret." *London Evening Standard*, 11 Oct. 2006.

Engel, Lehman. *Their Words Are Music: The Great Theatre Lyricists and Their Lyrics.* New York: Crown Publishers, 1975.

———. *Words with Music: Creating The Broadway Musical.* Updated and revised by Howard Kissel. New York: Applause Theatre and Cinema Books, 2006.

Everett-Green, Robert. "Nazi Music of 'Dishonour' Revived." *Globe and Mail*, 31 July 1993.

Ewen, David. *American Songwriters.* New York: H. W. Wilson, 1987.

Farber, Stephen. "*Cabaret* May Shock Kansas." *New York Times*, 20 Feb. 1972.

Farneth, David, ed. *Lenya the Legend: A Pictorial Autobiography.* Woodstock, N.Y.: The Overlook Press, 1998.

Feingold, Michael. "Lotte Lenya, 1898–1981." Obituary. *Village Voice*, 2 Dec. 1981.

Feuer, Cy, with Ken Gross. *I Got the Show Right Here.* New York: Applause, 2003.

Feur, Jane. *The Hollywood Musical.* Bloomington: Indiana University Press, 1982.

Flagler, J. M. "Cabaret." *Look*, Nov. 1966.

Flinn, Denny Martin. *The Great American Book Musical: A Manifesto/A Monograph/A Manual.* New York: Limelight Editions, 2008.

Foulis, Rhona. "Cabaret." *Culture Wars*, 16 Oct. 2006.

Frank, Michael. "Fred Ebb: *Cabaret*'s Lyricist on Central Park." *Architecture Digest*, Nov. 1995.

Franklin, Nancy. "The Gathering Storm." *New Yorker*, 6 April 1998.

Gänzl, Kurt. *The Blackwell Guide to the Musical Theatre on Record.* Oxford: Basil Blackwell Ltd., 1990.

Garber, Marjorie. *Vested Interests: Cross-Dressing and Cultural Anxiety.* London: Routledge, Chapman and Hall, 1992.

———. *Vice Versa: Bisexuality and the Eroticism of Everyday Life.* New York: Simon & Schuster, 1995.

Gardner, Paul. "Bob Fosse Off His Toes." *New York*, 16 Dec. 1974.

Gassner, John. *Dramatic Soundings: Evaluations and Retractions Culled from 30 years of Dramatic Criticism.* New York: Crown Publishers, 1968.

Gates, Gary Paul. "Broadway's Prince Charming." *Holiday*, April 1966.

Gilman, Richard. "I Am a Musical." *Newsweek*, 5 Dec. 1966.

Glover, William. "Jill Haworth 'Unprepared.'" *Newark Evening News*, 16 Oct. 1966.

Gordon, Mel. *Voluptuous Panic: The Erotic World of Weimar Berlin* (expanded edition). Los Angeles: Feral House, 2006.

Gottfried, Martin. *All His Jazz: The Life And Death of Bob Fosse.* New York: Bantam, 1990.

———. *Broadway Musicals.* New York: Abradale, 1984.

————. *"Cabaret." Women's Wear Daily,* 2 1 Nov. 1966.

Graeber, Laurel. "Stage Presence." *DNR The Magazine,* May 1986.

Green, Stanley. *Encyclopedia of the Musical Theatre.* New York: Da Capo,1976.

Grösz, George. *Ecce Homo.* Introduction by Lee Revens. New York: Jack Brussel, 1965.

Grubb, Kevin Boyd. *Razzle Dazzle: The Life and Work of Bob Fosse.* New York: St. Martin's, 1989.

Guernsey, Otis L., Jr., ed. *Broadway Song & Story: Playwrights/Lyricists/Composers Discuss Their Hits.* New York: Dodd, Mead, 1985.

————. *Curtain Times: The New York Theater, 1965–1987.* New York: Applause, 1987.

————. *Playwrights, Lyricists, Composers on Theater.* New York: Dodd, Mead, 1974.

Guidry, Frederick H. *"Cabaret Opens." Christian Science Monitor,* 1 1 Oct. 1966.

Gussow, Mel. "Harold Prince." *Newsweek,* 2 Dec. 1968.

Hale, Wanda. *"Exodus Teen Lover Yearns to see Bronx." New York Daily News,* 12 Feb. 1961.

Haun, Henry. "What Makes Hal Run." *New York Daily News,* 14 June 1987.

Hausam, Willy, ed. *The New American Musical: An Anthology from the End of the Century.* (Includes *Floyd Collins; Rent; Parade;* and *The Wild Party*). New York: Theatre Communications Group, 2003.

Hewes, Henry. "Not Quite a Camera." *Saturday Review,* 10 Dec. 1966.

Hipp, Edward Sothern. "Cabaret." *Newark Evening News,* 2 1 Nov. 1966. NYPL clipping folder.

Hirsch, Foster. *Harold Prince and the American Musical Theatre.* Cambridge: Cambridge University Press, 1989. Expanded edition with an updated foreword by Harold Prince. New York: Applause, 2005.

————. *Kurt Weill on Stage: From Berlin to Broadway.* New York: Alfred A. Knopf, 2002.

Hirsch, Samuel. "Musical *Cabaret* Opens with Lotte Lenya at Best." *Boston Herald,* 1 1 Oct.1966.

Hirschhorn, Clive. *The Hollywood Musical* (revised and updated). New York: Portland House, 1991.

Hischak, Thomas. *The Oxford Companion to the American Musical (Theatre, Film, and Television).* New York: Oxford University Press, 2008.

Ilson, Carol. *Harold Prince: From Pajama Game to Phantom of the Opera.* Ann Arbor: UMI Research Press, 1989.

Isherwood, Christopher. *Christopher and His Kind, 1929–1939.* New York: Farrar, Straus, Giroux, 1976.

————. *Diaries, Volume One: 1939–1960.* Edited and introduced by Katherine Bucknell. London: Methuen, 1996.

————. *Goodbye to Berlin.* London: Hogarth, 1939.

————. *Lost Years: A Memoir, 1945–1951.* Edited and introduced by Katherine Bucknell. New York: HarperCollins, 2000.

————. *Mr. Norris Changes Trains*. London: Hogarth, 1935.

Jackson, Arthur. *The Best Musicals from "Show Boat" to "Sweeney Todd."* New York: Crown Publishers, 1977.

Jacobs, Gerald. *Judi Dench: A Great Deal of Laughter*. London: Weidenfeld & Nicolson, 1985.

Jones, John Bush. *Our Musicals, Ourselves: A Social History of the American Musical Theatre*. Hanover, N.H.: Brandeis University Press, 2003.

Kael, Pauline. *Deeper into Movies*. New York: Atlantic Monthly Press, 1973.

Kakutani, Michiko. "Window on the World." *New York Times*, 26 April 1998.

Kander, John, and Fred Ebb, as told to Greg Lawrence. *Colored Lights: Forty Years of Words and Music, Show Biz, Collaboration, and All That Jazz*. New York: Faber and Faber, Inc., 2003.

Kasha, Al, and Joel Hirschhorn. *Notes on Broadway: Intimate Conversations with Broadway's Greatest Songwriters*. 1st Fireside Edition. New York: Simon & Schuster, 1987.

Kauffmann, Stanley. *Living Images: Film Comment and Criticism*. New York: Harper & Row, 1975.

Kelly, Kevin. "*Cabaret* Has the Makings of a Rare Musical." *Boston Globe*, 11 Oct. 1966.

Kehr, Dave. "Roll the Credits, Start the Music." *New York Times*, 14 Feb. 2003.

Kerr, Walter. "*Cabaret* Opens at the Broadhurst." *New York Times*, 21 Nov. 1966.

————. *Thirty Plays Hath November*. New York: Simon & Schuster, 1968.

————. "Today's Musicals: Green around The Girls?" *New York Times*, 4 Dec. 1966.

————. "Van Druten's 'Camera' Snaps a Berlin Scene." *New York Herald Tribune*, Dec. 9, 1951.

————. "When Best-Laid Plans Go Awry." *New York Times*, 15 Nov. 1987.

Kislan, Richard. *Hoofing on Broadway: A History of Show Dancing*. New York: Prentice Hall, 1987.

Kissel, Howard. "Rottin' Teuton." *New York Daily News*, 23 Oct. 1987. NYPL Clipping Folder.

Knapp, Raymond. *The American Musical and the Formation of National Identity*. Princeton, N.J.: Princeton University Press, 2005.

————. *The American Musical and the Performance of Personal Identity*. Princeton, N.J.: Princeton University Press, 2006.

Kretzmer, Herbert. "Good-time Girl Sally Has Another Success." *Daily Express*, 29 Feb. 1968.

Kuchwara, Michael. "Joel Grey Back in 'Cabaret' after 20 Years." Associated Press, 29 March, 1987.

"Landmark Symposium: *Cabaret*." *Dramatists Guild Quarterly* 19 (Summer 1982): 13–28.

Laufe, Abe. *Broadway's Greatest Musicals*. New York: Funk & Wagnalls, 1970.

Laurents, Arthur. *Mainly on Directing: Gypsy, West Side Story, and Other Musicals.* New York: Alfred A. Knopf, 2009.

Leigh, Wendy. *Liza: Born a Star.* New York: Dutton, 1993.

Lerman, Leo. "At the Theatre." *Dance Magazine,* July 1962.

Leve, James. *Kander and Ebb.* New Haven, Conn.: Yale University Press, 2009.

Lewis, Peter. "Sentiment and the Nazis Just Don't Mix." *Daily Mail,* 29 Feb. 1968.

Maloney, Alta. "*Cabaret* Sure to Arouse Broadway." *Boston Traveler,* 11 Oct. 1966.

Marcus, Frank. "Ich Bin Ein Berliner." *Plays & Players,* May 1968.

Marks, Peter. "Arena's 'Cabaret,' Heavy on the Makeup." *Washington Post,* 18 Sept. 2006.

Marowitz, Charles. "Cocktail Weenies." *Village Voice,* 25 Apr. 1968.

Mast, Gerald. *Can't Help Singin': The American Musical on Stage and Screen.* Woodstock: Overlook, 1987.

Masteroff, Joe. *Cabaret.* Vol. 2 of *Great Musicals of the American Theatre.* Edited, with an introduction and notes, by Stanley Richards. Radnor, PA: Chilton, 1976.

Masteroff, Joe, John Kander, and Fred Ebb. *Cabaret: The Illustrated Book and Lyrics.* Roundabout Theatre Company Production. Edited by Linda Sunshine. New York: Newmarket, 1999.

McClung, Bruce D. *Lady in the Dark: Biography of a Musical.* New York: Oxford University Press, 2007.

Miller, John. *Darling Judi: A Celebration of Judi Dench.* London: Weidenfeld & Nicolson, 2004.

———. *Judi Dench with a Crack in Her Voice: The Biography.* London: Weidenfeld & Nicolson, 1998.

———, ed. *Scenes from My Life.* London: Weidenfeld & Nicolson, 2006.

Miller, Scott. *From Assassins to West Side Story: The Director's Guide to Musical Theatre.* Portsmouth, N.H.: Heinemann, 1996.

Minnelli, Vincente, with Hector Arce. *I Remember It Well.* New York: Doubleday, 1974.

Mizejewski, Linda. *Divine Decadence: Fascism, Female Spectacle, and the Makings of Sally Bowles.* Princeton, N.J.: Princeton University Press, 1992.

Mordden, Ethan. *Better Foot Forward: The History of American Musical Theatre.* New York: Grossman/Viking, 1976.

———. *Broadway Babies: The People Who Made the American Musical.* New York: Oxford University Press, 1983.

———. "Celebrating America's Love of Show Biz." *New York Times,* 13 April 1997.

———. *The Happiest Corpse I've Ever Seen: The Last 25 Years of the Broadway Musical.* New York: Palgrave, 2004.

———. *The Hollywood Musical.* New York: St. Martin's, 1981.

———. *Movie Star: A Look at the Women Who Made Hollywood.* New York: St. Martin's, 1983.

———. *One More Kiss: The Broadway Musical in the 1970s.* New York: Palgrave Macmillan, 2003.

———. *Open a New Window: The Broadway Musical in the 1960s*. New York: Palgrave, 2001.

Morris, Mitchell. "*Cabaret*, America's Weimar, and Mythologies of the Gay Subject." *American Music* 22 (Spring 2004): 145–57.

Morrison, Hobe. "*Cabaret* Blatant, Vulgar; Few Attractive Qualities." *Morning Call*, 21 Nov. 1966.

Mostel, Kate, and Madeline Gilford, with Jack Gilford and Zero Mostel. *170 Years of Show Business*. New York: Random House, 1978.

Nachman, Gerald. "Color 'Cabaret' Joel Grey." *San Francisco Chronicle*, 15 May 1987.

Nadel, Norman. "Cabaret Fine New Musical." *New York World Journal Tribune*, 21 Nov. 1966. NYPL clipping folder.

———. "Hitler's Berlin in a Cabaret Mirror." *New York World Journal Tribune*, 4 Dec. 1966.

———. "The New York Harold." Interview with Harold Prince. *Theatre One* (International Theatre Institute of the U.S), 1969.

Nightingale, Benedict. "Cabaret." *The Times* (London), 11 Oct. 2006.

Norton, Elliot. "Musical Show *Cabaret* in Premiere at Shubert." *Record American*, 11 Oct. 1966.

Novick, Julius. "Schrecklich." *Village Voice*, 1 Dec. 1966.

Oliver, Edith. "It Goes." *New Yorker*, 26 May 1962.

Oppenheimer, George. "A Trio of Musicals." *Newsday*, 24 Dec. 1966.

———. "Painting Your Mood with Light." *Sunday Mirror Magazine*, 10 April 1955.

O'Toole, Fintan. "Under the Spell of a Stark 'Cabaret.'" *New York Daily News*, 20 March 1998.

Paglia, Camille. *Sexual Personae: Art and Decadence from Nefertiti to Emily Dickinson*. New Haven: Yale University Press, 1990.

———. *Vamps and Tramps*. New York: Vintage Books, 1994.

Patrick, John. "*Cabaret* Girl." *New York Sunday News*, 22 Jan. 1967.

Piazza, Paul. *Christopher Isherwood: Myth and Anti-Myth*. New York: Columbia University Press, 1978.

Powell, Dilys. *The Golden Screen: Fifty Years of Films*. Edited by George Perry. London: Pavilion Books Ltd., 1989.

Prince, Harold. *Contradictions: Notes on Twenty-six Years in the Theatre*. New York: Dodd, Mead, 1974.

Reed, Rex. "Liza's Doing *Cabaret* Like It Was." *Daily News*, 25 July 1971.

———. "Lotte Lenya." In *Do You Sleep in The Nude?* New York: New American Library, 1968.

Rich, Alan. "The Triumph of the Cliche." *New York World Journal Tribune*, 11 Dec. 1966.

Rich, Frank. "*Cabaret* and Joel Grey Return." *New York Times*, 23 Oct. 1987.

———. *Hot Seat: Theater Criticism for the New York Times, 1980–1993*. New York: Random House, 1998.

Rich, Frank, with Lisa Aronson. *The Theatre Art of Boris Aronson*. New York: Alfred A. Knopf, 1987.

Richards, David. "Willkommen, *Cabaret!*" *Washington Post*, 11 Sept. 1987.

Richards, Stanley, ed. *Great Musicals of the American Theatre*, vol. 2 (includes *A Little Night Music; Applause; Cabaret; Camelot; Fiorello!; Lady in the Dark; Leave It to me; Lost in the Stars; Man of La Mancha;* and *Wonderful Town*). Radnor, Pa., 1976.

Rizzo, Frank. "Kander and Ebb Still in Tune." *Variety*, 19 March, 2007.

Rorem, Ned. *Settling the Score: Essays on Music*. New York: Doubleday, 1989.

Sanders, Ronald. *The Days Grow Short: The Life and Music of Kurt Weill*. New York: Holt, Rinehart and Winston, 1980.

Seff, Richard. *Supporting Player: My Life upon the Wicked Stage*. New York: Xlibris, 2006.

Shorter, Eric. "Judi Dench a Spirited Sally Bowles." *Daily Telegraph*, 29 Feb. 1968.

Simon, John. "Play Reviewed." *Theater Arts*, Aug. 1962.

———. *Reverse Angle: A Decade of American Films*. New York: Clarkson N. Potter, 1982.

———. *Singularities: Essays on the Theater, 1964–1974*. New York: Random House, 1975.

———. *Uneasy Stages: A Chronicle of the New York Theatre, 1963–1973*. New York: Random House, 1973.

Solway, Diana. "The Odyssey of Joel Grey." *New York Times*, 18 Oct. 1987.

Sontag, Susan. *Against Interpretation and Other Essays*. New York: Farrar, Straus & Giroux, 1966.

———. *Under the Sign of Saturn*. New York: Farrar, Straus & Giroux, 1980.

Spencer, Charles. "A Dark and Decadent Sally." *Telegraph*, 11 Oct. 2006.

Spoto, Donald. *Lenya: A Life*. New York: Little, Brown & Co., 1989.

Steyn, Mark. *Broadway Babies Say Goodnight: Musicals Then and Now*. London: Faber and Faber, 1997.

———. "Ron Field." Obituary. *The Independent* (London), 13 Feb. 1989.

Stoop, Norma McLain. "Christopher Isherwood: A Meeting by Another River," *After Dark*, April 1975.

Sullivan, Dan. "Welcome to 'Cabaret'—For a New Generation." *L.A. Times*, 22 June 1987.

Summers, Claude J. *Christopher Isherwood*. New York: Ungar, 1980.

———. "Christopher Isherwood." In *Dictionary of Literary Biography, vol. 15: British Novelists, 1930–1959; Part 1, A–L*. Edited by Bernard Stanley Oldsey. Detroit: GaleResearch Co., 1983.

Sunshine, Linda, ed. *Cabaret: The Illustrated Book and Lyrics*. Roundabout Theatre Company Production. New York: Newmarket, 1999.

Suskin, Steven. *Opening Night on Broadway*. New York: Schirmer, 1990.

———. *The Sound of Broadway Music: A Book of Orchestrators and Orchestrations.* New York: Oxford University Press, 2009.

Swain, Joseph P. *The Broadway Musical: A Critical and Musical Survey.* New York: Oxford University Press, 1990.

Taubman, Howard. *The Making of the American Theatre.* New York: Coward McCann, 1965.

Taylor, Paul. "Circus of the Damned." *The Independent* (London), 20 Sept. 2006.

———. "First Night: Cabaret, Lyric Theatre, London." *The Independent* (London), 11 Oct. 2006.

Vallance, Tom. "Cabaret." *Focus on Film*, Summer 1972.

Van Druten, John. *I Am a Camera.* New York: Random House, 1952.

Violett, Ellen. "Name in Lights." *Theatre Arts*, Dec. 1950.

Wallach, Allan. "Harold Prince." *Newsday*, 3 Feb. 1980. NYPL clipping folder.

Wardle, Irving. "Broadway View of Berlin." *The Times* (London), 29 Feb. 1968.

Watt, Douglas. "Off the Track." *Sunday News*, 27 Feb. 1972.

Watts, Richard, Jr. "The Innocence of Sally Bowles." *New York Post*, 21 Nov. 1966.

Wiley, Mason, and Damien Bona. *Inside Oscar: The Unofficial History of the Academy Awards.* New York: Ballantine Books, 1987.

Wilk, Max. *They're Playing Our Song.* New York: Atheneum, 1973.

Wilson, Sandy. "Letter to Editor." *Dramatists Guild Quarterly* 19 (Winter 1983): 47.

Winsten, Archer. "*Cabaret* Glows at the Ziegfeld." *New York Times*, 12 March 1973.

Wolf, Matt. "American Musicals, as Tailored by the British." *New York Times*, 28 Aug. 1994.

———. *Sam Mendes at the Donmar: Stepping into Freedom.* London: Nick Hern Books, 2002.

Wolf, Stacy. *A Problem Like Maria: Gender and Sexuality in the American Musical.* Ann Arbor: University of Michigan Press, 2002.

York, Michael. *Accidentally on Purpose: An Autobiography.* New York: Simon & Schuster, 1991.

Zolotow, Sam. "*Cabaret* Angels Receive Refunds." *New York Times*, 22 Nov. 1966.

VIDEOTAPES

(Note: Taped for the Theatre on Film and Tape Project of the Lincoln Center Library, unless otherwise noted.) *The Dick Cavett Show*, with Harold Prince. 19 Feb. 1980; 20 Feb. 1980. PBS Channel 13, New York.

"Interview with Boris Aronson in Conversation with Garson Kanin." New York, 20 March 1975.

"Interview with John Kander: Raw footage." Interviewed by Michael Kantor. New York, 29 March 1999.

AUDIO TAPES

Amanda Dehnert Interviewed by Keith Garebian. 17 July 2009.
"Aural Tapestry: The Making of 'Cabaret.'" Radio Netherlands. Chris Chambers
    speaks with Keith Garebian and Peter Jelavich. Broadcast August 2002.

MANUSCRIPT COLLECTIONS

Fred Ebb Papers. 1927–2004. LPA Mss 2005-001, 1E and 9E. New York Public
    Library for the Performing Arts.
Hal Prince Papers. New York Public Library for the Performing Arts.

INDEX

Mankiewicz, Joseph, 134
Manson, Marilyn, 182
Mantle, Mickey, 99
Marcellino, Muzzy, 99
Marcus, Frank, 27, 131–32
Mardi Gras, 96
Marinetti, Filippo Tommaso, 51
"Mark in Your Pocket, A," 29, 73, 78
Marks, Peter, 190–91
Marowitz, Charles, 131
"Married," 34, 76, 83–84, 159, 166
"Married Reprise," 76
Marshall, Rob, 156, 168, 171–73
Martin, Anna Maxwell, 189–90
Martin, Ernest, 136
Martin, Mary, 124
Marx Brothers, 21
Master Builder, The, 45
Masteroff, Joseph, 16, 24–29, 31–33,
    39, 69–72, 76, 84, 88, 95–96, 100,
    103, 106, 113, 120, 123, 126,
    158–59, 173, 193, 196
Matchmaker, The, 15, 21
Maverick, 95
May, Elaine, 54
May Wine, 76
"Maybe Down That Street," 80
"Maybe This Time," 141, 153
Max (Maximilian), 102, 139–40, 153
McCandless, Stanley, 40
McCarthy, Sheila, 176
McClung, Bruce D., 20
McCormack, Eric, 177
McCullers, Carson, 11
McLellan, Nora, 186
McNicholl, B.T., 196
McRae, Carmen, 64
Medium, The, 40, 41
"Meeskite," 29, 83–84, 120, 126,
    158, 162
Meet Me in St. Louis, 151, 157
Meet the People, 94

Mehring, Walter, 52
"Mein Herr," 141, 143, 171, 172,
    185, 186
Meisner, Sanford, 95
Melville, Herman, 89
Mendes, Sam, 67, 71, 86, 164–68,
    171, 173–175, 179–81, 185,
    190–91, 194–196
Menotti, Gian Carlo, 40
Meredith, Burgess, 18
Merrick, David, 15, 64, 115
Meyerhold, Vsevolod, 38, 43–44
Mielziner, Jo, 17
Milian, Jose, 196
Miller, John, 128–29, 192
Miller, Scott, 28, 71, 82, 192
Mineo, Sal, 97
Minnelli, Liza, 65, 96, 106, 109, 133,
    141–143, 145–46, 148–49,
    154–156, 166, 169–70
Minnelli, Vincente, 142, 149–51
Miss Lonelyhearts, 56
Mrs. McThing, 12
Mitchell, Ruth, 105, 112
Mobley, Mary Ann, 99
"Money, Money," 141
"Money Song, The," 59–60, 73, 78,
    120, 140–41, 149, 153, 187, 189
Moore, Frank, 187
Mordden, Ethan, 73, 141
Morning Son, 64, 98
Morris, Mitchell, 144, 194
Morrison, Jim, 195
Mostel, Zero, 95
Moulin Rouge, 155–58
Mozart, Wolfgang Amadeus, 67
Murnau, F.W., 89
Murray, Peg, 120–21, 126
Music Man, The, 76
Musical Cabaret, 196
Musically Enhanced Reality Mode
    (MERM), 156–58